D0239753

THE WORLD CUP OF EVERYTHING

Also by Richard Osman
(and Alexander Armstrong)

The 100 Most Pointless Things in the World
The 100 Most Pointless Arguments in the World
The Very Pointless Quiz Book
The A–Z of Pointless
A Pointless History of the World

THE WORLD CUP OF EVERYTHING

RICHARD OSMAN

CORONET

First published in Great Britain in 2017 by Coronet
An Imprint of Hodder & Stoughton
An Hachette UK company

7

A CIP catalogue record for this title is available from the British Library

ISBN 9781473667266
eBook ISBN 9781473667280

Typeset in Celeste, Futura Round & Neutraface 2 Display by
Palimpsest Book Production Ltd, Falkirk, Stirlingshire

Printed and bound in Great Britain by Clays Ltd, St Ives plc

Hodder & Stoughton policy is to use papers that are natural, renewable and recyclable products and made from wood grown in sustainable forests. The logging and manufacturing processes are expected to conform to the environmental regulations of the country of origin.

Hodder & Stoughton Ltd
Carmelite House
50 Victoria Embankment
London EC4Y 0DZ

www.hodder.co.uk

CONTENTS

WORLD CUP OF EVERYTHING

Hello there, and a very warm welcome to *The World Cup Of Everything*! Inside these pages you will find the World Cup Of Chocolate, the World Cup Of Crisps, the World Cup Of Animals, the World Cup Of Christmas Films, and much, much more. And who wins? Well, you decide!

Ahead of you are fourteen different World Cup competitions. Each one has been meticulously prepared for you to vote on, and to argue about, with your family and friends. Though whether they will still be 'family and friends' after you've told them you think Skips are better than Wotsits, and that *Blackadder* is better than *Fawlty Towers*, is anybody's guess.

And if I were you I would set aside a whole afternoon for the Jaffa Cakes discussion in the World Cup of Biscuits.

On the cover of this book I say that it is '100 per cent interactive, if you have a pencil', and that's important. I want this book to be good, old-fashioned, laughing and joking, pen-and-paper fun. Adults, tell the kids to put down their tablets. Kids, tell the adults to put down their tablets. Everyone, don't tell your grandparents to put down their tablets, that's vital anti-arthritis medication.

It is a little-known secret of books, that the introduction is the last thing you write. I am writing this now, having literally just finished the book. I am happy to tell you that it's really terrific, and I think you're going to love it.

Of course it still has to be edited, so who knows what they'll chop out? If they don't include my controversial section about Fiona Bruce being an alien-lizard overlord, for example, or my theory that the Chuckle Brothers were behind the kidnap and disappearance of Shergar, then you'll know I've been censored.

★ HOW TO PLAY ★

Each World Cup has thirty-two competitors, and I have drawn them together in a series of 'battles'. For every single battle you must follow these complicated steps.

1. Get a pen.
2. Argue about crisps/biscuits/sharks.
3. Possibly have a drink.
4. Take a vote.
5. Fill in the wall chart with the winners of those votes with your pencil.

Everyone gets one vote each on all of the battles in this book. In the case of a tied vote, everyone should write down a score of between one and five, and the option with the highest overall score wins. If there is *still* a tie, I have suggested all sorts of ways to resolve this in the book, but if I were you I would toss a coin. Maybe even one of those new £1 coins if you want to be sophisticated.

Wall charts are available at the end of each chapter for you to fill in as you play along at home and fight it out with your family and friends. You can also download printable versions from worldcupofeverything.co.uk so you can keep on playing as many times as you like.

Alongside the voting I'm also going to tell you all sorts of interesting things about chocolate bars, sweets, sitcoms, Christmas films, booze, TV shows and much more.

For example, you will learn the answers to the following questions . . .

Who or what is the 'Nando' in Nando's?

Are Wagon Wheels really smaller than they used to be?

Which British crisps only became successful after they changed their disastrous original name?

Who gave away $500m in return for a second-hand VW Beetle?

What actually *is* sherbet?

What sitcom first used the title 'Only Fools and Horses'?

What is the connection between 'Mistletoe and Wine' and *Who Wants to Be a Millionaire?*?

What did Prince William do with 1,700 Rich Tea biscuits?

I hope you enjoy the book, it was honestly a treat to write. I know you have many hours of ridiculous, lovely, heartfelt, occasionally drunken, joyous, inconsequential but vitally important arguments ahead of you.

I used to create these World Cups as a child, to pass the long summer holidays. I loved making lists and running competitions. The very first World Cup I ran was the World Cup of Bands 1983, where Culture Club beat Spandau Ballet in the final. I wish I could pretend that I disagreed with the result, but, the truth is, I was the only voter.

I think that the twelve-year-old me might be a little surprised that I'm still doing the same thing thirty-five years later. But I hope he would be as proud of me as I am of him. I see him now, that quiet little boy with his pen and paper, lost in thought about whether Adam and the Ants were better than the Thompson Twins. This book is dedicated to him with my thanks.

WORLD CUP OF CHOCOLATE

So you are about to choose the best chocolate bar ever. I hope you are ready for the responsibility? I know that you will have put in the years of training and eating chocolate that are necessary to complete this task. I believe in you.

Now if I were you I would have a box of Celebrations and Miniature Heroes by your side, as well as the largest selection box you can find in Poundland. It surely can't do any harm to remind yourself what a Twirl tastes like. If you are a child and there is an adult involved in this vote who won't allow you to eat chocolate, then please call the police immediately.

When I asked the entire British public to decide on the World

Cup of Chocolate we received over a million votes and the eventual winner was the, frankly a bit boring, Dairy Milk. What is wrong with people? I mean, I don't mind a Dairy Milk, but the best ever? I'm sure you will come up with a far more worthy answer. Just make sure it's not Twix.

Chocolate is, of course, the best thing ever [citation needed]. It was invented, as a drink, by the Aztecs. They believed that the cacao seed was a gift from the god Quetzalcoatl, in much the same way that throughout the 1980s I believed that the Chocolate Orange was a gift from my auntie Jan. Chocolate was popularised in the UK by a series of Quaker families keen to promote a less sinful alternative to alcohol and tobacco. The names of these pioneers still resonate today: the Cadburys, the Rowntrees, the Terrys and the Frys. On the continent, men such as Henri Nestlé and Rodolphe Lindt were experimenting with adding milk to cocoa powder and learning how to mould chocolate into solid bars. It seems extraordinary that the names of these pioneer families still dominate the chocolate world today, although there was never anyone called Jean-Pierre Toblerone or Anna-Maria Kinder Surprise.

In 1847 Fry's produced the first chocolate bar as we would know it. My bet is that, exactly like today, it had 'sharing pack' written on the label but someone ate the whole thing by themselves. And, now, 170 short years later, it is time for you to decide on the greatest chocolate bar of them all.

Before we get down to business I have a few questions and challenges for you. I promise they are not mandatory; you can just go straight to voting on the World Cup if you want. But I have spent quite a lot of time thinking about them so if you see me in the street, at least pretend you filled them in.

★ CHALLENGE! ★

Okay, here's a challenge for you: guess the best-selling chocolate bars in the UK in 2016. They are all competitors in the World Cup of Chocolate. Give yourself one point if you name something on the list, and three points if you've put it in exactly the right position.

1. ____________________ **5.** ____________________
2. ____________________ **6.** ____________________
3. ____________________ **7.** ____________________
4. ____________________ **8.** ____________________

Answers at the back of the book.

★ ARGUMENT! ★

In my opinion these are the five worst chocolate bars available in the UK:

1. TOPIC
2. TWIX
3. BOURNVILLE
4. MILKY WAY
5. DRIFTER

We disagree with you Richard and, after a vote, we have decided that the worst chocolate bar is actually

----

(Please fill in your answer even though you are wrong and Topic is definitely the worst.)

★ CHALLENGE! ★

Naming chocolate bars is actually someone's job. Can you imagine that? You could sit in an office being paid a six-figure salary for just writing 'ChockStar? Cara-Mel Gibson? Ooh Ahh Nougat?' on a whiteboard while people nod.

So, as it is impossible to improve chocolate, except by adding more chocolate, I have chosen instead to come up with better names for some chocolate bars.

1. TOBLERONE - PROFESSOR SCHNITZEL'S CHOCOLATE MOUNTAINS
2. TWIRL - FLAKES IN JACKETS
3. LION - MEERKAT
4. ROLOS - CHOCOLATE POCKETS
5. SNICKERS - MARATHON

Okay, your turn. Your challenge is to come up with a new name for Bounty. Write down your answers secretly, then ask the best reader in your group, or the least drunk, to read them out and vote for the best. Done?

Yes, we did that, and we have decided that the best new name for Bounty is ____________ and this name was invented by ____________

Also, while we were arguing we also came up with a great new name for ______________ which is ______________

★ ARGUMENT! ★

Okay, what is the best-named chocolate bar? You are not allowed to choose Professor Schnitzel's Chocolate Mountains, but here are my top five:

1. CURLY WURLY – Even better in a Glaswegian accent.
2. MALTESERS – We used to call them 'small geezers'.
3. FLAKE – Does what it says on the tin.
4. DOUBLE DECKER – I don't eat one for ages, then three turn up at once.
5. FINGER OF FUDGE – No comment.

Again, Richard, you are wrong here. We have agreed, after some argument, that the best-named chocolate bar is ____________

Interestingly 'Brexit' would be a perfect name for a chocolate bar. I'm guessing it would have two fingers and it would be up to you what you do with them.

★ INTERESTING! ★

Some of our most famous chocolate-bar brands were introduced much longer ago than you might imagine. Here's a timeline of some of our favourites. I really know I'm a geek but I find this list fascinating. If you want to build some jeopardy into the proceedings, then one of you can take charge of the list and play a quiz called You'll Never Guess When Crunchies Were Invented!

1866 FRY'S CHOCOLATE CREAM
1905 DAIRY MILK
1908 BOURNVILLE
1908 TOBLERONE
1914 FRY'S TURKISH DELIGHT
1920 FLAKE
1923 MILKY WAY
1926 FRUIT & NUT

1928 REESE'S PEANUT BUTTER CUPS
1929 CRUNCHIE
1930 SNICKERS
1932 MARS
1935 KITKAT
1935 AERO
1936 MALTESERS
1937 SMARTIES
1937 ROLOS
1941 M&M'S
1948 FUDGE
1951 BOUNTY
1958 PICNIC
1960 GALAXY
1963 CREME EGG
1967 TWIX
1970 CURLY WURLY
1976 DOUBLE DECKER
1976 YORKIE
1976 STARBAR
1980 DRIFTER
1981 WISPA
1984 TWIRL
1985 BOOST

Makes you wonder what on earth the chocolate industry has been up to for the last thirty years.

OKAY, HERE WE GO: it's time for the World Cup of Chocolate. Don't forget, everyone votes for their favourite in each of these pairings to find the winners. Using your pen, write down the scores, then fill in each of the winners on your wallchart and begin the slow, chocolatey fight to the death. In case of a tie, either argue for a further twenty minutes or simply toss a chocolate coin.

1 MINSTRELS vs TWIX

Interesting match-up to kick us off. Already controversial to have chocolate sweets alongside traditional bars, but as you'll see in the World Cup of Sweets later on, I feel like this is where the likes of Minstrels, Maltesers, Smarties, M&M'S and Rolos belong. To be honest I'm more concerned about the Twix, which to my mind has such a thin layering of chocolate that it's barely a chocolate bar at all and is, dare I say it, actually a biscuit. No one agrees with me though, so here it is. My vote would go to Minstrels, but my vote doesn't count. Which will you choose?

VOTE, THEN WRITE YOUR WINNER IN BOX 1 ON THE CHART

2 DAIRY MILK vs BOUNTY

So Dairy Milk was the winner of the official Twitter World Cup of Chocolate in 2017. It is the oldest bar on the list and was originally going to be called 'Highland Milk' before the daughter of an early Cadbury's customer suggested 'Dairy Milk'. Dairy Milk famously stipulates that 'a glass and a half' of milk goes into each bar, without ever telling you how big those glasses are, therefore rendering the information meaningless.

The Bounty is sort of unique among chocolate bars, in that it has been around for over sixty years, yet no one else has bothered putting coconut in chocolate since. We've recently had endless brands of coconut water, coconut oil, coconut milk, but coconut chocolate only really exists in the form of a Bounty. Which I suspect means it's not very popular. Surely a win for Dairy Milk here?

VOTE, THEN WRITE YOUR WINNER IN BOX 2 ON THE WALLCHART

3 SMARTIES vs FRUIT & NUT

The big argument about Smarties was always whether the different colours actually tasted different. Well, up until 1958 there was a dark-brown Smartie (should the singular of Smarties be 'Smartie' or 'Smarty'? I've never had to think about that before) which contained dark chocolate, and a light-brown Smartie ('Smartie' just looks wrong) which was coffee flavoured. The orange Smarty (wait 'Smarty' looks wrong too) used to be made with orange chocolate, but now only has orange flavouring in the shell. All the other ones, including the blue ones introduced in 1988, taste identical, so it turns out that Ian Graham from my school was lying after all.

Fruit & Nut is no longer just called 'Fruit & Nut'. Since 2003 it has officially been called Dairy Milk Fruit & Nut, which is awful, but at least it's better than 'Highland Milk Fruit & Nut'. It had a surprise early exit in the official World Cup of Chocolate, but how will it perform in yours?

VOTE, THEN WRITE YOUR WINNER IN BOX 3 ON THE WALLCHART

CRUNCHIE vs LION

The Lion bar is a bit 'nothingy' to me but I felt I couldn't leave it out of the final thirty-two because I got a lot of grief for leaving it out in the official World Cup of Chocolate, and I am a firm believer in chocolate democracy ('Chocolate Democracy', by the way, would be a bad name for a new bar). The Crunchie breaks most of the rules of a popular chocolate bar by having a huge filling-to-chocolate ratio, and it also really, really, really gets stuck in your teeth. But there is still something undeniably great about it. But, listen, it's your choice.

Back when we discovered our beef burgers were full of horse meat I tweeted that I'd been furious to discover that my Lion bar was actually 50 per cent tiger. However, that is no longer a topical story so it wouldn't be good form to repeat that joke here.

VOTE, THEN WRITE YOUR WINNER IN BOX 4 ON THE WALLCHART

FREDDO vs KITKAT CHUNKY

Freddo is that tiny little chocolate bar shaped like a frog. It is half the price of a normal chocolate bar, but also half the size, so you have to buy two of them anyway, which rather defeats the object. They were invented in Australia in 1930 by Harry Melbourne, an eighteen-year-old employee of MacRobertson's confectionery company. The fact that they were originally Australian makes sense of the fact that they are called 'Freddo Frog' rather than 'Freddy Frog', and I will now always say 'Freddo' in an Australian accent, as if he's a new *Neighbours* character.

The key thing about a KitKat Chunky is to imagine what a four-finger KitKat would look like if it was made of four KitKat Chunkys. Like a delicious chocolate pan pipe. ('Chocolate Pan Pipe' would also be a very bad name for a new chocolate bar.)

VOTE, THEN WRITE YOUR WINNER IN BOX 5 ON THE WALLCHART

6 TOFFEE CRISP vs MILKY WAY

The adverts for Toffee Crisp used to have the slogan 'Somebody, Somewhere is Eating a Toffee Crisp', so I have tried to work out if this is true. After extensive research I have calculated that it takes an average of 131 seconds to eat a Toffee Crisp. Given that there are 31,536,000 seconds in a year that would mean Nestlé would have to sell 240,733 Toffee Crisps to ensure that one was being eaten at all times. This means selling just 660 Toffee Crisps a day across the whole of the UK. Even allowing for the fact that very few of these would be eaten at 4 a.m., I am willing to accept that their slogan is acceptable, unlike 'A Mars a Day Helps You Work, Rest and Play'. Who has a Mars bar to help them to sleep? Please don't answer that question honestly.

I am also willing to accept the Milky Way slogan 'The Treat You Can Eat Between Meals Without Ruining Your Appetite', because they're so tiny and boring you could eat thirty and still go to Nando's afterwards.

VOTE, THEN WRITE YOUR WINNER IN BOX 6 ON THE WALLCHART

7 STARBAR vs SNICKERS

I am a great believer in Starbars, although I fear I'm fighting a losing battle. I think they have the combination of chocolate, chew and crunch just right, and that they led the way to every single restaurant in Britain having salted caramel on their menu. The Starbar was doing salted caramel back in the 1970s; so deal with that, Jamie Oliver. You know all about Snickers of course, but here's a simple way to win £10 off anyone over the age of thirty-five. Simply bet them £10 they can't tell you what the Snickers bar was originally called. They will laugh smugly and say 'Marathon', at which point you ask for your £10, as Snickers were originally called 'Snickers', named after the family horse on the farm run by the Mars family in the 1920s. It was renamed 'Marathon' in the UK because they wanted to suggest it was a health bar. Which, just to confirm, it isn't.

VOTE, THEN WRITE YOUR WINNER IN BOX 7 ON THE WALLCHART

8 FOUR-FINGER KITKAT vs M&M'S

Forrest Mars Sr, the son of Frank Mars the founder of the Mars company, saw British soldiers eating Smarties during the Spanish Civil War, then totally nicked the idea, took it back to the US and invented M&M'S. During the Second World War these were sold exclusively to the military, and now over 400 million of them are produced every day. Beat that, Toffee Crisp. In 1997 the most common colour of M&M was brown, with the least common being blue. By 2007 that had completely reversed, with blue now the most common and brown the least. I honestly find this interesting, but I recognise you've probably already moved on to Wispa vs Toblerone by now.

KitKat was introduced by our friends Rowntree's in the mid-1930s under the name 'Chocolate Crisp' but was quickly renamed 'KitKat' after everyone realised that 'Have a break, have a Chocolate Crisp' didn't scan.

VOTE, THEN WRITE YOUR WINNER IN BOX 8 ON THE WALLCHART

WISPA vs TOBLERONE

Ouch, this is a very tough pairing. The Wispa was introduced as a direct competitor to Aero. It disappeared in 2003, replaced by Dairy Milk Bubbly (the what now?) before being brought back in 2007 after an Internet-led campaign.

The Toblerone is the second-biggest-selling chocolate bar in the world, behind Snickers, believe it or not. In 2016 Toblerone caused extreme controversy when they changed the design of their bar in the UK. There are now bigger gaps between the chocolate peaks, meaning the new Toblerone looks less like a chocolate bar and more like a bike rack.

VOTE, THEN WRITE YOUR WINNER IN BOX 9 ON THE WALLCHART

10 CREME EGG vs DOUBLE DECKER

Another close battle here. Cadbury's Creme Eggs were originally Fry's Creme Eggs when they were introduced in 1963. When I initially started researching Creme Eggs I accidentally typed 'Crime Egg' into Google, so I now know an awful lot about Venero Frank 'Benny Eggs' Mangano, the apparently infamous underboss of the Genovese crime family.

Fortunately I didn't replace an 'e' with an 'i' when I was researching the Double Decker.

VOTE, THEN WRITE YOUR WINNER IN BOX 10 ON THE WALLCHART

11 FLAKE vs MARS

How on earth did they have the technology to invent the Flake in 1920? It looks like the sort of thing that NASA would invent. Famously, it was the only chocolate bar advertised being eaten in the bath, despite actually being the worst possible chocolate bar to eat in the bath. The Aero is probably the best chocolate bar to eat in the bath because of its buoyancy.

The Mars bar is the seventh-best-selling chocolate bar in the world, but when did you actually last want one? Apart from right now because I've just mentioned it.

VOTE, THEN WRITE YOUR WINNER IN BOX 11 ON THE WALLCHART

12 YORKIE vs MALTESERS

I am going to come clean: Maltesers would be the winner in my own personal World Cup of Chocolate. They did actually make the final in the official competition, only to be beaten by the dreaded Dairy Milk. Maltesers were originally advertised as 'energy balls' to be sold to 'slimming women'. It has long been my ambition to create a packet consisting of half Minstrels and half Maltesers, like a bag of Revels with all the rubbish ones taken out. I'd call my creation 'Maltinstrels' but, as yet, no one has agreed to make them. I guarantee I would not be marketing them to 'slimming women'.

Yorkie was invented at the Rowntree's factory in York, which seems obvious, but Maltesers weren't invented in Malta. In much the same way that Mars bars weren't invented on Mars but Galaxy was invented in the Galaxy.

VOTE, THEN WRITE YOUR WINNER IN BOX 12 ON THE WALLCHART

13 FRY'S TURKISH DELIGHT vs ROLOS

Fry's Turkish Delight is the most exotic bar on our list, and also the one that you definitely haven't eaten for at least twenty-five years. They still make them, still sell them and, for the purposes of research, I am eating one this very second and it's delicious. 'Full of Eastern promise' as the adverts used to say, although 'Full of Eastern European promise' would be more apt as they are now manufactured in Poland.

If you want to know the official scientific name for the shape of a Rolo it is a 'frustum'. Do you love anyone enough to give them your last chocolate-covered, caramel-centred frustum?

VOTE, THEN WRITE YOUR WINNER IN BOX 13 ON THE WALLCHART

14 TWIRL vs CARAMEL

I first ran the World Cup of Chocolate in 2012 and in that year the Twirl was the winner, but it was knocked out by Maltesers in the 2016 semi-finals. I love a Twirl; it's the bar that the Twix always dreamed of being. It's smooth, intense, chocolatey, a great conversationalist, able to play the piano, speaks seven languages, great with kids, once had trials for Fulham, always recycles, never . . . wait where was I? Ah yes, vote for Twirl.

Dairy Milk Caramel? Well, it's only been around since 1976 despite the fact that it's just a Dairy Milk with a bit of caramel in it. How on earth did Cadbury's invent the Flake fifty-six years before they invented this?

VOTE, THEN WRITE YOUR WINNER IN BOX 14 ON THE WALLCHART

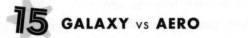

15 GALAXY vs AERO

Galaxy is known as 'Dove' in the USA, which immediately makes me wonder what Dove is known as over there? Starburst? Anyway, Galaxy is Mars' direct competitor to Dairy Milk, but was knocked out by Dairy Milk in the semi-finals of the official World Cup of Chocolate 2016. It does a really strong job holding together the diverse elements in a box of Celebrations and I can strongly recommend the Salted Caramel Galaxy they recently launched (which would never have happened without the pioneering work of the Starbar).

Weirdly the Mint Aero was launched thirty-five years before the Chocolate Aero. It's still the best though. No one has ever done mint and chocolate as well as the good people at Aero, not even After Eight. Actually, forget that, Mint Viennetta is better than Mint Aero.

VOTE, THEN WRITE YOUR WINNER IN BOX 15 ON THE WALLCHART

Match 16 is the wild-card match. If you feel that there are competitors you love that I've left out of The World Cup of Chocolate then you can write them in here. A few chocolate bars I felt weren't worthy of inclusion include Topic (obvz), Picnic, Drifter, Chocolate Orange bar, Kinder Surprise, Munchies and Boost. Or you may have your own weird favourite. At this point your dad will say: 'They should bring back Texans/Fuse bars/Spiras', depending on his age. Simply draw your two favourite absentee bars together here and take a vote.

VOTE, THEN WRITE YOUR WINNER IN BOX 16 ON THE WALLCHART

CHOCOLATE

THE WORLD CUP OF EVERYTHING

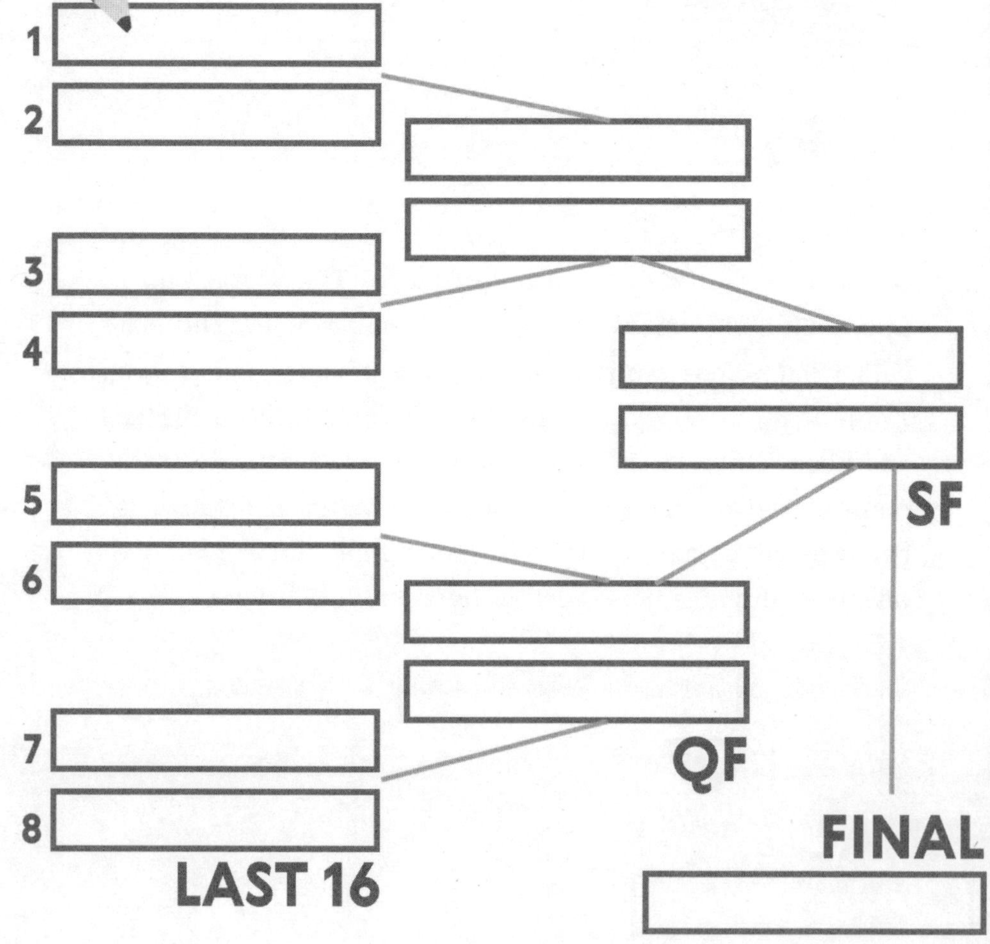

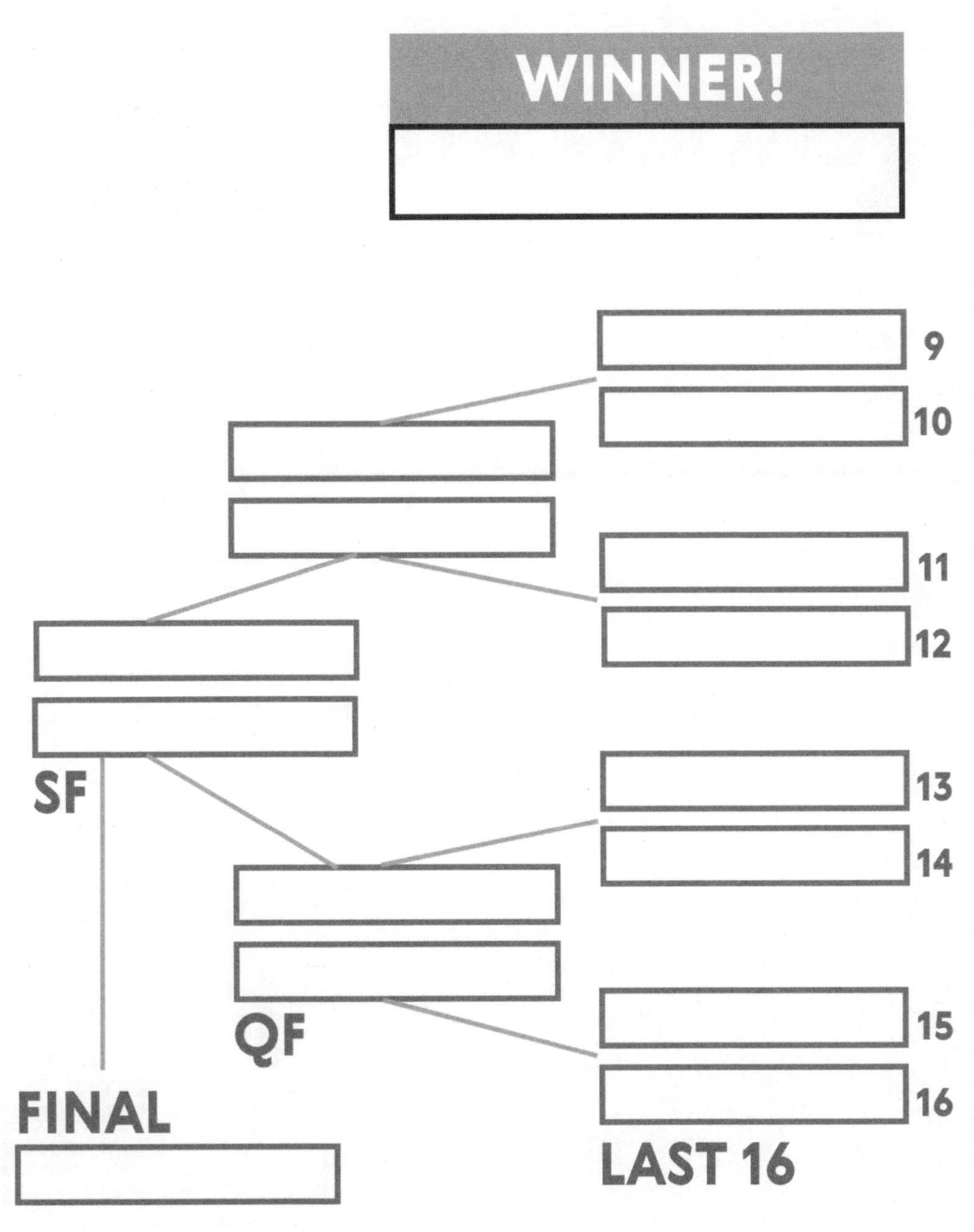
WINNER!
9
10
11
12
SF
13
14
QF
15
16
FINAL
LAST 16

WORLD CUP OF ANIMALS

How on earth can we choose the best animal? What's the best tactic here?

Maybe we could choose the smartest animal? Chimpanzees supposedly have enormous brainpower, and they certainly all had facial hair long before we decided to think it was cool. But then look at the mess they made trying to get that piano up those stairs? Equally, dolphins are often said to possess great intelligence, yet they have lived in water for millions of years and still haven't invented the SodaStream. We are also told that a middle-aged pig can be as smart as a three-year-old human, but, respectfully, both of my kids were three-year-old humans at one point and you'd be hard pushed to be more stupid. Honestly Ruby, if you *really* think I've stolen your nose then magically put it back again, then you are not someone we should be using as a measure of intelligence. Sheep are said to have better memories than humans, and I suppose that's true, as I've never seen one lose a pen. Elephants also never forget, which is why if you ever borrow a lawnmower off an elephant make sure you return it. Elephants are really good to go to the cinema with because if you ever wonder where you've seen an actor before, they just lean over and whisper 'He played CJ's boyfriend in season 2 of *The West Wing*.' Though there's a slight downside, which is that they eat an awful lot of popcorn. The sad truth is that humans are far and away the cleverest animals, and we're not intelligent at all, so what does that tell us about animals? I know you're sitting there right now thinking that your dog or cat is intelligent, but why not ask them to make you a cup of tea and see how far that gets you?

So maybe we could choose the most useful animal? Dogs are useful. They can be guide dogs, therapy dogs, guard dogs, sheepdogs, sniffer dogs, train-driver dogs, dentist dogs and management-consultant dogs. Cows are useful for dairy products and for jumping over moons. Horses used to be useful, but then we invented cars and lorries and combine harvesters and electricity. So now they are pretty much obsolete, and largely stand in fields in the same way that abandoned fridges sometimes sit in people's front gardens. Pigeons are useful. They have always been at the cutting edge of technology. Not only were they used in wartime as an early and remarkably effective form of email, but they were also the first animals to tweet. We have rats that can detect landmines, eels that are unlocking the secrets of electricity, and goats that teach Pilates to senior citizens at very reasonable rates. ('How flexible are you? Well. I can't do Tuesdays.' My favourite joke ever.) But the truth is that by far the most useful animal of all is the bee. Without bees fertilising our crops, the human race would die out in five years. Anyone want to vote for bees in the World Cup of Animals? I thought not. Really the only thing we think about bees is 'Well, at least you're not wasps.'

No, we all know how you're going to choose your World Cup of Animals winner. You're going to go for the cutest one. Good news for dogs, cats, meeerkats and penguins; bad news for hippos and warthogs.

Before we begin, here are some light warm-up exercises.

★ CHALLENGE! ★

Here are some clues to famous people, all of whom have an animal somewhere in their name. Name the famous people please, in a quiz I am calling 'The Weakest Mink', hosted by Cat Deeley and Richard Herring.

1. Action-man TV host appointed Britain's Chief Scout in 2015 ____________

2. One of the most successful sports stars of all time, christened with the name Eldrick ____________

3. Co-hosted the Brit Awards with Mick Fleetwood in 1989 ____________

4. Announced she was standing against Jeremy Corbyn in the Labour leadership election of 2016 ____________

5. Friend of Dec ____________

6. Footballer voted FIFA Player of the Year for the first time in 2009 ____________

7. Greek physician known as the 'Father of Modern Medicine' _____________

8. Author whose home, Hill Top, in Cumbria is now a museum _____________

9. Republican Speaker of the House of Representatives 1995–99 _____________

10. Singer once married to the model Heidi Klum __________

Answers at the back of the book.

★ CHART! ★

This is a list of Britain's most popular pets. Actually not most popular, just most numerous. In 2016 Britain had the following pets.

1. 20 MILLION fish kept in ponds. (Not really pets in my opinion. If you can't stroke it, it isn't a pet.)

2. 15 MILLION indoor fish. Again not a pet. A pet is something you should be able to take for a walk in the park in an attempt to pull other single pet owners. Try that with a freshwater guppy.

3. 8.5 MILLION dogs! At last, a proper pet.
4. 7.5 MILLION cats! You can't take them for a walk in the park, but you can show pictures of them at work and pretend to have a sensitive side.
5. 800,000 rabbits. You'd think there would be more, given how they breed.
6. 600,000 domestic fowl. That's chickens and ducks. You can always tell if a friend is going through a crisis because they decide to get chickens in their back garden. It is not 'back to nature' or 'self-sufficiency'; it is 'a cry for help'.
7. 700,000 guinea pigs. They eat them in Peru you know.
8. 600,000 budgies. Something, something, something 'going cheep'.
9. 400,000 hamsters. Though over 300,000 of these have been brought home from school for the weekend.
10. 300,000 lizards. My kids had a lizard called Beyoncé.

★ PET SOUNDS!★

We are used to our animals going 'baa' or 'woof' or 'oink' but animals make very different noises in different countries. Can you answer these questions, in a quiz I'm calling 'Moo-niversity Challenge', with your host, Jeremy Quacksman.

1. In Germany, which animal says 'GRUNZ'? ____________
2. In Turkey, which animal says 'VRAK'? ____________
3. In Sweden, which animal says 'IIIK'? ____________
4. In Iceland, which animal says 'VOFF'? ____________
5. In Japan, which animal says 'MAU MAU'? ____________
6. In Spain, which animal says 'BEEE BEEE'? (clue: it isn't a bee) ____________
7. In Italy, which animal says 'PORTOBELLO'? ___________
8. In Denmark, which animal says 'KYKYLIKY'? __________

Despite what number 5 might look like, I haven't put cat on the list because they pretty much say 'miaow' wherever you go. That's why cats travel abroad so much while you're at work.

Answers at the back of the book.

★ CHALLENGE! ★

Can you guess the top five cat and dog names in Britain last year? It is extraordinary how much crossover there is with the most popular children's names of last year. An incredible forty-one names in the top 100 dog names were also in the list of the top 100 girls' and boys' names. And surely some of the others, like Sparky, Rascal and Zeus, should be making an appearance any time soon.

DOGS

1. M _ _

2. B _ _ _ _

3. M _ _ _ _

4. M _ _ _ _ _

5. J _ _ _

CATS

1. M _ _ _ _

2. C _ _ _ _ _ _ _

3. T _ _ _ _ _ _

4. P _ _ _ _

5. O _ _ _ _

This might be a good time to let you know that the eleventh most popular cat name of last year was Trevor.

Answers at the back of the book.

LET THE WORLD CUP OF ANIMALS BEGIN. I think this might throw up serious arguments, in the same way as a cat throws up a fur ball (i.e. regularly and requiring an awful lot of cleaning up afterwards). Have your arguments, make your decisions and, in the event of a tie, ask a parrot.

1 HAMSTER vs TIGER

Almost all domestic hamsters are either Syrian, Russian or Chinese. You can tell if your hamster is Russian because when you come downstairs in the morning you'll find it has annexed the rabbit hutch next door. Every single pet Syrian hamster in existence today is descended from one brother–sister pair captured in Aleppo in 1930. If there was a Syrian hamster edition of *The Jeremy Kyle Show* it would be carnage.

At the beginning of the twentieth century there were around 100,000 tigers in the wild. According to a global census in 2016 there are now just 3,890. So if your school has a pet tiger which it lets you take home at the weekend, it is very bad news if it dies. Don't even try to go to Pets at Home to get a replacement and hope your child's teacher won't notice.

WRITE YOUR WINNER IN BOX 1 ON THE WALLCHART

2 WHALE vs CAT

In a real-life fight between a cat and a whale, the winner would very much depend on the field of combat. If the battle took place underwater, the whale would win, but if the battle took place in your next-door neighbour's tree then my money is on the cat. Though your cat would make an awful racket dragging the whale through your cat flap to proudly show you what he'd done. Don't forget though: this World Cup is not about who would win in a fight; it's more of a popularity contest. So basically, would you rather have a cat or a whale curled up on your lap while you're watching *Midsomer Murders*?

It is a well-known fact that most animals like to wear clothes that they rhyme with. For example, cats wear hats and whales wear veils.

WRITE YOUR WINNER IN BOX 2 ON THE WALLCHART

3 SHEEP vs EAGLE

Eagles are powerful and majestic creatures, even the bald ones. They are the primary predators of the avian world and have even been known to kill sheep. Their eyesight is three times sharper than that of humans, so if you ever lose your keys then you know who to call. Be aware though that even if you have a new HD TV they will complain about the picture.

Eagles are happiest in the air, but are also comfortable on

the ground, scavenging for food. Sheep are happiest on the ground but are also comfortable in the air, where everybody mistakes them for clouds. There are over 1 billion sheep in the world, though no one knows the exact number because scientists always fall asleep before they get to the last one.

WRITE YOUR WINNER IN BOX 3 ON THE WALLCHART

4 GOLDFISH vs MEERKAT

Anyone over forty will back me up on this; we didn't use to have meerkats. They seem to have been invented sometime around 1998 by David Attenborough in an attempt to make wildlife documentaries 47 per cent cuter. They are constantly vigilant for predators (chiefly snakes and birds of prey), they spend much of every day underground in huge networks of tunnels, and they invented car insurance.

Goldfish were first domesticated in China over a thousand years ago, and famously thrive in small plastic bags from 1970s fairgrounds. For the Chinese, goldfish were highly valued and were always kept outside in ponds. They would occasionally be displayed indoors in glass bowls to bring good luck on special occasions, which is where we get the Western tradition of keeping goldfish in indoor bowls. This practice is now banned in many countries. Goldfish have notoriously poor memories, with many failing in scientific tests to remember their mum's birthday, or recognise a picture of Olly Murs. The oldest goldfish ever was Tish, from Thirsk in North Yorkshire. He lived to the age of forty-three and put his good health down to regular early-morning swims.

WRITE YOUR WINNER IN BOX 4 ON THE WALLCHART

5 RABBIT vs GORILLA

First things first: how many times do you think Chas & Dave mention the word 'rabbit' in their song 'Rabbit'? *Forty-two times.* I am definitely going to use that fact in a quiz one day. If you ever let pet rabbits into your house they will chew through the television cable and kill you or, even worse, make you miss *Gogglebox*. All domesticated rabbits are European rabbits, which you can tell because they have thin moustaches, smoke Gauloises, and have better workplace pay and conditions than you.

Before he invented meerkats, gorillas were David Attenborough's big gimmick. Gorillas are highly intelligent, can make and use tools, have strong family bonds and seem capable of thinking about the past and the future. They are also long-lived, especially in zoo environments. The oldest recorded gorilla was Colo, who lived at Columbus Zoo and Aquarium (predominantly the 'zoo' bit I'm guessing). Colo lived until the age of sixty, thus becoming the first gorilla in history to travel on the bus for free after 9.30.

WRITE YOUR WINNER IN BOX 5 ON THE WALLCHART

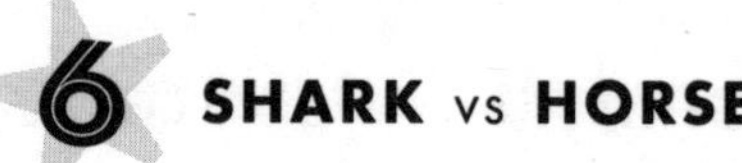

6 SHARK vs HORSE

'Shark vs Horse' is another contest that would pull in pretty big ratings if TV executives got hold of it. Cold-blooded, predatory killers, their dead eyes hunt the weak and defenceless, their nostrils scent blood, and their tiny brains feel no pity or remorse. But enough about TV executives; let's talk about sharks. The first sharks appeared an incredible 420 million years ago, shortly followed by the first ever documentary about sharks on the Discovery Channel. There are over 470 species of shark, the vast majority of which are harmless to humans. On average there are 4.3 deaths per year from unprovoked shark attacks. It's the .3 that sounds the most painful.

Horses are extraordinary animals and can form very strong bonds with human beings. They do still have three main uses. They are often used in various forms of physical and emotional therapy; are used by police officers to get a better view at football matches; and are used by bookmakers to steal my money.

If a horse ever behaves badly, they make it do dressage.

WRITE YOUR WINNER IN BOX 6 ON THE WALLCHART

7 GIRAFFE vs HEDGEHOG

Don't think I've forgotten that all animals rhyme with clothing. For example, a giraffe likes to wear a scarf and hedgehogs wear wedge clogs.

The best thing about giraffes is that they're so tall they're the only animal you can see at London Zoo without having to buy a ticket.

The foot of a giraffe is up to four times the size of a human foot and so a giraffe treading on a hedgehog would feel almost identical pain to a human treading on a piece of Lego.

WRITE YOUR WINNER IN BOX 7 ON THE WALLCHART

8 HIPPO vs BUDGIE

'Hippopotamus' comes from the ancient Greek for 'river horse', which makes them absolutely perfect for water polo. Hippos are notoriously aggressive and unpredictable but, despite this, attempts were made to introduce them to the USA in 1910. It was thought that releasing hippos into the bayous of Louisiana would help to clear the water hyacinth that was choking the rivers, and that they would also provide a plentiful supply of meat. According to a report in the *New York Times,* hippo meat tastes like 'lake cow bacon'. The bill was not passed.

Budgerigars are the third most common pet in the world after dogs and cats. They can be taught to whistle and to speak a few rudimentary words. Therefore it is only their inability to brandish red cards that disqualifies them from becoming Premier League referees.

WRITE YOUR WINNER IN BOX 8 ON THE WALLCHART

9 OWL vs BEAR

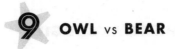

There are seven main types of owl you can find on the British mainland. There's the little owl, invented in the 1970s by the Japanese to replace the clunky and cumbersome large owl. There's the barn owl, or as it's now more commonly known the 'light & spacious 4-bedroom barn-conversion owl'. There are the short-eared owl and the long-eared owl, which are very easy to tell apart unless they are wearing hats. The tawny owl is the one that makes the familiar 'too-whit-too-whoo' call, although this behaviour has recently been banned on a lot of owl building sites. The snowy owl is very rare and, since the advent of global warming, is starting to be replaced by the slushy owl. Finally there is the European eagle owl, which was recently voted out by 52 per cent of the other owls and is currently waiting on a decision about its visa.

Brown bears are healthier to eat than white bears, due to having more fibre. The healthiest bears of all to eat are wholemeal bears. In summer brown bears can double their weight, adding up to 400lb of fat. I know that feeling.

WRITE YOUR WINNER IN BOX 9 ON THE WALLCHART

10 PENGUIN vs COW

The largest penguin species is the emperor penguin. Incidentally, emperor penguin is a really cool name for a penguin, but a really uncool name for an emperor. Penguin eggs are very small and are therefore a really disappointing alternative to Chocolate Buttons eggs at Easter.

Cows have the enormous misfortune to be delicious without being cute. For all we know, meerkats are delicious, but you could never kill them because of the way they stand on their hind legs and look around as if they can't believe their bus hasn't arrived yet.

I'm afraid there is no way a cow is going to beat a penguin in this competition. Everybody loves penguins. Imagine if a penguin waddled into your house right now. You'd be delighted. Surprised too, but delighted. Now imagine if a cow walked into your house right now. You would open a window and try to shoo it out while trying to find the Cow Spray.

Sometimes a waddle of penguins will disguise themselves as a cow when they want to carry out a bank robbery.

WRITE YOUR WINNER IN BOX 10 ON THE WALLCHART

11 GUINEA PIG vs GIANT PANDA

Guinea pigs are not pigs and do not come from Guinea. Even weirder than that, the French call them 'Indian pigs', although they are still not pigs, and they're not from India, and the Germans call them 'little sea pigs', although they don't live in the sea and aren't pigs (and the Germans *used* to call them '*Merswin*' which means 'dolphin'). The Chinese, who tend to be pretty good at this sort of thing, call them 'mouse pigs', which actually works pretty well, even though they are neither mice nor pigs. If you want to call them what they actually are, then a more honest name would be Peruvian gerbil or Chilean chinchilla.

Giant pandas are sort of like cute cows, so we have no idea how they taste. The Chinese government lease them out for up to $1 million a year to foreign zoos. Edinburgh Zoo is currently home to two, leading to the single most extraordinary political fact of our era. Namely that there are now more giant pandas in Scotland than there are Labour MPs.

WRITE YOUR WINNER IN BOX 11 ON THE WALLCHART

12 DOG vs CHICKEN

A dog's sense of smell is 10,000 times more sensitive than a human's, so if you think it's bad when your dog passes wind, imagine what it's like for them. Their hearing is also four times better, which is why they look at you so knowingly when you pass wind and blame it on them. Kubla Khan owned over 5,000 dogs, so must have had a very big car. Hitler owned two dogs, which was awkward for him as he only had one ball.

There are over 19 billion chickens in the world and over 20 billion fried-chicken shops in South London.

WRITE YOUR WINNER IN BOX 12 ON THE WALLCHART

13 KOALA vs LION

It is obligatory for anyone visiting Australia to have their photo taken with a koala. Everyone from Queen Elizabeth to One Direction to Vladimir Putin has been pictured cuddling the cute marsupials. A koala famously urinated on Liam and Harry from One Direction, winning it legions of fans worldwide, though the koala held by Vladimir Putin very wisely behaved itself and so is still alive today.

The most famous lion of all is the MGM lion, used in the logo at the beginning of all MGM movies since 1924. The logo has actually featured seven different lions. The first MGM lion of all was Irish. Slats was born in Dublin Zoo in 1919 and was quickly followed by Jackie, Telly, Coffee, Tanner, George, and, since 1957, Leo. Leo, still used by MGM today, was born in Royal Burgers' Zoo in the Netherlands. The coolest lion of them all was Jackie. Jackie appeared in over 100 movies, including all the Johnny Weissmuller *Tarzan* films, and also survived two train crashes, one earthquake and a studio explosion.

WRITE YOUR WINNER IN BOX 13 ON THE WALLCHART

14 PIG vs CLOWNFISH

You have to admit that the pig is a versatile animal. Foodstuffs made from pigs include bacon, ham, wafer-thin ham, gammon, pork chops, chorizo, pepperoni, pork scratchings, Smoky Bacon crisps, ribs, spare ribs, baby back ribs, pork belly, crackling, suckling pig, salami, Cumberland sausage, pancetta, Spam, and Marks & Spencer's Percy Pigs. The only pig in no danger of being eaten any time soon is Peppa Pig, who made over $200m in merchandising revenue alone in 2016.

Clownfish, with their distinctive orange, black and white colouring, were made famous by Marlin and Nemo in *Finding Nemo*. Before then they struggled to get work. Clownfish have developed a way to live among the venomous tentacles of the sea anemone, in much the same way as I developed a way to live in my first flat-share in Kentish Town in the early 1990s. The coolest thing about clownfish is that they are protandrous hermaphrodites, meaning they are gender-fluid and alternate between being male and female at some point in their lives. Scientists have discovered that while they are in a female phase they earn up to 20 per cent less.

WRITE YOUR WINNER IN BOX 14 ON THE WALLCHART

15 RHINO vs CHIMPANZEE

Chimpanzees are humankind's closest living relative, sharing up to 98.6 per cent of our DNA. There are some differences of course. Their mating act lasts between ten and fifteen seconds, while ours is around half that. Also, chimpanzees live off a diet of insects, honey, bark and leaves, but then so does Gwyneth Paltrow.

I realise that I may not have fully convinced you that animals like to wear clothes that they rhyme with, and I'm probably not going to change your mind at this late stage by suggesting that rhinos wear chinos.

WRITE YOUR WINNER IN BOX 15 ON THE WALLCHART

16 _______________ VS _______________

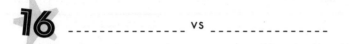

So which animals have I forgotten? Fill in your two wild-card choices here. Python? Flamingo? Robin? Wombat? Warthog? Stoat? Chinchilla? Fox? Lemur? Crocodile? Anteater? Otter?

It's worth noting that, on this list, stoats wear coats, anteaters wear windcheaters and a fox likes to wear socks, smocks and a choice of frocks.

WRITE YOUR WINNER IN BOX 16 ON THE WALLCHART

ANIMALS

THE WORLD CUP OF EVERYTHING

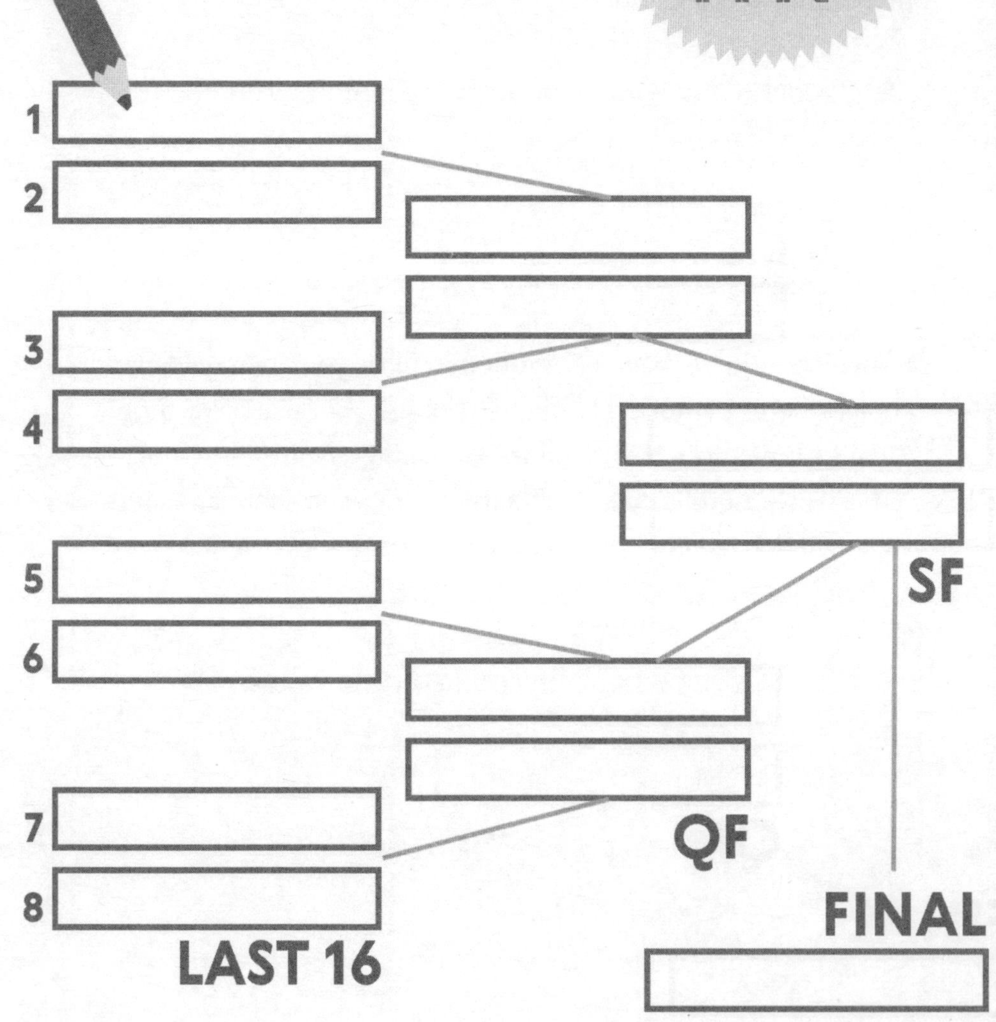

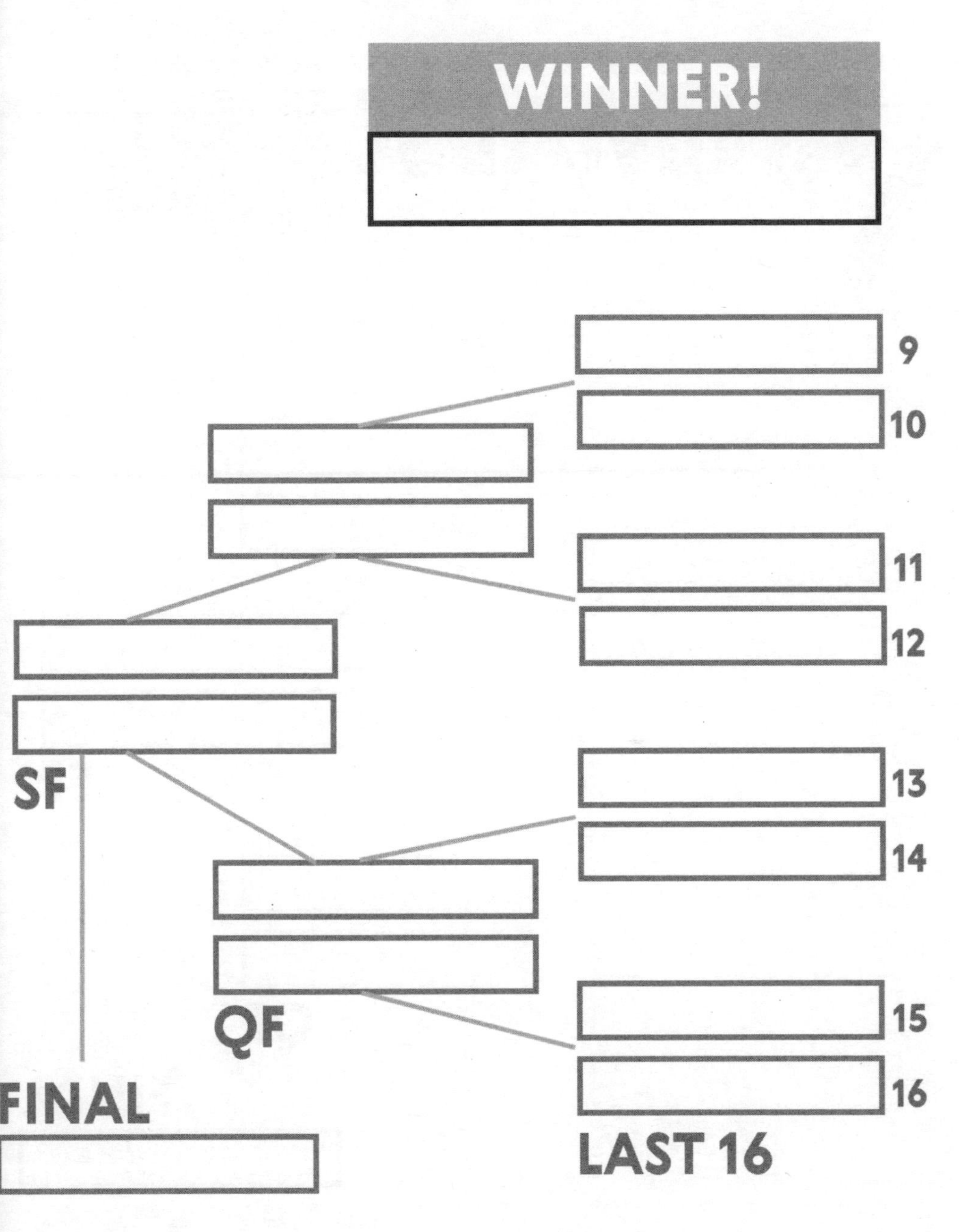
WINNER!
9
10
11
12
SF
13
14
QF
15
16
FINAL
LAST 16

WORLD CUP OF CRISPS

The time has come to vote on packs
Of corn/potato/maize-based snacks.
Who likes Wotsits? Who likes Quavers?
Who likes Walkers' countless flavours?
What's the best of this fair bunch?
Pickled Onion Monster Munch?
Could Chipsticks shine? Will Pringles dazzle?
Does everybody like a Frazzle?

Will the snacking championships
Be won by Discos, Squares or Skips?

Will Cheese & Onion be forsaken
For Worcester Sauce? For Smoky Bacon?
Perhaps we'll see a big surprise?
Nik Naks? Pom-Bears? Scampi Fries?
Some will win while others blunder
(I frankly fear for Golden Wonder).

The time has come to vote on groups
Of Kettle Chips and Hula Hoops;
To think of bribes or other ploys
To win this thing for Steak McCoy's;
To argue, fight and issue vetoes,
When Uncle Keith defends Doritos;
To counter underhand shenanigans
Fixing votes for Roast Beef Brannigans.

And once the cup is done and halted
And one crisp reigns supreme, exalted,
To prove your taste cannot be faulted,
Don't choose Walkers Ready Salted.

★ CHALLENGE ★ ★ AND ARGUMENT! ★

These are the top ten best-selling Walkers crisps flavours in the UK. In the brackets next to their name is the position they should really be in, if we lived in a sane and rational world. Feel free to take a vote amongst yourselves too!

1. READY SALTED (10)
2. CHEESE & ONION (5)
3. SALT & VINEGAR (1)
4. STEAK & ONION (4)
5. SMOKY BACON (2)
6. ROAST CHICKEN (6)
7. PRAWN COCKTAIL (3)
8. PICKLED ONION (8)
9. TOMATO KETCHUP (9)
10. BBQ RIB (7)

★ CHINESE CHALLENGE! ★

Below are ten flavours of Lay's crisps you can buy in Chinese supermarkets. Five of them are real, five are ludicrous inventions. Well, they're all ludicrous inventions really, but five of them are real ludicrous inventions.

1. CUCUMBER
2. GIANT PANDA
3. MYSTERY FLAVOUR
4. ROASTED SQUID
5. TOMATO CHICKEN
6. DRY PIG NOSE
7. BLUEBERRY
8. SOUR BLACK BEAN CHUTNEY
9. NUMB & SPICY HOT POT
10. EEL & ONION

Answers at the back of the book.

★ CHALLENGE! ★

Here are the dictionary definitions of ten words that are also a type of crisp. Welcome to 'Name That Crisp!' with Roy Walkers and Sylvester McCoys.

1. Large hoops spun round the body by gyrating the hips, for play or exercise ____________
2. Induces a state of being very tired in a nervous or slightly anxious way ____________
3. Musical notes half as long as crotchets ____________
4. Events where people dance to modern recorded music for entertainment, or places where this often happens ____________
5. Does not do or does not have something that is usually done or that should be done ____________
6. Small decorative objects, especially in a house _________
7. Objects or people whose name you have temporarily forgotten or do not know ____________

8. A Scottish clothing company started in 1815 ___________

9. Multiplies a number by itself ____________

10. Smooth yellow cheeses in 1959 British car ____________

Answers at the back of the book.

★ INFORMATION! ★

It is always nice to hear good news, and I am very happy to tell you of an area where the United Kingdom leads the world. We eat more crisps per person than every other country in the world! Give each other a high-five, before swiftly sitting down again to catch your breath. The average Brit eats roughly 3kg of crisps every year. Which other nations grace the world's top ten crisp consumer countries? Here's the full list:

1. UNITED KINGDOM
2. AUSTRALIA
3. IRELAND
4. NEW ZEALAND
5. NORWAY

6. USA
7. FINLAND
8. SWEDEN
9. ISRAEL
10. CANADA

It is fairly simple to conclude that if you speak English, even the Australian form of it, then you like crisps. This may be because lots of European countries (I'm looking at you, Germany) still insist on selling only Ready Salted or Paprika-flavoured crisps.

SO TIME TO VOTE IN THE WORLD CUP OF CRISPS. Thirty of Britain's finest salted snacks, plus two chosen by you. Worth noting that strictly speaking every single one of these battles is a crunch decision. If there is a tie then decide the winner with a Pringle-tube sword fight.

1 WOTSITS vs READY SALTED HULA HOOPS

Wotsits were launched in 1970, as was I. Over the years we have spent a lot of time together. 'Wotsit fingers', that giveaway orange staining, is the childhood equivalent of 'nicotine fingers'. In the good old days they made Wotsits in Prawn Cocktail and BBQ flavours, as well as Whopping Wotsits (big ones), Weenie Wotsits (small ones), Wafflers Wotsits (waffly ones), and even Frozen Wotsits (don't even ask). Since 1970 Wotsits have become healthier, leaner and fresher and, in that regard, they have aged an awful lot better than me.

Hula Hoops have a similar history to Wotsits. They were first sold in 1973 by KP, and over the years we have spent a lot of time together. Putting Hula Hoops on your fingers is the childhood equivalent of getting married. Beyoncé's line 'if you liked it then you should have put a ring on it' was about Jay-Z's love of Salt & Vinegar Hula Hoops. They have also had a number of variations over the years, such as Big Os (big ones), Shoks (small ones) and Frozen (still don't ask, but you can get them at Iceland if you are really curious). I have chosen to go with the most popular flavour, Ready Salted, rather than the actual best ones, BBQ Beef or Salt & Vinegar. But cross out the flavour with a pen if you fancy; I won't tell anyone.

WRITE YOUR WINNER IN BOX 1 ON THE WALLCHART

2 WALKERS CHEESE & ONION vs CHIPSTICKS

When Walkers created a promotional campaign renaming Salt & Vinegar as Salt & Lineker, and Cheese & Onion as Cheese & Owen, almost everybody in the country thought they were the only person to suggest to Walkers that Smoky Bacon should become Smoky Beckham. The fact that it didn't suggests that Beckham said no to the idea. Michael Owen obviously said yes because he is nowhere near as rich as David Beckham, and Gary Lineker said yes because he has been held captive in the Walkers' basement for the last twenty years.

Chipsticks were created by one of the great names in British snack history, Smith's. Smith's was founded by Frank Smith and Jim Viney shortly after the end of the First World War, and initially started trading from the garage of Smith's house in Cricklewood. Smith's were eventually sold to Nabisco, and then to PepsiCo, who withdrew all of their potato crisp lines in favour of another of their brands, Walkers. Some snacks still retain the Smith's branding though, and the wonderful Salt & Vinegar Chipstick is one of them.

WRITE YOUR WINNER IN BOX 2 ON THE WALLCHART

DORITOS CHILLI HEATWAVE vs MINI CHEDDARS

Doritos were, genuinely, invented at Disneyland in Anaheim, California, during the early 1960s. The company-owned restaurant would take any surplus tortillas at the end of each day, fry them up and add seasoning. Archibald West, a vice president at the Frito-Lay company, noted their popularity at Disneyland, and struck a deal to begin manufacturing Doritos nationwide. In 1994 Frito-Lay launched a two-year market-research study into Doritos, involving 5,000 crisp-eaters. At the end of the two years, Doritos were made 20 per cent larger, 15 per cent thinner and, crucially, had their sharp corners rounded off. The whole redesign exercise cost over $50 million. Which sounds a lot but, given that Doritos had sales of $1.2 billion in 1993, they could probably afford it.

Are Mini Cheddars a crisp? Well, you buy them in the crisp aisle with the crisps (this is like Jaffa Cakes all over again), they come in all sorts of flavours, and you get them in your school lunchbox. When this debate raged on Twitter, one of my wisest correspondents suggested a law.

If it counts as a packet of crisps in the Boots Meal Deal, then it's a crisp.

WRITE YOUR WINNER IN BOX 3 ON THE WALLCHART

PICKLED ONION MONSTER MUNCH vs SQUARES

And so we meet the winners of the Twitter World Cup of Crisps: Pickled Onion Monster Munch. They were launched by Smith's crisps in 1977 as 'The Prime Monster', a weak pun on 'Prime Minister' that, for some reason, the kids of Britain failed to go crazy for. In 1978 the decision was made to relaunch the snack under the new name 'Monster Munch'. I am going to go on record as saying that this was the single wisest decision in snack history. Monster Munch are now sold under the Walkers brand.

Squares are another Smith's invention to have been rebadged as Walkers. Squares were invented because scientists were concerned that children weren't hurting the roofs of their mouths as often as they should be.

WRITE YOUR WINNER IN BOX 4 ON THE WALLCHART

NICE 'N' SPICY NIK NAKS vs WALKERS SALT & VINEGAR

The Nik Nak is an 'extruded corn snack' launched by Sooner Snacks in 1981. It launched with four flavours: Nice 'n' Spicy,

Rib 'n' Saucy, Pickle 'n' Onion and Scampi 'n' Lemon. Scampi 'n' Lemon were justly famous for being the smelliest crisp in the history of snacking. Nik Naks were bought by Golden Wonder in the late 1980s, then sold to United Biscuits, who in turn sold them on to a company I had not previously heard of, but now want to work for: the Intersnack Group.

Walkers was founded by Henry Walker in Leicester in 1948 and, though it was sold to the American Frito-Lay company in 1989, their Leicester factory remains the biggest crisp-production plant in the world, producing over 11 million bags of crisps a day.

WRITE YOUR WINNER IN BOX 5 ON THE WALLCHART

6 TAYTO CHEESE & ONION vs STEAK McCOY'S

If you want to talk about true crisp pioneers then I'm afraid Henry Walker and Frank Smith have nothing on Joe 'Spud' Murphy, the founder of Ireland's Tayto Crisps. In the mid-1950s Murphy, along with one of his chief scientists, Seamus Burke, started experimenting with adding flavouring to crisps during the production process. Up to that point, crisps only came flavoured with salt, and even that had to be added after opening the packet. Not only did Joe Murphy and Seamus Burke succeed in their quest, but literally the first two flavours they created were Cheese & Onion and Salt & Vinegar, still the two most popular crisps flavourings over sixty years later.

According to their former owner, United Biscuits, McCoy's are 'the only overtly male-targeted crisp brand', which hadn't occurred to me before. They are the Yorkie or Coke Zero of crisps.

WRITE YOUR WINNER IN BOX 6 ON THE WALLCHART

FRAZZLES vs SPICY TOMATO WHEAT CRUNCHIES

You really have to take your hat off to whoever was working in product design at Smith's crisps in the mid-1970s. Just two years before creating the magnificent Monster Munch, they also came up with Frazzles. Also, a special shout-out to Leslie Ivey, a tool-maker at Smith's West London factory, who built the very first machine to put the iconic stripes on a Frazzle. Not all heroes wear capes. Quite apart from being iconic and delicious, Frazzles are suitable for vegetarians.

Wheat Crunchies performed surprisingly well in the Twitter World Cup, knocking out both Discos and Walkers Prawn Cocktail. They were another invention of Sooner Snacks in the early 1980s. Tragically I have just discovered that they no longer make individual packs of Worcester Sauce Wheat Crunchies. Wake up Britain!

WRITE YOUR WINNER IN BOX 7 ON THE WALLCHART

8 POM-BEARS vs SOUR CREAM & CHIVE PRINGLES

Pom-Bears also put up a sterling performance in the Twitter World Cup, knocking out Walkers Roast Chicken and also defeating the king of posh crisps, Tyrrells Salt & Vinegar. If you like eating tiny, nude, potato bears, then they are the snack for you.

The shape of Pringles – a hyperbolic paraboloid – and the tube in which they are still sold, were both developed by Procter & Gamble research scientist Fredric Baur between 1956 and 1958. So proud was Baur of this work that when he passed away in 2008, his ashes were, genuinely, buried in a Pringles tube. Which goes to prove that even when you pop off, you can't stop.

WRITE YOUR WINNER IN BOX 8 ON THE WALLCHART

 9 DISCOS vs WALKERS READY SALTED

Discos are the most salt and vinegary crisps in history. It's like they were mild-mannered, unassuming crisps, just going about their business, until one day they were bitten by some radioactive salt and vinegar at a crisp factory, and it gave them superpowers. Eat a packet of Discos and your lips will hurt for days.

Walkers Ready Salted crisps are the best-selling crisps in Britain, which I find extraordinary. 'Ready Salted' isn't even a flavour; it's an absence of a flavour. Don't let Ready Salted Walkers win the World Cup of Crisps. It would be like letting Sugar Flavour win the World Cup of Ice Cream or Flour Flavour win the World Cup of Biscuits.

WRITE YOUR WINNER IN BOX 9 ON THE WALLCHART

10 SKIPS vs GOLDEN WONDER CHEESE & ONION

While Smith's crisps were busy developing Monster Munch and Frazzles, KP Snacks were also making snack history, with the 1974 launch of Skips. They didn't actually invent Skips, but started to sell them under licence from the Japanese pharmaceutical and confectionery company, Meiji Seika. You know,

Meiji Seika, the makers of Hello Panda biscuits and Yan Yan chocolate dips? No, me neither. To think that in just seven years from the start of the 1970s, Britain had been introduced to Wotsits, Skips, Frazzles and Monster Munch. The 1970s were for crisps what the 1990s were for the Internet.

I felt I had to include Golden Wonder for purposes of nostalgia. In the 'Golden Age of the Crisps' (1970s, as just discussed) they were the big hitters, the dominant brand, the IBM of crisps. But they were crushed by the Google, Apple and Facebook of Walkers, and had to be rescued from administration by Tayto in 2006. The shift between Golden Wonder and Walkers also led to the greatest cultural shift of twentieth-century Britain, namely Salt & Vinegar crisps going from blue packets to green packets, and Cheese & Onion changing from green packets to blue packets. In terms of impact, it dwarfs decimalisation, Brexit and when Robbie first left Take That.

WRITE YOUR WINNER IN BOX 10 ON THE WALLCHART

11 PICKLED ONION SPACE RAIDERS vs WALKERS SMOKY BACON

Riding the end of the 1970s crisp boom were KP's Space Raiders. They cost 10p when introduced, and unbelievably stayed at exactly the same price for the next twenty-seven years. When the price went up to 15p in 2007, KP executives received death threats. Each crisp is in the shape of an alien head, and the Pickled Onion Space Raiders were originally green, until EU food-colouring laws forced a change. Now we are out of the EU, I think reverting back to the original colour of Space Raiders should be a bigger priority than reverting back to blue passports.

Walkers started out as a butcher's shop, and it wasn't until after the Second World War that meat rationing forced them to diversify. Managing director R.E. Gerrard had noted the burgeoning popularity of potato crisps and decided to shift the company's focus. From that very moment an empire was born. Smoky Bacon seems a fitting tribute to Walkers' origins, even though, strictly speaking, they are vegetarian.

WRITE YOUR WINNER IN BOX 11 ON THE WALLCHART

12 ROAST BEEF MONSTER MUNCH vs WALKERS THAI SWEET CHILLI SENSATIONS

The shape of Monster Munch is designed to represent a monster's feet and toes, rather than, as some people believe, the eye and eyelashes of a monster. I honestly don't think that the eyelashes of a monster are ever its scariest feature. Perhaps if they were swords or lasers? Or if they'd forgotten to take last night's mascara off? Anyway, all these years you've been biting off monsters' toes, not monsters' eyelashes. Monster Munch launched a line of soft drinks in the 1980s. It was about as successful as if Vimto had started making crisps.

Sensations are Walkers successful attempt to break into the 'posh crisps' market. Posh crisps are different to normal crisps because they enable you to pay much more money for roughly the same thing. They also enable you to eat an entire packet in front of *Line of Duty* and feel sophisticated, rather than ashamed and regretful. Thai Sweet Chilli Sensations got all the way through to the quarter-finals in the Twitter World Cup, losing out narrowly to Walkers Cheese & Onion.

WRITE YOUR WINNER IN BOX 12 ON THE WALLCHART

13 QUAVERS vs BRANNIGANS ROAST BEEF & MUSTARD

If I were to ask you when Quavers were launched you would confidently say the 1970s, but you'd be wrong. Quavers were actually launched in 1968, the first of the big corn and maize snacks that remain with us today. That means that scientists invented Quavers roughly a year before scientists managed to land a man on the moon. It is not historically recorded, but one imagines that the team at NASA were inspired by the lab team at Smith's crisps.

According to the KP Snacks website, a Mr Brannigan, an Irish shopkeeper, took his 'popular crisps' to America to sell on a market stall, and they proved an 'instant hit'. However, I can find no independent source for this, unless you count the picture of the jolly 'old time' shopkeeper on the front of the packets as evidence. Quite apart from the fact that KP don't even seem to know Mr Brannigan's first name, I am even less inclined to believe this romantic origin myth when KP Snacks go on to say: 'now the crisps that still carry his name are a firmly established favourite, particularly in the on-trade and foodservice sectors'.

WRITE YOUR WINNER IN BOX 13 ON THE WALLCHART

14 McCOY'S SALT & MALT VINEGAR vs WALKERS PRAWN COCKTAIL

The name 'McCoy's' is inspired by the common expression 'the real McCoy', meaning something genuine and unique. Brilliantly there are four different explanations of where the phrase 'the real McCoy' comes from, and no one can agree on which one is genuine.

Gary Lineker has been the face of Walkers crisps since 1994, one of the longest and most successful endorsement campaigns in advertising history. It is not known exactly how much money he has made from his various deals over the years, but even the very first contract he signed with Walkers back in 1994 was worth £200,000. So let's assume it's a lot.

WRITE YOUR WINNER IN BOX 14 ON THE WALLCHART

15 SEA SALT & CRUSHED BLACK PEPPERCORNS KETTLE CHIPS vs DORITOS COOL ORIGINAL

By the name, you can tell that Kettle Chips are an American invention, first made by Cameron Healy in Salem, Oregon, in 1982. However, the name is misleading in one way, because they are not actually made in a kettle, they are made in a factory on the outskirts of Norwich. Kettle Chips are posh crisps, in the same way that Ferrero Rocher are posh chocolates, and Viennetta is posh ice cream.

I have already mentioned that Archibald West was the man who popularised Doritos in the US. Incredibly, much like Fredric Baur and his Pringles tube, when West died in 2011 he had crushed Doritos crumbled into his grave.

WRITE YOUR WINNER IN BOX 15 ON THE WALLCHART

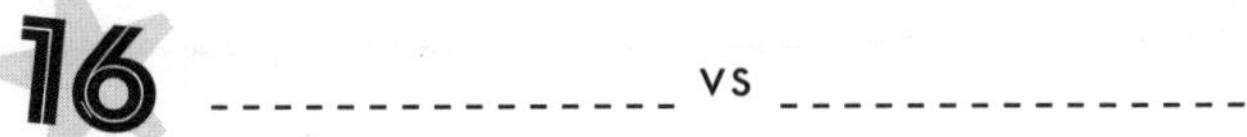

Here's your wild-card battle, and you have plenty to choose from. Just a few of the snacks I've missed out include: Walkers Roast Chicken; Tyrrell's entire range of posh crisps; Spicy Tomato Snaps; Popchips, Pringles Texas BBQ Sauce; Salt & Vinegar and, if you absolutely must, Original Salt & Shake; French Fries; Burton's Fish 'n' Chips; the superior flavours of Hula Hoops; the other manly flavours of McCoy's, such as Sizzling King Prawn and Mexican Chilli; or even Scampi Fries if you're feeling adventurous. And of course, depending on where you are, you may well want to include some of the crisp heroes from your area, such as Mackie's, Seabrook and Tayto. But please, no Paprika, even if you are German.

WRITE YOUR WINNER IN BOX 16 ON THE WALLCHART

CRISPS

THE WORLD CUP OF EVERYTHING

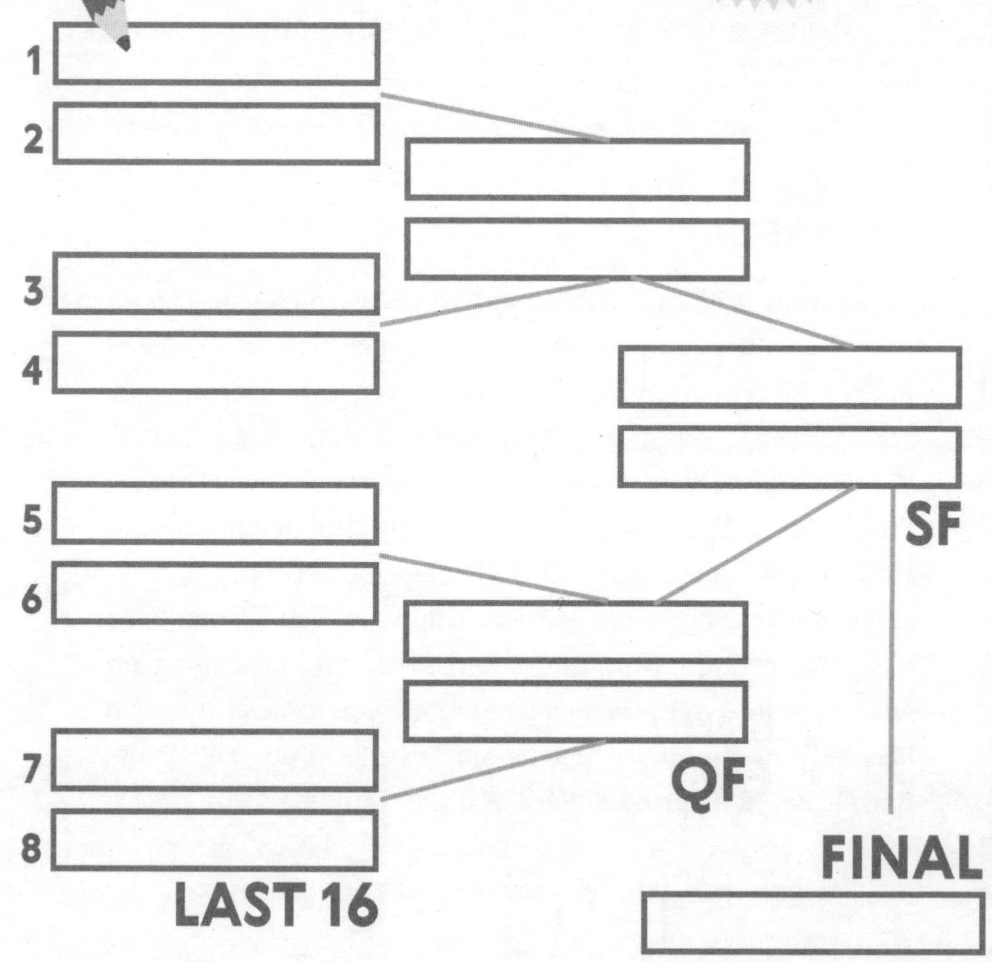

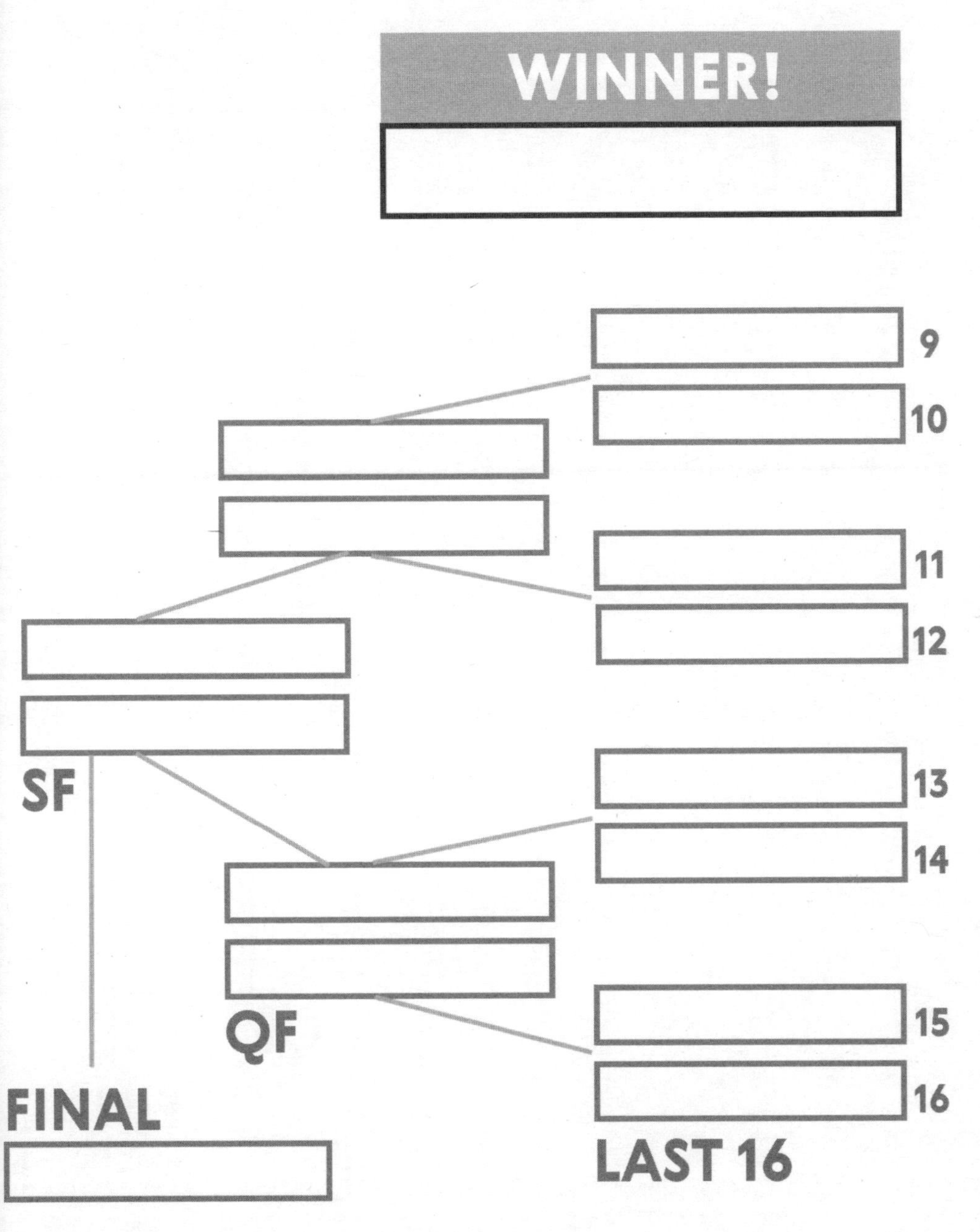

WINNER!
9
10
11
12
SF
13
14
QF
15
16
FINAL
LAST 16

WORLD CUP OF RESTAURANTS

When you walk into Nando's, do they ask 'The usual, Keith?' Is Domino's listed before 'Mum' on your speed-dial? Have you ever been to a Harvester before? You *have*? Then I think you are ready for the World Cup of Restaurants.

When I was young we simply didn't have restaurants. Maybe in London they did, but nobody lived in London in those days. British Home Stores had a canteen, and once a year, on my nan's birthday, we would go to a carvery, but a world of McDonald's, Zizzi and Pizza Hut was pure science fiction. Imagine if you'd told us about sushi? It would have blown our minds. Raw fish on a conveyor belt? Yeah, right, and who's President? Donald Trump?

But there are now endless opportunities to avoid cooking and washing up. If you are lazy enough, you can even get your meal delivered to your door. Or if not your door, then the door of someone in the next street, because the guy on the motorbike is new and, for some reason, they don't trust him with a phone. The only effort left in the whole process is actually eating the food, and someone will soon come up with an app that will do that for you. I should warn you that, even though it sounds plausible, Grindr is not that app.

For the World Cup of Restaurants I have used a fairly loose definition of 'restaurant', but I have only included restaurants you would find the length and breadth of the country. So, for example, Heston Blumenthal is not represented here, but Colonel Sanders is. If Heston ever opens up a Kentucky Steam-Bathed Chicken, he can make the list. Though I bet Heston would make you eat the actual bucket too.

I've included anywhere you might sit down, or anywhere you might reasonably order a takeaway from. Basically anywhere you can buy a hot meal without having to cook it. I have also included a very select pair of establishments which bend the definition of 'restaurant' but which are used in such a way that they just about qualify. Or, to put it in a way that people from the South and the North will understand, I have included Pret A Manger and Greggs.

Again, I have a few little lists and quizzes, and things I would consider fun, but you are free to disagree.

★ CHALLENGE! ★

Time for a quiz I call 'I Honestly Don't Have a Clue How Old Greggs is!'

Can you place the following eight restaurants in the order of when their first ever branch opened worldwide? McDONALD'S, PIZZA EXPRESS, GREGGS, NANDO'S, JAMIE'S ITALIAN, KFC, YO! SUSHI and HARRY RAMSDEN'S.

1. 1928 ____________
2. 1939 ____________
3. 1940 ____________
4. 1952 ____________
5. 1965 ____________
6. 1987 ____________
7. 1997 ____________
8. 2008 ____________

One point for each restaurant in the right year! Answers at the back of the book.

★ ARGUMENT! ★

Here is a series of my opinions that you will disagree with. Argue among yourselves, then take a vote.

BEST BURGER – Five Guys Bacon Cheeseburger
No Richard, you loon, it is actually ____________

BEST PIZZA – Domino's Pepperoni Passion
You are a joke Osman; the answer is ____________

BEST NANDO'S FLAVOUR – Lemon & Herb
Ahahahahahahahahahaha! No, it's ____________

BEST PASTRY-BASED SNACK – Greggs Jumbo Sausage Roll
Agreed

BEST THING TO HAVE WITH CHIPS – Only vinegar
Incorrect; it is ____________ and ____________ and maybe ____________ too.

★ CHALLENGE! ★

We all know the excitement of turning up in a foreign city, maybe for a stag do or to hunt for a missing golden amulet, spotting a McDonald's and finding out that the menu is *slightly different* to the UK. Here are ten dishes you might find in McDonald's restaurants around the world. Five of them are absolutely real, and five of them are entirely made up by me. Unless McDonald's read this and immediately decide to buy the rights to them.

McFalafel - Egypt
Squid McNuggets - Japan
Fig Mac - Lebanon
Mung Bean Ice Cream - Hong Kong
Beef Torpedo - New Zealand
McD Chicken Porridge - Malaysia
McToast - Greece
Double-fried McPizza Burger - USA
McGuineaPig Sandwich - Chile
Stroopwafel McFlurry - Netherlands

Answers at the back of the book.

★ ARGUMENT! ★

Are the following things in restaurants acceptable or unacceptable? I have given my opinion too. Start arguing . . . now!

PINEAPPLE ON A PIZZA – Absolutely unacceptable. You wouldn't put pepperoni in a fruit salad.

RED WINE WITH FISH – Acceptable. Any booze with any food is fine by me. Gin with chips, vodka with saveloys, WKD with Viennetta, I'm not fussy.

ORDERING TWO CHILD MEALS INSTEAD OF ONE ADULT ONE – Acceptable. Sometimes they don't have fish fingers and smiley faces on the adult menu so this is your only option.

NOT ORDERING CHIPS AND THEN STEALING SOMEBODY ELSE'S CHIPS – Absolutely 100 per cent unacceptable. This is the worst thing you can do in a restaurant. Except for not ordering pudding and then stealing someone else's pudding.

HAVING A MIX OF COKE, SPRITE AND FANTA FROM THE MACHINE – Not just acceptable, but compulsory.

SENDING FOOD BACK BECAUSE THERE IS SOMETHING WRONG WITH IT – Completely acceptable but, thanks to being British, not something I have ever done or will ever do. I wouldn't do it even if I was Liam Neeson in *Taken* and all I had to do to save my family was to mention to a waiter that my lasagne was still frozen in the middle.

OKAY, HERE WE GO: it's time for the World Cup of Restaurants. Don't forget, everyone votes for their favourite in each of these pairings to find the winners. Using your pen, write down the scores, then fill in each of the winners on your wallchart. In case of a tie, either argue for a further twenty minutes or order pizzas from two separate restaurants and see which arrives first.

1 McDONALD'S vs CAFÉ ROUGE

The Chicken McNugget was invented in 1979 by McDonald's first 'executive chef' Rene Arend. Within four years of the

McNugget being introduced, McDonald's was the second-largest buyer of chickens in the world (the largest was some guy in Sunderland; no idea what he was up to). According to McDonald's, the McNugget comes in four distinct shapes: the bell, the bow-tie, the ball and the boot. Lucky they don't come in five distinct shapes, as they are running out of things beginning with 'B' that McNuggets look like.

Café Rouge probably also has an 'executive chef', but as he or she didn't invent the McNugget we don't know their name.

WRITE YOUR WINNER IN BOX 1 ON THE WALLCHART

2 PIZZA EXPRESS vs HARVESTER

Pizza Express is now over fifty years old and has over four hundred UK restaurants. In the evening it is the perfect place to watch people on awkward first dates desperately trying to ignore the enormous pepper grinders, while at lunchtime it is the ideal spot to watch parents of toddlers regret their decision to have children.

Harvester is most famous for its all-you-can-eat salad carts. Hey Harvester, call me back when you've got an all-you-can-eat Chocolate Orange cart.

WRITE YOUR WINNER IN BOX 2 ON THE WALLCHART

3 LOCAL INDIAN vs GIRAFFE

Everyone has a favourite Indian restaurant, and everyone always has exactly the same meal when they go there. It is a rite of passage whenever you move to a new area: the first time the woman on the phone at your local Indian recognises your voice. It is proof that you have successfully integrated into your new community. Be honest, if you died, your local Indian takeaway would probably be the first people to raise the alarm.

If you don't have a Giraffe in your area, this match-up is going to look bizarre. But I promise it is a restaurant. It was briefly owned by Tesco for reasons best known to themselves, and it has branches from Inverness to Bournemouth. I suspect that Giraffe will do better in World Cup of Animals than in World Cup of Restaurants.

WRITE YOUR WINNER IN BOX 3 ON THE WALLCHART

4 WAGAMAMA vs IKEA CAFÉ

Wagamama has pulled off one of the greatest tricks in the history of the restaurant trade. When you first go there they let you know that it is traditional in Asian cuisine to serve food when it is ready, so all the dishes will come out at different times. You, of course, think this is quite wonderful and authentic, and it adds to your enjoyment of noodles with a boiled egg floating in it. Therefore they have successfully sidestepped the single most difficult aspect of running a restaurant, which is getting everyone's meals to arrive at the same time. It is genuinely clever. Even as you finish your Chicken Katsu Curry before your son's Chilli Chicken Ramen has arrived, you still congratulate yourself on enjoying a traditional Japanese dining experience. Even though you are in Basingstoke and you've had to order another Diet Coke just to have something to do while he's eating.

IKEA calls its café a restaurant, but then IKEA has a workbench called a 'Fartfull' and a computer desk called a 'Jerker', so we shouldn't always trust them. I do love the IKEA café though. After an hour of weeping, forgetting what you came in for and then panic-buying coat hangers, it's nice to settle down to a plate of meatballs or smoked and dried elk sausage.

WRITE YOUR WINNER IN BOX 4 ON THE WALLCHART

GREASY SPOON vs DOMINO'S

A battle that really highlights the socio-economic and geo-political changes in how Britain likes to get fat. The traditional greasy-spoon café is dying out in huge numbers as its customers also die out in huge numbers. But you simply can't beat all-day breakfasts, builder's tea, white bread and butter, bacon sandwiches and beans with everything. Whether you're hungover or about to start drinking, just finished a hard day's work or just about to start one, there surely can be nothing better.

In 1960 James and Tom Monaghan bought DomiNick's pizza restaurant in Michigan. They soon had three restaurants and decided to rebrand them as 'Domino's' (the three dots on the logo represented the three restaurants and they originally planned to add extra dots for each new restaurant). At this point, James decided the business was getting in the way of his day job as a postman, so he sold his half of the business to Tom for a second-hand Volkswagen Beetle. Tom ran the business for the next thirty-eight years, until he sold his share for over $1 billion. Oops.

WRITE YOUR WINNER IN BOX 5 ON THE WALLCHART

 NANDO'S vs CHIQUITO

Sometimes it's easy to see how you can make money in the restaurant business. Everybody likes burgers, everybody likes pizza; just do that better or cheaper than other people, buy half of the business from your brother in return for a car, and retire with a billion dollars. But what if you were a Portuguese sound engineer in 1987 and you walked into a restaurant called Chickenland in a Johannesburg suburb and enjoyed how they'd cooked your chicken in a Mozambican sauce called peri-peri. Would you spot the opportunity? Well, that's exactly what Fernando Duarte did. I say Fernando; he was, of course, 'Nando' to his friends.

Chiquitos is the UK's best-known Tex-Mex chain and I have never been in one. But I promise I will. There's one in Cambridge, but it's right next to a Nando's so I've never felt the need.

WRITE YOUR WINNER IN BOX 6 ON THE WALLCHART

 ALL-YOU-CAN-EAT BUFFET vs CARLUCCIO'S

All-you-can-eat buffets originated in – surprise, surprise – Las Vegas, but are now huge business in the UK. One of the key advantages is that many of them now do a range of different cuisines (I am using the word 'cuisine' loosely here). Why go for a Chinese or an Indian or Italian when you can go to all of them at once? And why choose to eat from a menu? Simply choose to eat the whole menu.

In Carluccio's, for example, you can have a lovely ravioli with sage, butter and Parmesan. But you can't have it with chicken tikka, egg-fried noodles, sesame prawn toast and chips on top. I mean, you do the maths right?

WRITE YOUR WINNER IN BOX 7 ON THE WALLCHART

8 BELLA ITALIA vs LOCAL CHIPPY

I worked with a very young James Corden many years ago and he had, until recently, been working as a waiter at the High Wycombe Bella Italia (or Bella Pasta as it was then; a lot has changed). He said that whenever a customer would ask him to 'thank the chef' for their meal, he would reply that they had no chef but he would pass on the thanks to whoever was on 'food assembly' that day. But, equally, I remember that some of my daughter's first ever steps were taken in the Bella Pasta in St Albans, and that makes me a bit teary. She is now eighteen and really, really good at walking, so another change there.

The local chippy is very, very hard to beat though. At my local chip shop when I was a kid you could have the regular cod, haddock or plaice but they also served huss. It occurred to me that I have never heard that name since, so I just looked it up. It's a small shark!!!! I was eating shark!!!!! Why didn't they call it *that*? Oh man, all these years and I never realised I used to eat shark and chips.

I think you know where my vote is going on this one.

WRITE YOUR WINNER IN BOX 8 ON THE WALLCHART

BURGER KING vs PRET A MANGER

The very first Burger King was opened after Keith Kramer and Matthew Burns visited the first ever McDonald's in the 1950s, and there are now over 15,000 Burger Kings worldwide. However, Burger King was not set up by an actual king, has no members of royalty on its current board, and the crowns they give out at children's parties are fake and have very little actual monetary value. Very disappointing. No wonder they call it the home of the whopper.

Pret A Manger has around 400 branches, including forty-three in New York, sixteen in Hong Kong, fourteen in Paris – where they find the name *very* boring – but only two in the whole of Wales. There are also currently more branches of Pret A Manger in Dubai than there are in Northern Ireland. There is no news of how the Northern Irish are currently coping without £3.49 rocket and crayfish sandwiches. Belfast alone has seven Burger Kings though, so I suspect they're okay.

WRITE YOUR WINNER IN BOX 9 ON THE WALLCHART

10 ZIZZI vs WELCOME BREAK

Zizzi is yet another chain of Italian restaurants. It's amazing that the Italians pretty much invented pasta and pizza. They surely have the greatest carbohydrate versatility of any country. It is no surprise that there are countless Italian and pizza chains up and down the UK but almost no French ones. Even Café Rouge is English. The French have long prided themselves on being the international centre of fine dining, but despite centuries of exposure to it, the British have simply never taken French food to their hearts. I mean, we like baguettes, but that's about it. Sorry France.

There are thirty-five Welcome Breaks in the UK, all at motorway service stations, and their headquarters are, perhaps inevitably, in Newport Pagnell. Motorway service areas are the ideal place to take a rest, stretch your legs and refuel both your vehicle and yourself. Other things you can do in motorway service stations include accidentally driving into the coach parking bit and feeling intimidated, paying way too much for a packet of Skips, not being able to go to the toilets because your route is blocked by French exchange students playing arcade machines, and wondering which of the tired men you see slumped over a coffee and a ham baguette will go on to kill.

WRITE YOUR WINNER IN BOX 10 ON THE WALLCHART

11 KFC vs GBK

The battle of the initials. The USP of KFC is AOK. Eat too much, though, and your BMI will be OMG. KFC is the second-largest fast-food chain in the world after McDonald's, thanks in no small part to its widespread success in China, which is now KFC's largest single market. I have eaten in the KFC in Shanghai and, if you visit, I would recommend having the chicken.

GBK, or Gourmet Burger Kitchen, was set up by a gang of expat New Zealanders and was the first of the new wave of artisan burger joints to make it big. Other notable New Zealand exports include Phillip Schofield. I recently read that, come the apocalypse, New Zealand will be the best place to flee to, so maybe it's worth visiting GBK now so you can get used to the food.

WRITE YOUR WINNER IN BOX 11 ON THE WALLCHART

12 **HUNGRY HORSE** vs **PIZZA HUT**

Hungry Horse is a chain of over 200 pub-restaurants in the UK with a family-friendly atmosphere, and at one point had a burger on its menu called the Double Donut, which contained almost 2,000 calories. But did it ever sell shark and chips? It probably did, yes.

Pizza Hut is the largest pizza chain in the world, with over 15,000 branches, including many in China and even one in Iraq. I have to say that I prefer Domino's, so I am not a frequent visitor. Expect that to change though if I ever get that job on *Iraqi Countdown*.

WRITE YOUR WINNER IN BOX 12 ON THE WALLCHART

13 YO! SUSHI vs GREGGS

Well, your vote on this one is going to say an awful lot about the type of people you hang out with. I would be firmly on the side of Greggs, but I see the fun appeal of a Yo! Sushi. So really my perfect restaurant would be a Greggs with a conveyor belt. And the conveyor belt could go through an oven to keep everything warm. Now I come to think about it, I'm going to open one myself and call it Dough! Sushi.

WRITE YOUR WINNER IN BOX 13 ON THE WALLCHART

14 WIMPY vs JAMIE'S ITALIAN

Yes, there are still Wimpys in the UK. In fact, at last count there were eighty-one. You will be glad to hear that they still serve their famous Bender in a Bun and there is no sign of pulled pork or salted caramel anywhere. If you go on their website you can even become a franchisee, and by this time next year you could be running your very own Wimpy which, let's face it, would be a great story at parties.

Jamie's Italian is more expensive than Wimpy and, at last

visit, was not serving Bender in a Bun. But you can have a Truffle Shuffle Pizza, which probably amounts to the same thing. You can also order a Prosciutto Board, which I think they should rename Oliver's salArmy.

I honestly don't know what I would vote on this one.

WRITE YOUR WINNER IN BOX 14 ON THE WALLCHART

15 LOCAL CHINESE vs FRANKIE & BENNY'S

When the National Lottery first started in the 1990s we used to select our numbers based on our favourite dishes from the local Chinese. We never won anything, but on that first draw in 1994 if you lived in Kentish Town and you liked 3. Sweet & Sour Pork Balls in Batter, 5. King Prawn Curry, 14. Chinese Greens in Oyster Sauce, 22. Deep Fried Bean Curd, 30. Chicken Fried Rice and 40. a Lilt, you would have won £10 million.

On the Frankie & Benny's website you can read the heart-warming story of ten-year-old Frankie leaving Sicily in 1924, and meeting Benny in New York's Little Italy, with the two boys eventually taking over Benny's family's neighbourhood restaurant in 1953. Which is nice, but Frankie & Benny's is actually owned by Restaurant Group PLC and they opened their first restaurant in Leicester in 1995. Still, they do pipe in Italian language lessons to the loos, which is pretty cool.

WRITE YOUR WINNER IN BOX 15 ON THE WALLCHART

Match 16 is the wild-card match. If you feel that there are competitors I've left out of the World Cup of Restaurants then you can write them in here. A few establishments you might consider include your local kebab shop or Chicken Cottage. There are no Thai or Caribbean restaurants on the list. So you could either write those in above or you could launch a UK-wide chain of Thai or Caribbean restaurants and make a fortune. I have an idea for a Thai-Australian fusion restaurant that shows the football. It's called Thai Me Kangaroo Down Sport.

WRITE YOUR WINNER IN BOX 16 ON THE WALLCHART

RESTAURANTS

THE WORLD CUP OF EVERYTHING

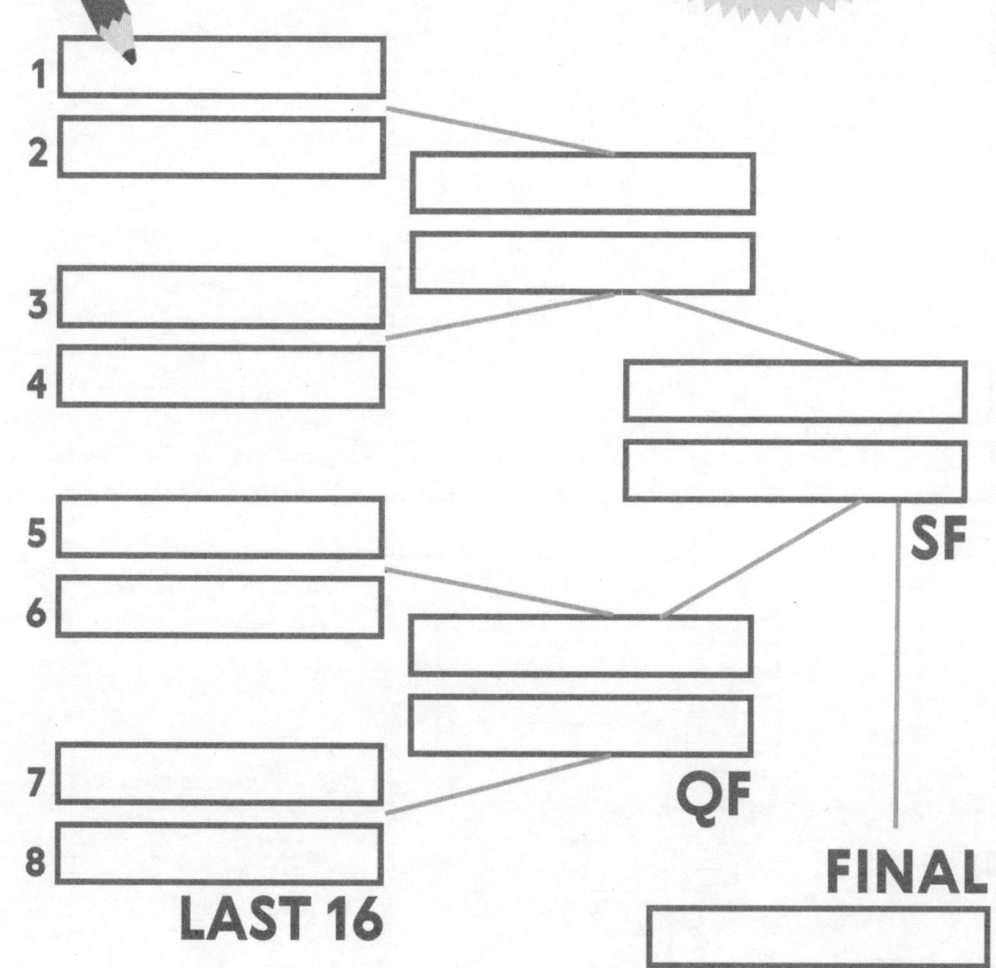

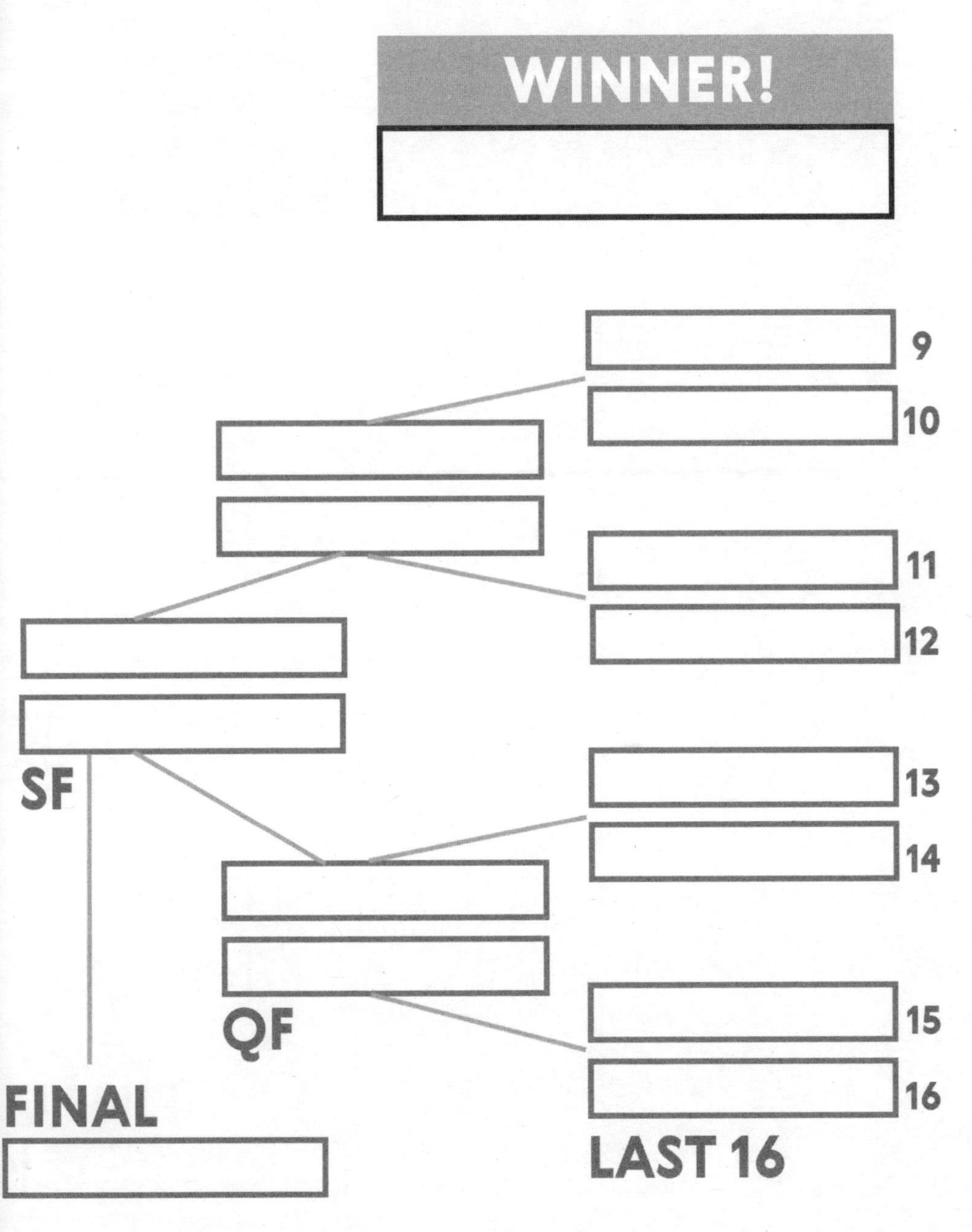
WINNER!
9
10
11
12
13
14
15
16
SF
QF
FINAL
LAST 16

WORLD CUP OF BRITISH BANDS

There are some things that the British are definitely the best in the world at.

Off the top of my head we are the best in the world at playing snooker, eating crisps, queuing for anything, defeating fascism, eating scones, getting sunburnt, aerospace technology, apologising when things aren't our fault, drinking milky tea, walking dogs even though it's raining, daytime quiz shows, bespoke tailoring, financial services, writing about wizards, applauding when someone drops a tray in a restaurant, binge drinking, avoiding eye contact on public transport, sense of fair play, winning world wars as and when they crop up, inventing Mint Viennetta, watching programmes about posh but brilliant detectives, not taking ourselves too seriously, keeping calm, carrying on, having a Royal Family, discussing the weather, going out dressed for yesterday's weather, becoming borderline-obsessed with weather presenters, paying our tax, loving animals, tutting, darts, playing Americans in films, losing gracefully, loving the underdog, country pubs, theatre, building Stonehenge, watching tennis for two weeks a year, fighting for our Health Service, whisky, fish and chips, Sunday roasts, managing to turn breakfast into a 2,000-calorie meal, standing in the right place on escalators, spying, planning Hatton Garden jewellery heists in our seventies, making apple crumble, writing Elizabethan plays, developing and then largely believing in the theory of evolution, inventing the Internet, the steam engine, passenger trains, chocolate bars, the telephone, the light bulb, the thermos flask, the tank, the television, the jet engine, the Chocolate Orange, the automatic kettle, *Downton Abbey* and the Chuckle Brothers.

But above all, the one thing the British are best at in the world is music. We are the undisputed kings and queens. Take a look at the incredible talent on display in the World Cup of British Bands, and then reflect on the fact that in the last sixty years the only bands the rest of the world has really given us are Van Halen, A-Ha and those two guys who did 'Macarena'.

★ CHALLENGE! ★

I have run the names of a number of classic, and not so classic, British bands through the French Google Translate. But who are the ten bands below? I have ranked them from easiest to hardest, so if you find yourself struggling with the first clue it might be time to stop drinking. This little gang have had over 180 UK top ten hits and thirty-five number one singles between them.

1. MODE DEPECHE
2. MANOEUVRES D'ORCHESTRE DANS LE NOIR
3. TETE DE RADIO
4. EST DIX-SEPT
5. HUMIDE HUMIDE HUMIDE
6. BEBES DE SUCRE
7. LES PIERRES QUI ROULENT
8. PREND CA!
9. JEU FROID
10. PREDICATEUSE DU RUE MANIAQUE
11. LE TRAITEMENT
12. PETIT MELANGE

13. BROUILLER
14. LES FORGERONS
15. COUDE

Answers at the back of the book.

★ ONE-HIT WONDERS! ★

Below is a list of ten UK hit singles that proved to be far and away the biggest hit for the British bands involved. I have given you the initials of the songs, followed by the initials of the band, the year the song was released and its highest chart position.

1. MMAMCAD by BAM (number 1 in 1978)
2. VKTRS by TB (1 in 1980)
3. TJ by TV (3 in 1980)
4. TOAO by CH (1 in 1991)
5. I by S (1 in 1994)
6. S by BZ (1 in 1996)
7. T by C (2 in 1997)
8. YW by WT (1 in 1997)

9. BOA by C (1 in 1998)
10. JCBS by N (1 in 2005)

Answers at the back of the book.

★ ARGUMENT! ★

Which is the greatest American band of all time? British bands are obviously better than bands from all other countries. However, I did start having a little think about which American bands would hold their own in this company. There are strong arguments for the Beach Boys, of course, or someone boring like The Doors. How about some classic US metal bands like Guns N' Roses. Metallica or Aerosmith? Britain has never produced a hip-hop band with the fierce brilliance of Public Enemy; R.E.M. are kind of the American Smiths; Red Hot Chili Peppers are kind of the American Shakin' Stevens. I also thought about Talking Heads, The Ramones, Blondie, Velvet Underground, Sly and The Family Stone or The White Stripes. So what would your choice be? Taking everything into consideration, my vote for the greatest US band of all time is . . . Nirvana.

Richard, once again you have shown you are not to be trusted. The greatest American band of all time is, in fact, ----------------

★ INFORMATION! ★

These are the record sales of the biggest-selling British acts in history. For this chart I've also included solo performers, because I thought it was interesting.

1. THE BEATLES (400m estimated worldwide record sales)
2. ELTON JOHN (350m)
3. LED ZEPPELIN (320m)
4. QUEEN (300m)
5. CLIFF RICHARD (260m)
6. THE ROLLING STONES (210m)
7. PINK FLOYD (200m)
8. GENESIS (150m)
8. PHIL COLLINS (150m)
10. DAVID BOWIE (145m)

Other UK acts to sell over 100 million records include The Who, Shirley Bassey, The Dave Clark Five, Paul McCartney, Rod Stewart, Deep Purple, Status Quo, Iron Maiden, Dire Straits, Depeche Mode, George Michael, the Pet Shop Boys and Adele.

SO, IT'S NOW TIME FOR THE WORLD CUP OF BRITISH BANDS. Do feel free to turn this whole exercise into an impromptu karaoke session. If votes are tied at any point, the first person to recite the entire chorus of 'Agadoo' by Black Lace gets the casting vote.

1 WHAM! vs BLUR

Wham! released the best-selling single in the history of the UK charts never to go to number one. 'Last Christmas' has so far sold over 2 million copies in the UK. Incredibly it was also the biggest-selling single in the history of the Japanese charts never to reach the top ten, the biggest-selling Christmas single in German chart history despite only peaking at number four, and has sold almost 1 million copies in the USA without ever climbing higher than a chart position of fifty. In the UK it was kept off the number one slot on its original release by 'Do They Know It's Christmas?'. Not only did George Michael also sing on that song, but he and Andrew Ridgeley donated all of the proceeds from 'Last Christmas' to Ethiopian famine charities. One of many classy acts from this class act.

This will be a tough battle for Blur to win, but they have a long and illustrious history of almost endless success. They managed to beat Oasis in the battle of Britpop, they've won five Brit Awards, eleven NME Awards, an Ivor Novello Award, seven Q Awards and even two Smash Hits Awards. In a rare slip, drummer Dave Rowntree was a defeated Labour parliamentary candidate in 2010, but this failure was more than offset by bassist Alex James winning Best Goat's Cheese at the 2008 British Cheese Awards for his Farleigh Wallop.

WRITE YOUR WINNER IN BOX 1 ON THE WALLCHART

While an unheralded Pink Floyd were recording their first album *The Piper at the Gates of Dawn* at Abbey Road Studios, The Beatles were recording *Sgt. Pepper's Lonely Hearts Club*

Band just down the corridor. *The Piper at the Gates of Dawn* sold fairly well, but could never match the might of *Sgt. Pepper*, which went on to sell a staggering 32 million copies. Staggering, that is, until you consider that Pink Floyd went back into Abbey Road Studios six years later to record *Dark Side of the Moon*, which proceeded to spend over 800 weeks on the Billboard album chart, selling 45 million copies and becoming the third-biggest-selling album of all time. Only Michael Jackson's *Thriller* and AC/DC's *Back in Black* have sold more.

One Direction entered *X Factor* in 2010 as five individuals. Simon Cowell pretended to ditch all of them from the solo category, and then magically decided to put them together as a group. They were defeated on *X Factor* by Matt Cardle and Rebecca Ferguson, but this didn't seem to hold them back. Their first single sold over 4 million copies in the US alone, their first four albums all debuted at number one in the UK and the US, and their 2013 album *Midnight Memories* was the biggest-selling album of the year worldwide, despite only being released in November. By 2016 *Forbes* magazine ranked them as the second-highest-earning celebrities in the world. Presumably behind Alexander Armstrong.

WRITE YOUR WINNER IN BOX 2 ON THE WALLCHART

PET SHOP BOYS vs IRON MAIDEN

The Pet Shop Boys are the most successful duo in the history of British music. In this regard they are fortunate that Jedward are Irish.

Iron Maiden have recorded nearly forty albums since forming in 1975, and their success rate remains sky-high. Their 2015 album *The Book of Souls* reached number one in twenty-four countries, including the UK. It was the best-selling album of the year in Croatia, an accolade that even One Direction couldn't match. Following a car accident while recording their *The Number of the Beast* album, producer Martin Birch received a bill from the garage of exactly £666. He refused to pay it until they added another £1 on top.

WRITE YOUR WINNER IN BOX 3 ON THE WALLCHART

THE CLASH vs COLDPLAY

The Clash posed one of the great questions in rock history: 'Should I Stay or Should I Go' However, even a cursory look at the lyrics shows you that the question is idiotic. Joe Strummer clearly states that if he goes, there will be trouble, then goes on to mention that, were he to stay, it would be double.

If I go, there will be trouble
And if I stay it will be double.

Well then, with all due respect Joe, you should go, because it will only be half the trouble. I know you don't want to do either, we all get that, but you got yourself into this situation and you acknowledge that one option is twice as bad as the other one. End of song.

Coldplay, of course, famously sang that they not only never meant to cause you trouble, but also that they never meant to do you wrong. Unlike The Clash they then had enough sense not to add . . .

Oh, and if I ever caused you double
Oh, it'd be the end of the song.

Coldplay were originally called Starfish, and I'm afraid you must come up with your own jokes for that.

WRITE YOUR WINNER IN BOX 4 ON THE WALLCHART

5 FIVE STAR vs THE BEATLES

Sure, The Beatles have had seventeen UK number one singles, more than anyone else, fifteen UK number one albums, more than anyone else, sold over 400 million records worldwide, more than anyone else, and spent over 1,300 weeks on the Billboard music charts, more than anyone else, but have they ever released a song as good as 'System Addict'? Well yes, but I have to write *something* here.

Believe me, there will be households where Five Star win this battle, so please give this one due consideration. Play the whole of *Revolver, Sgt. Pepper, Abbey Road* and *The White Album,* and then play 'Rain or Shine' by Five Star. Wait for an hour and then tell me which one you're whistling.

WRITE YOUR WINNER IN BOX 5 ON THE WALLCHART

6 PULP vs THE PRETENDERS

Pulp's breakthrough single 'Common People' starts with the famous line about a mystery student with a thirst for knowledge, who studied sculpture at St Martin's College.

This line was about a genuine encounter Pulp singer Jarvis Cocker had during his student days at Central St Martins College of Arts & Design. For years, no one had been able to confirm the identity of the mystery Greek student, but in 2015, when Yanis Varoufakis rose to prominence as the maverick Greek finance minister, it was widely reported that the mystery woman in the song was his wife, Danae Stratou, former St Martin's College student, heir to the Stratos textile family fortune, and internationally renowned artist. What was less clear was whether anything in the song was true, but who can resist rhyming 'knowledge' with 'college'?

Chrissie Hynde has been the one permanent fixture in The Pretenders for nearly forty years, and is responsible for an almost endless stream of enduring pop hits in that time, from 'Brass in Pocket' and 'I'll Stand By You' to '2000 Miles' and 'Don't Get Me Wrong'. In the late 1970s Hynde worked in Vivienne Westwood and Malcolm McLaren's King's Road clothes shop and, in an attempt to get a UK visa, persuaded Johnny Rotten to marry her. When Rotten got cold feet and pulled out, Sid Vicious volunteered to take his place. When they turned up at the registry office the following morning, they found it was shut, and their plan to return the following day was scuppered due to Sid Vicious having to make a court appearance. You wouldn't get that sort of trouble with Ed Sheeran.

WRITE YOUR WINNER IN BOX 6 ON THE WALLCHART

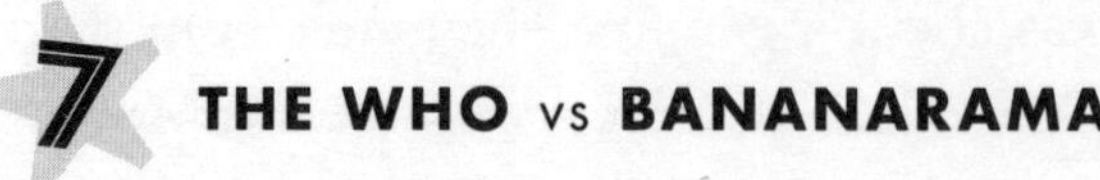

7 THE WHO vs BANANARAMA

If 'Last Christmas' was the best-selling single in UK chart history not to reach number one, The Who must be the most successful band in UK chart history never to have had a number one single at all. Despite twenty-five top forty hits and fourteen top ten hits, The Who never hit the top spot. 'Pinball Wizard' was number five, 'Substitute' was number four, and, even more cruelly, 'My Generation' and 'I'm a Boy' were both number two (kept off number one by 'The Carnival is Over' by The Seekers, and 'Distant Drums' by Jim Reeves).

Things don't get any rosier when we consider Bananarama. Despite being one of the most successful all-female bands in history, not only did Bananarama never reach number one, they also never reached number two. They had eight top five hits, and even their Comic Relief cover of 'Help' only reached number three. So next time Andrew Ridgeley complains that 'Last Christmas' was never number one, he will get no sympathy from his ex-partner, Keren Woodward of Bananarama.

WRITE YOUR WINNER IN BOX 7 ON THE WALLCHART

 DEPECHE MODE vs TAKE THAT

I'm aware that this is getting ridiculous now, but Depeche Mode have also had fourteen top ten hits, but have never managed to get higher than number *four*. They've hit this spot three times. To give you an idea of the immense longevity of Depeche Mode, when 'People are People' was number four in 1984, the three acts above them were Lionel Richie, Shakin' Stevens and the Thompson Twins, while when 'Precious' hit number four in 2005 the three acts above them were the Sugababes, Robbie Williams and The Pussycat Dolls.

If it's number one singles you're looking for then Take That are your boys and, after they re-formed, your men. Twelve number one singles over twenty-one years. Gary Barlow has had number one singles in a five-piece, four-piece and three-piece version of Take That, and as a solo artist. Unfortunately he just missed out on a number one as a duo when his collaboration with Robbie Williams hit number two. 'Shame' was the rather apt name of that song.

WRITE YOUR WINNER IN BOX 8 ON THE WALLCHART

 THE STONE ROSES vs DURAN DURAN

When The Stone Roses were recording their first album *Stone Roses* they were each being paid £10 a week by their record label Silvertone. The record was written, recorded and released at breakneck speed. By the time of their second album, *Second Coming*, the boys had signed to Geffen Records for £20 million, and been paid an immediate advance of £2.3 million. For some reason this album was not written, recorded and released at breakneck speed; in fact it took nearly five years. Parts of *Second Coming* were recorded at Bury's Square One Studios where their pizza-delivery boy was Mark Potter, later the guitarist in Elbow.

Duran Duran had two UK number one singles, and if I gave you an hour you would not guess them. Feel free to try though; answers at the end of this paragraph. But speaking of number ones, they recorded 'A View to a Kill' – still the only Bond theme ever to hit number one in the US – and even more impressively, keyboardist Nick Rhodes co-produced the stone-cold classic 1980s number one 'Too Shy' by Kajagoogoo. And Duran Duran's two number one singles? 'Is There Something I Should Know?' and 'The Reflex'. Very well done if you got that at home.

WRITE YOUR WINNER IN BOX 9 ON THE WALLCHART

10 THE KINKS vs SUGABABES

Over the years The Kinks have had three number one singles, ('You Really Got Me', 'Tired of Waiting for You' and 'Sunny Afternoon').

The Sugababes meanwhile have had six number one singles ('Freak Like Me', 'Round Round', 'Hole in the Head', 'Some Other Song I Don't Recognise', 'Seriously, *Six* Number One Singles' and 'Feel Free To Google This If You Don't Believe Me').

WRITE YOUR WINNER IN BOX 10 ON THE WALLCHART

11 DIRE STRAITS vs THE ROLLING STONES

While Dire Straits were recording their *Brothers in Arms* album on the Caribbean island of Montserrat, Sting was on holiday there and popped into the recording sessions. Pretty much for fun, and riffing on his own song 'Don't Stand So Close to Me', he added the 'I want my MTV' refrain, to the beginning of 'Money for Nothing'. He didn't ask for a writing credit, but his publishers insisted on it and, considering the album went on to sell 30 million copies and 'Money for Nothing' went to number one in the US, he's probably fairly pleased that they did.

The Rolling Stones have had eight UK number one singles,

which, to put it into some perspective, is two more than the Sugababes. The four current members of The Rolling Stones – Jagger, Richards, Watts and Wood – have racked up some pretty spectacular statistics of their own. Between the four of them, they are 296 years old, have had twenty children spanning forty-eight years, and now have seventeen grandchildren and one great-grandchild.

WRITE YOUR WINNER IN BOX 11 ON THE WALLCHART

12 SOUL II SOUL vs ROXY MUSIC

Soul II Soul grew out of Jazzie B's 1980s sound system. Within just two years they sold over a million copies of their breakthrough single 'Keep on Movin'', over 4 million copies of their album *Club Classics Vol. One* and had a UK number one and Grammy Award-winning single with 'Back to Life'. Jazzie B's real name is Trevor Beresford Romeo, and his son Mahlon Romeo is a professional footballer playing for Millwall and internationally for Antigua and Barbuda. The daughter of one of Soul II Soul's singers, Melissa Bell, is 2008 *X Factor* winner Alexandra Burke. Burke had the first million-selling UK single by a solo female artist, but, at the time of writing, has never played for Millwall.

When Brian Eno joined Roxy Music in 1971 he was interested in the idea of synthesisers, but played no actual musical instruments. Despite this, he has since produced a string of million-selling albums for artists such as U2 and Coldplay, and most notably he wrote the six-second start-up music for Microsoft Windows. He later admitted that he wrote it on a Mac.

WRITE YOUR WINNER IN BOX 12 ON THE WALLCHART

13 JLS vs OASIS

JLS stands for 'Jack the Lad Swing', one of the worst band names in British chart history. Other terrible band names include Prefab Sprout, Limp Bizkit, Bananarama, Orchestral Manoeuvres in the Dark, Spandau Ballet and Kajagoogoo. Scientists have proved that the second-worst band name of all time is The Beatles.

Oasis is also a pretty bad name. They were named after the Oasis Leisure Centre in Swindon, spotted by Noel Gallagher on a tour poster. And whose tour was the poster advertising? The band for which Noel Gallagher used to roadie, and the proud owners of the worst band name of all time, the Inspiral Carpets.

WRITE YOUR WINNER IN BOX 13 ON THE WALLCHART

14 RADIOHEAD vs EURYTHMICS

With hit singles like 'Creep', 'My Iron Lung', 'Paranoid Android', 'Knives Out', 'Burn the Witch' and 'Pop is Dead', Radiohead are in great demand for children's parties.

The Eurythmics' only number one single was 'There Must Be an Angel (Playing with My Heart)' and its chorus contained some very misleading lyrics. It is absolutely vital to note that, whatever the Eurythmics would ask you to believe, if you walk into an empty room, and suddenly your heart goes boom, it is not an orchestra of angels playing with your heart; it is in fact a serious cardiac episode and you must seek medical help immediately.

WRITE YOUR WINNER IN BOX 14 ON THE WALLCHART

15 SPICE GIRLS vs THE SMITHS

At last the battle you've all been waiting for. The Spice Girls released just eleven singles and an incredible nine of them reached number one, including three consecutive Christmas chart-toppers, which I bet you can't name. In all, that means that an incredible 82 per cent of their singles reached number one.

Of The Smiths' twenty UK chart hits, none went to number

one, including no consecutive Christmas chart-toppers. In all, that means an incredible 0 per cent of their singles reached number one. I would have loved a Smiths' Christmas number one; perhaps 'This Charming Snowman', 'How Soon is Snow?' or 'Heaven Snows I'm Miserable Snow'. While the Spice Girls were famously known by nicknames like Scary, Sporty and Baby, The Smiths were known by the nicknames Morrissey, Johnny, Thingy and Thingy.

WRITE YOUR WINNER IN BOX 15 ON THE WALLCHART

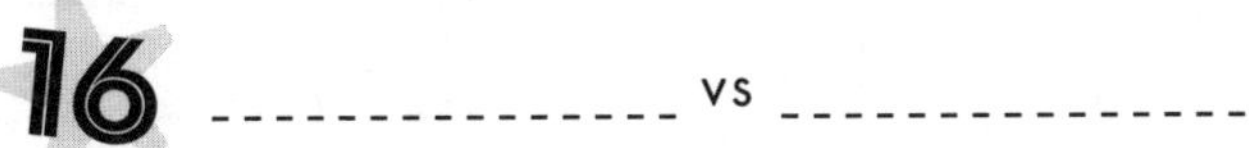

Okay, here's the wild-card round. Who have I missed out? I mean Kajagoogoo clearly, but who else? The Sex Pistols, Adam and the Ants, Spandau Ballet, The Cure, Happy Mondays, Def Leppard? Pretty much anyone except for Black Lace and Kasabian.

WRITE YOUR WINNER IN BOX 16 ON THE WALLCHART

BRITISH BANDS

THE WORLD CUP OF EVERYTHING

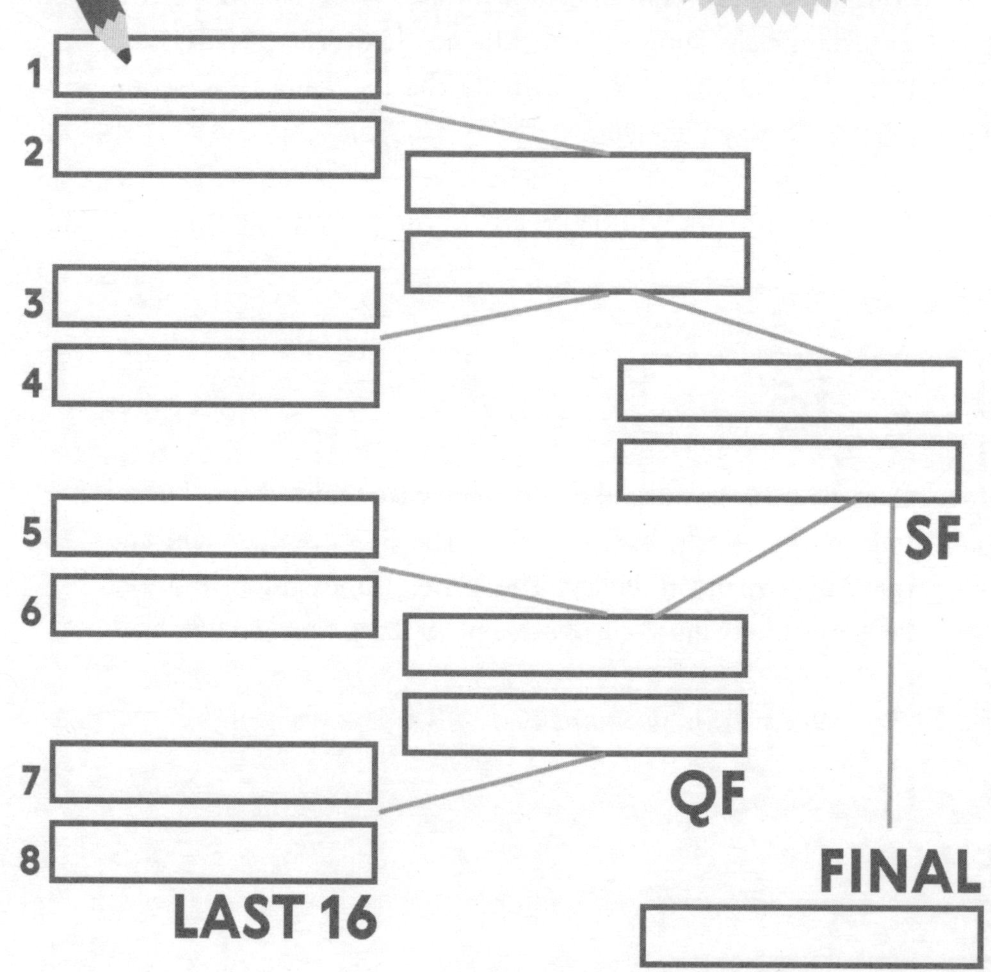

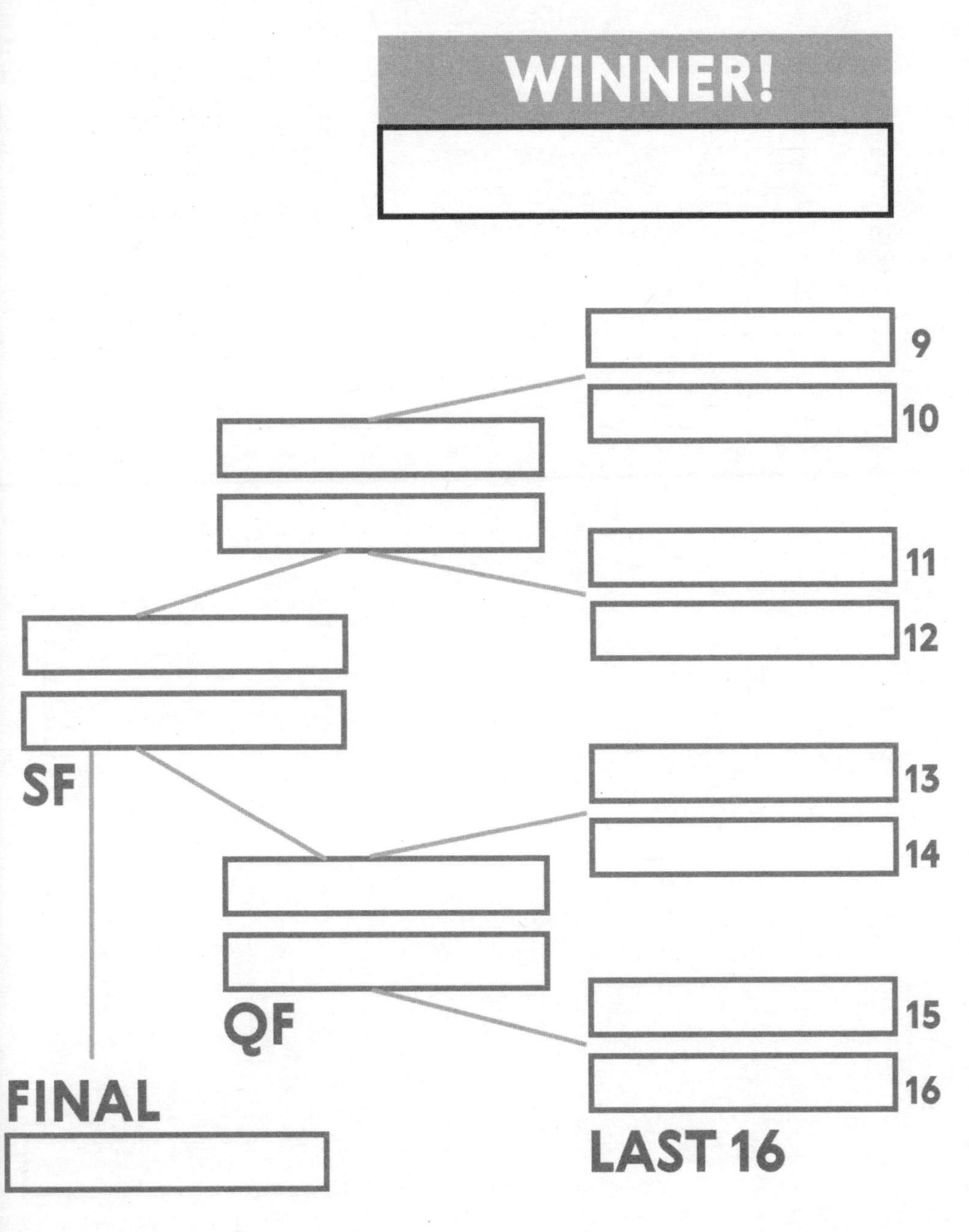
WINNER!
9
10
11
12
13
14
15
16
SF
QF
FINAL
LAST 16

WORLD CUP OF SWEETS

It's time to play the World Cup of Sweets
To choose the greatest sugary treats
As we revisit childhood shops
With flying saucers, acid drops,
Sherbet stuffed in cardboard tubes,
Jelly babies, cola cubes,
Sherbet lemon, chocolate lime
(The easiest sweet of all to rhyme),
Drumsticks, BlackJacks, penny chews,
They made us a Toffo we couldn't refuse.
All these sweets were childhood fixtures
(Also wine gums, dolly mixtures).

But who will win this championship?
Something old like sherbet dip?
I'm *sure* that retro sweets can do it.
Fruit Gum? Allsort? Maybe Chewit?
Those days they seem so long ago
We hadn't heard of Haribo;
We didn't have these new recruits
Like Starburst (clearly Opal Fruits);
Skittles were unknown to us
As we sucked Spangles on the bus.
These days there's a lot of pressure
On Love Heart, Tic Tac and Refresher.

So time to get your forces mustered.
Strawberry/cream and rhubarb/custard.
By the end there'll be one winner
And you won't have room for dinner.
Enjoy the vote, enjoy the sweeties;
I hope you don't get diabetes.

★ CHALLENGE! ★

What sweets were these advertising slogans used to advertise? I think we can all agree that the weirdest is number five. Do, please, be very careful with number eight.

1. DON'T FORGET THE _____________ MUM!
2. BET YOU CAN'T PUT A ____________ _____________ IN YOUR MOUTH WITHOUT CHEWING.
3. IT'S THE FIZZ THAT GIVES YOU WHIZZ!
4. HOOTS MON! THERE'S A MOOSE LOOSE ABOOT THIS HOOSE.
5. THE TOO GOOD TO HURRY MINTS.
6. DOUBLE WRAPPED TO KEEP THE FLAVOUR IN AND THE DIRT OUT.
7. ____________, TASTE THE RAINBOW!
8. PUT A ____________ IN YOUR MOUTH AND GET A BANG OUT OF LIFE.

9. A MAN'S GOTTA CHEW WHAT A MAN'S GOTTA CHEW.

10. KIDS AND GROWN-UPS LOVE IT SO, THE HAPPY WORLD OF _ _ _ _ _ _ _ _ _ _ _ _

Answers at the back of the book.

★ THE SWEETS SMELL ★ ★ OF SUCCESS! ★

Sweets are big business. Below are a few figures which prove exactly how big.

$4.2bn – The total estate left by Haribo boss Hans Riegel Jr upon his death in 2013. That is an awful lot of Tangfastics.

£50m – The price that H2 Equity Partners paid in 2012 for sweet company Hancocks. And who are Hancocks? You've never heard of them, so how can they be worth £50 million? Well, they're Britain's largest supplier of

Pick 'n' Mix sweets. Hancocks began business with a single sweet shop in Loughborough in 1962.

£390,000 – The price paid at a charity auction for the final piece of gum chewed by Sir Alex Ferguson as Manchester United manager.

£14,500 – Another auction price, this time for the last ever bag of Woolworths Pick 'n' Mix. The bag, containing fizzy cola bottles, rhubarb & custards, strawberry bonbons, white mice and pineapple cubes, was filled by Woolworths manager Ed Adams as he closed his Bromley store for the last time.

£20 – What Fortnum & Mason in London charge for a single jar of flying saucers!

£1.65 – The price per 100g of Pick 'n' Mix in my local Vue cinema. That's twice as expensive as Britain's poshest food, quinoa. Though Pick 'n' Mix is at least thirty times tastier, so it's actually a bargain.

5p – The current price of Fruit Salads and BlackJacks, the original penny chews of the 1970s. That represents an inflation rate since 1970 of 500 per cent. The average house price in that time has risen from £5,600 to over £250,000, an inflation rate of over 4,300 per cent. If penny chews had risen in value at the same rate as houses, then a single Fruit Salad sweet would now cost you 43p. So if anyone reading this decided to invest all of their money in penny chews in 1970 instead of buying a house, you made a bad, if delicious, choice.

★ ARGUMENT! ★

Here is the definitive order of the best Fruit Pastilles flavours. In my opinion. And I'm sure in your opinion too, as you seem pretty smart to me.

1. Blackcurrant
2. Lime
3. Lemon
4. Strawberry
5. Orange

If you honestly think that orange is the best flavour and blackcurrant the worst, then please get in touch. We could set up an elaborate illegal exchange scheme where I swap my orange Fruit Pastilles for your blackcurrant Fruit Pastilles in a poorly lit underground car park in Nantwich. Or we could go legit and invent an app that puts disenfranchised sweet lovers in touch with each other. We could call it Sweet Tin-der.

★ CHALLENGE! ★

Which of these are genuine messages that have been written on Love Hearts sweets, and which have I just made up? Five are real and five fake.

1. GROW UP
2. LEAVE THE EU
3. SKYPE ME
4. JUST SAY NO
5. I LIKE YOUR HAIR
6. I HAVE REPORTED YOU TO HR
7. LUV U 24/7
8. I FANCY YOUR MUM
9. YOLO
10. I AM BEING HELD PRISONER IN THE LOVE HEARTS FACTORY, PLEASE SEND HELP.

Answers at the back of the book.

Love Hearts did actually run a competition in which you could have your own message printed on a Love Heart. One of the winners was 'I LUV U ALAN', which must surely take the prize for the most niche Love Heart ever.

SO, SHALL WE BEGIN THE WORLD CUP OF SWEETS? Don't forget, this one has never been tested on the British public, so you are true pioneers. Argue freely and vote wisely. In case of a tie, each take individual Love Hearts and the first one to pull out I LUV U ALAN gets the casting vote.

FLYING SAUCERS vs JELLY BABIES

If you type the words 'Are flying saucers . . .' into Google, the first four auto-complete suggestions are.

Are flying saucers . . . vegan? – Yes they are. They are literally just coloured rice paper and sherbet. Absolutely no beef whatsoever.

Are flying saucers . . . gluten-free? Again yes, though I am struggling to imagine a scenario where that information might be vital. It's never come up on any Bear Grylls show I've watched.

Are flying saucers . . . fattening? No they are not. Each flying saucer contains just four calories. This might be the most extraordinary information I have ever heard. I am going to launch the flying saucer Diet. You could eat 400 flying saucers every day and stay under the recommended daily calorie intake for an average man. Just make sure you're eating plenty of greens.

Are flying saucers . . . real? Of course they are, otherwise how could Fortnum & Mason charge you twenty quid for them? If you are contemplating my Flying Saucer Diet, then I suggest Poundland might be a better bet.

The first known advert for jelly babies was produced by Riches Confectionery of Duke Street, London, in 1885, but they are believed to have been invented by the firm of Thomas Fryer in Nelson, Lancashire, in the 1860s. They were originally known as 'Unclaimed Babies'. Delicious. The best-selling UK jelly babies are made by Bassett's, and they name all the different-coloured babies. In case you were wondering who you've been eating all this time, it's Bubbles, Baby Bonny, Boofuls, Brilliant and Bumper.

WRITE YOUR WINNER IN BOX 1 ON THE WALLCHART

 FRUIT SALAD vs HARIBO TANGFASTICS

Off the top of your head tell me what two flavours make up a Fruit Salad sweet. Congratulations if you said raspberry and pineapple. We already know that if the price of Fruit Salads had risen at the same rate as house prices they would now cost 43p. But if they had risen at the same rate as shares in Apple, then each Fruit Salad sweet would now cost you £8,127. And presumably you'd also have to update it every two months and store it in a cloud.

Haribo was founded by Hans Riegel in Bonn (Ha . . . ri . . . bo) in 1922, when he invented the first ever gummi bear. They invaded the US in the 1980s (Haribo, not gummi bears) and the UK in the 1990s. Far and away the best Haribo are Tangfastics. Sour sweets have become a real phenomenon in the last twenty years. The ingredient that turns sweets into sour sweets is called 'sour sanding' and, as a fan, I'm delighted to read that it can cause '*irreversible dental erosion*'. Haribo also own another of my favourite sweets, Maoam chews. To quote Maoam's own website: '*Maoam gibt es in verschiedenen Geschmacksrichtungen*', so it's good to get that cleared up.

WRITE YOUR WINNER IN BOX 2 ON THE WALLCHART

 3 REFRESHERS vs RHUBARB & CUSTARD

For anyone new to the UK, there is a correct way to eat Refreshers.

1. Carefully run a finger under the join of the multi-coloured outer sleeve, discarding it to leave just the green foil wrapper.
2. Delicately unfold the foil wrapper at one end and loosen along the length of the tube.
3. Tip entire contents into your mouth in one go, then trudge reluctantly to your double maths lesson.

Refreshers are made by Swizzels Matlow at their factory in New Mills, Derbyshire. It is the closest thing in the UK to Willy Wonka's factory. As well as Parma Violets and Love Hearts, Swizzels Matlow also make a series of other sweets I now really want to try, including Climpies, Fizzers, Fruity Pops and Fun Gums. They have a river of pure chocolate running through the centre of the factory.*

Rhubarb & custard sweets contain neither rhubarb nor

* They don't. Although they *have* invented bubble gum that changes flavour**

** They haven't. But I bet it's still a cool factory.

custard. Strictly speaking they should have been called 'tartaric acid & liquid glucose' sweets, but they might not have sold quite so well, and also that would have been a terrible name for a cartoon.

WRITE YOUR WINNER IN BOX 3 ON THE WALLCHART

SHERBET LEMONS vs WERTHER'S ORIGINAL

Sherbet lemons are the favourite sweet of Albus Dumbledore, and of all right-thinking people everywhere. They would be my choice of winner in the World Cup of Sweets. Although that has made me think: what actually is sherbet? You know? I mean seriously, what is it? I've already found out that it's vegan and gluten-free but I am clueless apart from that. I'm going to make it my mission to find out what it is, and by the time we get on to the sherbet dip later in the competition I will let you know.

And here's another mystery. The adverts for Werther's Original make great play of nostalgia, evoking memories of kindly grandfathers buying Werther's treats from old-fashioned sweet shops for wide-eyed children. All very moving except that Werther's Original were unavailable outside Germany until the early 1990s, so what was that elderly German guy doing buying you sweets in the 1950s, and how did he overcome the stringent German import bans of the era? Something doesn't add up in your family, I'm afraid.

WRITE YOUR WINNER IN BOX 4 ON THE WALLCHART

5 COLA CUBES vs LOVE HEARTS

I used to buy a quarter of cola cubes, or kola kubes if you want to be all hipster about it, from Broad Street Stores in Cuckfield on my way home from school every day. I've just looked on Google Maps and Broad Street Stores no longer exists. All trace has gone, and it has been replaced by a new-build house. I would say two things to the owners of that house. First, that shop was a very happy one, and I hope that the same happiness shines through into your home; and second, you need to put your bins out, because everyone else on Broad Street on Google Maps has put theirs out and you haven't.

I would truly love to know if anyone has ever proposed using the 'MARRY ME?' Love Heart, and how long that marriage lasted. I would also love to know if any embattled dictator has ever met the rapid advance of invading Allied troops with the 'I SURRENDER' Love Heart.

WRITE YOUR WINNER IN BOX 5 ON THE WALLCHART

SKITTLES vs FRUIT PASTILLES

US confectionery companies like to exploit their brands mercilessly. Over the years Skittles have genuinely launched all of the following: Tropical Skittles, Wild Berry Skittles, Tart-n-Tangy Skittles, Skilled Skittles (Skittles that 'look like athletes'. Okay.), Skittles Confused (no kidding), Sour Skittles, Crazy Sour Skittles, Smoothie Mix Skittles, Ice Cream Skittles, Carnival Skittles, Skittles Unlimited, Double Sour Skittles, Extreme Fruit Gum Skittles (I condemn the spread of Fruit Gum Extremism), Mint Skittles, Extra Chewy Mint Skittles, Chocolate Skittles (I probably would have thought of Chocolate Skittles before I thought of Skittles that 'look like athletes'), Chocolate Mix Skittles, Liquorice Skittles, Citrus Skittles, Fresh Mint Skittles ('Fresh' Mint Skittles? Now I'm worried about the Mint Skittles.), Skittles Sensations, Fizz'd Fruits Skittles, Skittles Blenders, Skittles Riddles, Skittles Darkside (Really?), Skittles Brightside (Phew!) Dessert Skittles, Orchard Skittles (note

Dessert Orchard would be a good name for a racehorse) America Mix Skittles, Cauldron Skittles, Flavour Mash-up Skittles and Sweet & Sour Skittles.

UK confectionery companies are a bit cooler and Rowntree's just sometimes do Fruit Pastilles in a bigger bag.

WRITE YOUR WINNER IN BOX 6 ON THE WALLCHART

7 COCONUT MUSHROOMS vs PINEAPPLE CHUNKS

Who on earth thought of coconut mushrooms? You might as well have strawberry parsnips or liquorice cabbages.

Pineapple chunks are identical to cola cubes except they contain delicious artificial pineapple flavouring instead of delicious artificial cola flavouring. They are sometimes called pineapple cubes, and in New Zealand are covered in chocolate and called pineapple lumps. Note, nowhere are they called pineapple broccoli.

WRITE YOUR WINNER IN BOX 7 ON THE WALLCHART

8 WHITE MICE vs WINE GUMS

Just like normal mice, white mice are either chocolate or strawberry flavoured and you can eat them in the cinema.

Charles and Tom Maynard set up the Maynards sweet company from the kitchen of their home in Stamford Hill, London, in 1880. In 1909 Charles Maynard's son, Charles Jr, invented wine gums, but took some time persuading his father, a strict Methodist and teetotaller, that they didn't contain any wine. Which does make you wonder why he called them wine gums in the first place. Though it seems to have worked out okay in the long run. Each sweet used to be printed with a name: PORT, SHERRY, CHAMPAGNE, GIN (which isn't even a wine, Charles; what are you on mate?) BURGUNDY or CLARET, but Maynards no longer do this. Who knows why? Probably Brussels.

WRITE YOUR WINNER IN BOX 8 ON THE WALLCHART

9 FRUIT GUMS vs PEAR DROPS

Rowntree's Fruit Gums are almost entirely inedible and were considered the single greatest source of income for 1970s British dentists.

Pear drops are either yellow or pink and they famously smell exactly like those pens that teachers use to write on whiteboards. Their distinctive smell is due to a combination of isoamyl acetate and ethyl acetate (that's the distinctive smell of pear drops, not of teachers). Confusingly, isoamyl acetate is actually a banana flavouring. After learning that, I just ate one and, you know what, you can kind of tell. Give it a go.

WRITE YOUR WINNER IN BOX 9 ON THE WALLCHART

10 POLO vs STARBURST

Polo were invented in 1948 by Rowntree's employee John Bargewell at their York factory. Each Polo is 1.9cm in diameter and has a 0.8cm-diameter hole. They called it Polo because it sounded like 'polar' and suggested cool, icy freshness. It is worth noting that the Pole also now has a hole in it.

Starburst were introduced into the UK by Mars in 1960, and were named through a public competition. Their original name, Opal Fruits, was suggested by Peter Phillips (not that one) and won him £5. The original Opal Fruits flavours were lemon, lime, orange and strawberry. In the UK, the lemon and lime flavours were soon combined in order to make room for the blackcurrant flavour. Interestingly, while blackcurrant is the best Fruit Pastille it is actually the worst Opal Fruit. Since Opal Fruits became Starburst in the mid-1990s, they went all uncool and American, and have launched countless other flavours including apple, banana, blackberry, blueberry acai (what have we become?), cherry, cherry-lime, fruit punch, grape, honeydew, kiwi, kiwi-banana, mango-melon, passion fruit, pineapple, pina colada, plum, raspberry, raspberry-pomegranate, tangerine and watermelon. Well done America. I bet they even asked Peter Phillips to send his fiver back.

WRITE YOUR WINNER IN BOX 10 ON THE WALLCHART

11 LIQUORICE ALLSORTS vs DRUMSTICK

Bassetts Liquorice Allsorts have a mascot, Bertie Bassett, made entirely from the sweets that he supposedly makes. What does this tell us about Bertie Bassett? He's such a raging narcissist that he takes one look at his own body and assumes people would enjoy eating it? Or that he's a Hannibal Lecter-style psychopath who delights in growing dismembered body parts and feeding them to children? It has to be one or the other. I do like Liquorice Allsorts – supposedly invented when an early Bassetts salesman dropped a tray of sweet samples, mixing them randomly – but Bertie Bassett's reign of terror must be ended.

Drumstick lollies are all well and good, but we all know they are essentially just a Fruit Salad on a stick. Drumstick is to Fruit Salad what a shish kebab is to a nice steak.

WRITE YOUR WINNER IN BOX 11 ON THE WALLCHART

12 FIZZY COLA BOTTLES vs CHEWITS

Fizzy cola bottles are always my first choice at a Pick 'n' Mix. Pick 'n' Mix fizzy cola bottles are infinitely superior to Haribo fizzy cola bottles. I go to the cinema a great deal, but I do sometimes wonder if I'm a genuine film fan or whether I just really, really like Pick 'n' Mix.

Adverts for Chewits in the 1970s and 80s starred a monster who would eat various buildings, none of which proved as chewy as a Chewit. Perhaps most famous among them was Barrow-in-Furness bus depot. The name of the monster was the Monster Muncher. How on earth did they get away with ripping off that name from Smith's crisps you might wonder? Well the truth is, it was the other way round. The first Chewits advert aired in 1976 and Monster Munch crisps were launched in 1977. Uh oh, I sense a multibillion-dollar lawsuit.

WRITE YOUR WINNER IN BOX 12 ON THE WALLCHART

13 SHERBET DIP vs PARMA VIOLETS

Hey, I found out what sherbet is! I promised you I would, and I did. You really want to know? Okay, here goes. Sherbet is a mix of tartaric, citric or malic acid, with sodium bicarbonate or magnesium carbonate (or a blend of the two), with large amounts of sugar added to disguise how awful that tastes. Good eh? The sherbet dip, or sometimes Sherbet DipDab, adds to the fun by letting you dip a lollipop made with corn syrup and soya lecithin into your malic acid and magnesium carbonate.

That still sounds more appetising than Parma Violets, however. Who is eating these? People who don't actually like sweets is who. If you want a sweet that tastes of flowers and soap, then Parma Violets are for you.

WRITE YOUR WINNER IN BOX 13 ON THE WALLCHART

14 HARIBO STARMIX vs JELLY BEANS

The Starmix contains all the classic Haribo sweets, none of which I like. There are bears, fried eggs, hearts, rings and cola bottles. Sweets are so weird when you see them written down like that. Bears and fried eggs?

The first-discovered mention of 'jelly beans' was in 1861 when Boston confectioner William Schrafft urged people to send his jelly beans to soldiers fighting in the American Civil War. Marks & Spencer seem to have stopped making their Sour Jelly Beans, which were my absolute favourite. If you work for Marks & Spencer and you're reading this, you know what to do.

WRITE YOUR WINNER IN BOX 14 ON THE WALLCHART

15 CHOCOLATE LIMES vs TIC TAC

Also, if you work for Marks & Spencer, or any confectionery company, I love chocolate limes, but I think you should also make chocolate lemons. I would also be very happy to eat chocolate strawberries, but I recognise there might be trademark infringements if you wanted to make chocolate oranges.

Seriously though, a bag of chocolate limes and chocolate lemons, have a think about it.

Guess who makes Tic Tac? It's Ferrero, the home of Ferrero Rocher. Try building a pyramid of Tic Tac at the next ambassador's party and see where it gets you. The Ferrero factory in Cork produces over a billion Tic Tac every year. Also, the Tic Tac factory makes a really cool sound if you shake it up and down.

WRITE YOUR WINNER IN BOX 15 ON THE WALLCHART

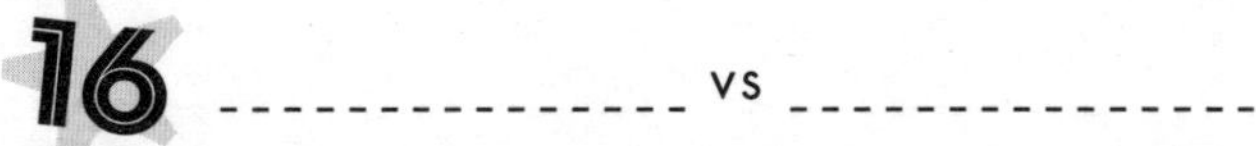

The wild-card battle. What sweets have I missed out? American hard gums? Aniseed balls? Acid drops? Dolly mixtures? Jazzles? Fizzles? Lozzles? Strawberry swizzles? Nozzles? Shizzles? Dibdazzles? Whizzles? Wazzles? Super Sour Watermelon Wazzocks? I have made some of those up.

WRITE YOUR WINNER IN BOX 16 ON THE WALLCHART

SWEETS

THE WORLD CUP OF EVERYTHING

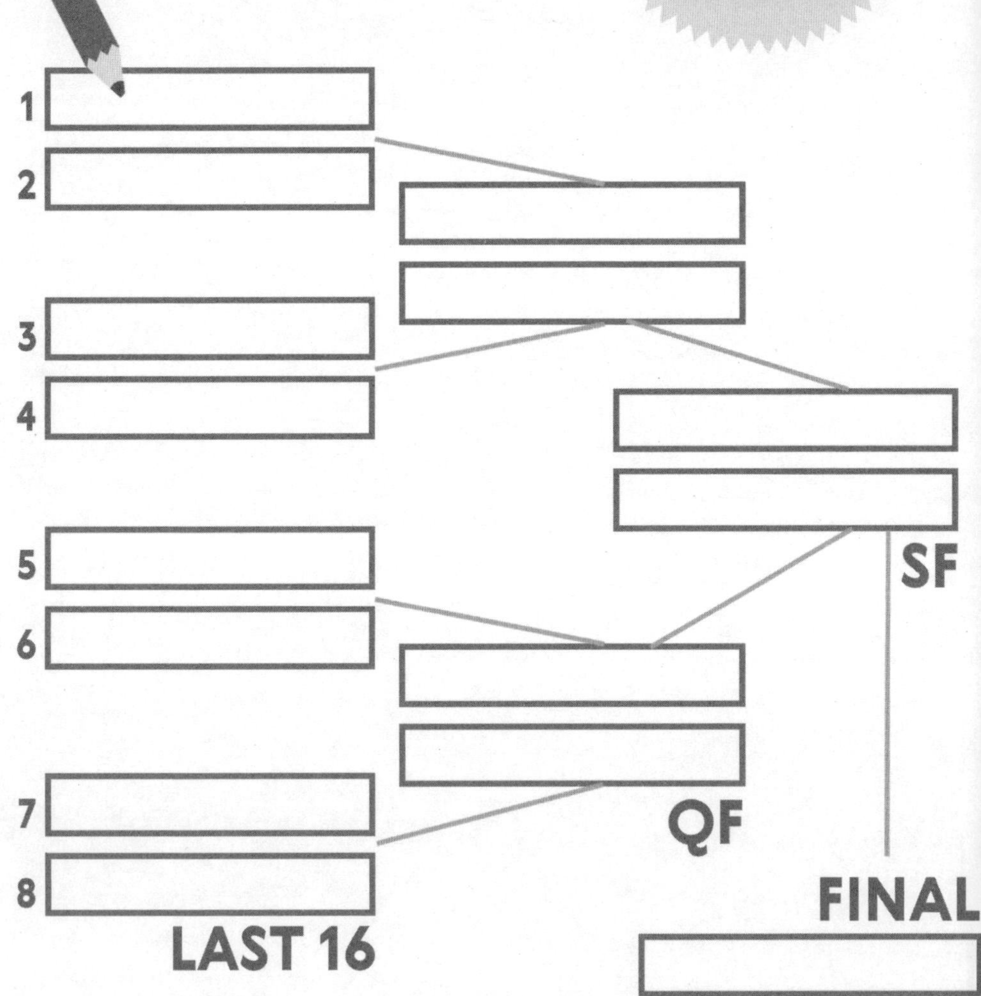

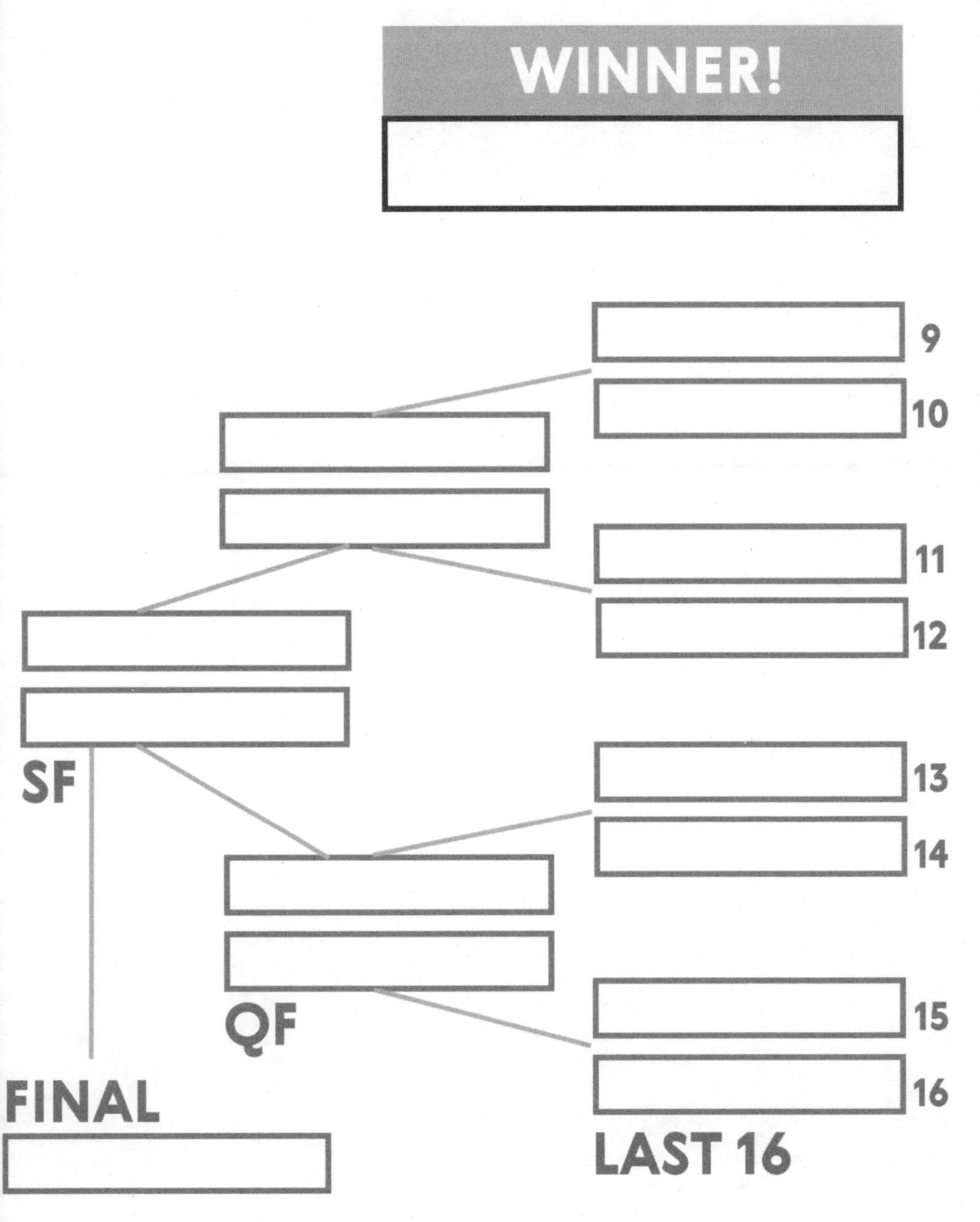

WINNER!
9
10
11
12
SF
13
14
QF
15
16
FINAL
LAST 16

WORLD CUP OF AMERICANS

The Americans themselves tried to settle the matter of the greatest ever American in a 2005 TV show poll. However, in further evidence that you shouldn't always trust America to vote for things, in that poll Ronald Reagan was voted the greatest American of all time. Not only that, but George W. Bush beat Elvis and the Wright Brothers. And who's that finishing one place above Muhammad Ali? Why it's Lance Armstrong. Goodness only knows what would have happened if Kim Kardashian had been around in 2005. With all that in mind I thought it might be worth having another crack at it?

Americans come in all shapes and sizes: tall and short, old and young, fat and slightly fatter. They pronounce things wrong, they spell things wrong, they all carry guns, none of them have passports, they've never elected a female President or Vice President and they think that Hershey's is chocolate. They think that crisps are chips, chips are fries, jam is jelly, jelly is jello, pants are trousers, bums are butts, and bumbags are fannypacks. They say 'math' instead of 'maths' and they use the leftover 's' to turn 'sport' into 'sports'.

But, they also brought us *Star Wars*, manned flight, the electric light bulb, Tina Fey, rock and roll, barbecues, hip-hop, *The Simpsons*, Denzel Washington, Google Maps and pretending to land on the moon. They've also made us laugh more often than any nation in history, both intentionally and unintentionally.

Here's a question that can win you a few quid down the pub or in the staff room. Or maybe even in the waiting room at the clinic? (It's really none of my business how you choose to live your life, and I'm sure that rash is nothing.) What is the most dangerous profession in the USA? It's not police officer, soldier, astronaut or firefighter. The most dangerous profession in the USA is President. Of the forty-five men who've held the post, four have been murdered while in office, giving the US Presidency a mortality rate of nearly 9 per cent.

America is a beautiful, dumb, spectacular, incendiary soap

opera of a country, a giant mash-up of cultures you simply can't tear your eyes away from. We've lost count of the times we've sat agog wondering 'what have they done *now*'? But when America gets it right, then boy does it get it right.

In honour of those times I have gathered together thirty prominent figures from American history (well, twenty-nine and Taylor Swift) and you can provide the final two. It is a list that actually makes you stop and think about the USA and the brilliance, the innovation, the quiet braveness and, perhaps more than anything, the sheer entertainment value of this nation which sometimes appears be a theme park of all human life. Or maybe a movie about a theme park of all human life, starring David Hasselhoff and Miley Cyrus.

But who is the greatest non-Kardashian American of them all? You decide.

First though, you know the drill: a few little challenges for you to ignore.

★ CHALLENGE! ★

Can you name the twenty biggest-selling music acts in the history of the US from just their initials? Some are soloists, some are bands, but they've all sold over 50 million records in the US alone. This is according to the Recording Industry Association of America, which began compiling records, literally, in 1958. I would say this one will be slightly easy for the older reader, so why not suggest playing it competitively against your kids?

1. TB
2. GB (good luck with this one)
3. EP
4. LZ
5. E (I thought this should have a T in front of it, but it doesn't)
6. BJ
7. MJ
8. EJ
9. PF
10. ACDC (there is a slight clue here)
11. GS (hardest on the list)
12. BS
13. A
14. TRS
15. BS (a different one to number 12)
16. M
17. MC

18. M (a very different one to 16)
19. WH
20. VH

Answers at the back of the book.

★ ARGUMENT! ★

Who's best, the UK or the US? I have given my judgement on a series of areas. Please discuss and feel free to disagree.

TV – So many good US dramas and sitcoms, but we're getting pretty good at that ourselves and I think our news, documentary and entertainment programming just edges this for the **UK**.

FILMS – Just looking through my favourite movies of all time and seeing so much Scorcese, Woody Allen, *Shawshank*, Pixar, *Spinal Tap* and more. This has to go to **USA**.

FOOD – Burgers and barbecues and southern-fried chicken. Forgive me but **USA**.

POLITICIANS – When we get it wrong in the UK we only tend to get it a bit wrong and we eventually swing back the other way. We have, believe it or not, one of the healthiest, least-corrupt political systems in the world. I mean, we're not Sweden or something, but we're better than the craziness and naked avarice of Washington DC. A win for the **UK**.

SPORT – I am of the deeply controversial opinion that baseball is better than cricket, and I'm a huge fan all round of US sports. But let's not forget that they still don't really take football seriously and, much more importantly, they don't have darts or snooker over there. No thanks. A win for the **UK**.

ATTITUDE TO GUNS – The **UK**.

HEALTHCARE SYSTEM – The **UK**.

MOUNTAINS/DESSERTS/OCEANS ETC. – The **USA**.

CARS – I don't really know anything about cars but I know that the cars in *Grease* were cooler than our Austin Maxi. The **USA**.

MUSIC – The USA never produced a band to match East 17, fact! **UK**.

I make that 6–4 to the UK. Are you more or less patriotic than me?

★ CHALLENGE! ★

In which US cities would you have found all of the following professional sports teams in 2017?

1. JETS, METS, KNICKS ____________
2. CUBS, BULLS, BEARS ____________
3. INDIANS, BROWNS, CAVALIERS ____________
4. BRAVES, HAWKS, FALCONS ____________
5. LAKERS, DODGERS, CHARGERS ____________
6. CELTICS, RED SOX, BRUINS ____________
7. ROCKETS, ASTROS, TEXANS ____________
8. STEELERS, PIRATES, PENGUINS ____________
9. SEAHAWKS, MARINERS, SUPERSONICS ____________
10. REDSKINS, WIZARDS, CAPITALS ____________

Answers at the back of the book.

★ CHALLENGE! ★

In the short passage below are FIFTY words that the British and Americans would spell differently. Can you spot them all?

He was in the lecture theatre, on the second storey of the annexe his organisation had provided for the programme. Stroking his grey moustache he finally prised open the matt aluminium artefact. Inside was exactly what he had dreamt: a horde of marvellous jewellery. Holding his favourite piece, a jewelled axe, in the centre of his vice, he analysed it, using the skilful judgement that was his speciality. In that moment he knew he had learnt the cypher.

You could tell by his behaviour that every fibre of his being was aflame. He instantly understood he had to be travelling soon if he was to be the saviour of his nation. His aeroplane was refuelling, the snow-ploughs clearing the runway. He threw on body-armour over his woollen pyjamas (good to keep cosy in defence of your country). He knew he would receive no acknowledgement for his valour. He ran the half-kilometre to his plane, checked the

tyres and the brake discs, still smouldering from the emergency landing. He simply had to leave before his authorisation was cancelled. He checked his victuals – a doughnut, a few liquorice sticks – and with grim humour climbed aboard.

He knew the future of civilisation depended on the manoeuvre he was about to make.

Answers at the back of the book.

OKAY, HERE WE GO: IT'S TIME FOR THE WORLD CUP OF AMERICANS. Don't forget, everyone votes for their favourite in each of these pairings to find the winners. Using your pen, write down the scores, then fill in each of the winners on your wallchart. In case of a tie, either hold an absurdly complicated electoral college vote which sees the person with the fewest votes win, or simply ask Vladimir Putin who he would like to win.

OPRAH WINFREY vs TOM HANKS

Oprah Winfrey is sometimes called the American Jeremy Kyle. Let's see if that's true.

Oprah was born into poverty in rural Mississippi and, through hard work, talent and charisma, is now worth $2.9 billion, has a salary of $75 million a year, has been awarded the Presidential Medal of Freedom and has degrees from Duke and Harvard Universities. Jeremy Kyle was born in Reading, his dad was personal assistant to the Queen Mother. He studied History and Sociology at Guildford and now spends every morning shouting at a guy who has slept with his brother's girlfriend, then stolen his dog, or very occasionally the other way round. Hmmmmm.

Good luck against Oprah, Tom Hanks. I do have a recommendation though. I think that *Captain Phillips* is just about the best film of the twenty-first century, so if you haven't seen it I think you might enjoy it. It is about Somali pirates, not about Princess Anne's first husband.

WRITE YOUR WINNER IN BOX 1 ON THE WALLCHART

MUHAMMAD ALI vs BARBRA STREISAND

Well, what a match-up this is. I can't help thinking that if this battle was in a boxing ring, then Muhammad Ali would have the advantage, with his superior reach and footwork, and the fact that he was a professional boxer. In a concert hall, however, Streisand would come into her own, as her vocal power and years of stage and screen experience would surely prove more than a match for Ali. You are going to have to use your skill and judgement to decide your winner. If it helps, then I will point out that, due to a cut-and-paste error, Barbra Streisand was born Cassius Clay and Muhammad Ali was once married to Elliott Gould.

WRITE YOUR WINNER IN BOX 2 ON THE WALLCHART

NEIL ARMSTRONG vs MICHAEL JACKSON

Essentially the only question you need to ask yourself here is: 'Who did the best moonwalk?'

WRITE YOUR WINNER IN BOX 3 ON THE WALLCHART

DONALD TRUMP vs HILLARY CLINTON

I know this has recently been covered in some depth elsewhere, but I just wondered if you had a different opinion? It is a secret of the book trade that books have to be finished several months before publication so I can't begin to imagine what Donald Trump is up to as you read this. I suppose if you are reading this at all it is a good sign, and basic civilisation, sanitation and electric light still remain. My predictions, as I write, of what the future holds would be . . .

a) He has resigned. I don't know what would precipitate this, as I'm guessing that even if he killed the Pope he would still cling on.

b) North Korea and America are at war, and if we're honest we're not entirely sure of who to support.

c) He's in *Celebrity Big Brother*.

d) Vladimir Putin has taken his rightful place as World Emperor and I for one welcome his strong yet compassionate leadership and thank him for sparing us.

WRITE YOUR WINNER IN BOX 4 ON THE WALLCHART

5 ELEANOR ROOSEVELT vs TINA FEY

Eleanor Roosevelt is probably the closest the USA has ever had to a female President. She was by her husband FDR's side throughout his four terms of Presidency, making speeches on his behalf, writing newspaper columns frequently disagreeing with him on policy matters, and having huge influence over the politics of her country. After FDR's death, Eleanor Roosevelt lobbied for the USA to join the United Nations and became its first representative. She played a major role in the drafting of the Universal Declaration of Human Rights, and in 1999 was named in the top ten of Gallup's poll of 'The Most Admired People of the Twentieth Century'. I know what you're thinking: she sounds a lot like Melania Trump.

Tina Fey was the star, producer and writer of the single greatest sitcom of all-time *30 Rock* and was named in the top ten of Gallup's poll 'The People Richard Osman Would Most Like to Somehow Have Married of the Twenty-first Century'.

WRITE YOUR WINNER IN BOX 5 ON THE WALLCHART

 BEYONCÉ vs THE WRIGHT BROTHERS

Without Beyoncé, one of the greatest music talents of the twenty-first century, we wouldn't have had any of the following iconic moments of pop history – 'Survivor', 'Bills, Bills, Bills', 'Bootylicious', 'Crazy in Love', 'Single Ladies (Put a Ring on It)', 'Halo' or 'Lemonade'.

However, without those great pioneers of aviation, the Wright Brothers, we wouldn't have had the following iconic moment of pop history: 'I Believe I Can Fly' by Keith Harris and Orville.

Just decide who you'd rather see at Glastonbury and cast your vote accordingly.

WRITE YOUR WINNER IN BOX 6 ON THE WALLCHART

 SUSAN B. ANTHONY vs THOMAS EDISON

Two people who brought light to darkness. Susan B. Anthony is the American suffragette who fought for the rights of US women all her life and was eventually rewarded with the passing of the 19th Amendment to the US Constitution giving women the right to vote. It is known, in her honour, as the

'Anthony Amendment'. In 1979 she appeared on the dollar coin, the first woman ever to appear on US money.

For his part Edison invented light bulbs, which are often used in polling stations. For all I know, he might also have invented the short stubby pencil you vote with too. He certainly invented a lot of stuff (phonograph, iron ore separator, SodaStream, Boots Advantage Card, etc.)

WRITE YOUR WINNER IN BOX 7 ON THE WALLCHART

8 ABRAHAM LINCOLN vs WILL SMITH

This match-up comes down to which of these famous quotes resonates with you the most.

> **'Four score and seven years ago our fathers brought forth on this continent, a new nation, conceived in Liberty, and dedicated to the proposition that all men are created equal.'**

Or

> ***'Four score and seven years ago, my life got flipped, turned upside down. And I'd like to take a minute, just sit***

right there, I'll tell you how our fathers brought forth on this continent, a new nation, conceived in Liberty and how I became the Prince of a town called Bel-Air.'

Too close to call for me.

WRITE YOUR WINNER IN BOX 8 ON THE WALLCHART

FRANK SINATRA vs MARILYN MONROE

'My Way' by Frank Sinatra was for many years the most popular song played at British funerals. And as Sinatra croons about having few regrets, about having done things his own way, without exemption, you just know that at least one person there is thinking: 'Yes, I know you did Geoff; that's why you got married and divorced three times, you were fired from your accountancy firm for refusing to learn how to use a computer, and you were banned from the Kettering branch of Costa for bringing your own flask.'

Marilyn Monroe famously did things her way. Brought up in a succession of foster homes and orphanages, she married at the age of sixteen and began working in a munitions factory. But within just ten years she became a worldwide movie star and one of the richest and most bankable actors in Hollywood history. She was trouble and troubled but, as the most famous line of her most famous film puts it, 'Nobody's perfect'.

WRITE YOUR WINNER IN BOX 9 ON THE WALLCHART

10 BARACK OBAMA vs MICHELLE OBAMA

I know this is mean, but I couldn't resist it. I mean, we all have a favourite member of every couple we've ever met don't we? Whether it's Joyce and Ray from across the road, or Brad Pitt and Angelina Jolie (my choices, for the record, would be Brad Pitt and Joyce). But Barack vs Michelle seems tricky. So this exercise might help you decide. I think it's best to imagine that you have just gone out onto your balcony in a Spanish holiday apartment complex, and the Obamas are on the balcony next door. You wave and exchange a few pleasantries each morning, say awkward hellos as you bump into each other at communal volleyball and the Kids' Club drop-off. Then, on about night four as you walk into the resort restaurant, Barack catches your eye and beckons you over. You share a very friendly dinner, chat about the kids, discuss why sangria always tastes so amazing in Spain but you never drink it at home, and drunkenly force Barack to reveal the nuclear launch strike codes. You then feel you should invite them to share a nightcap on your balcony, but when they've left, you can't really discuss them in case they hear. So you pass each other a note saying which one of them you got on with best.

Simply vote for whoever you would write on that piece of paper.

WRITE YOUR WINNER IN BOX 10 ON THE WALLCHART

TAYLOR SWIFT vs BENJAMIN FRANKLIN

Benjamin Franklin famously said: 'In this world nothing is certain but death and taxes', forgetting to add '. . . and that if you're on a train the Wi-Fi won't work but they'll still charge you for it'. He was one of America's Founding Fathers and invented the lightning rod and bifocal spectacles. He also conducted a very famous experiment that involved flying a kite in a storm, the exact details of which we are a little sketchy on, but we basically all sort of assume that he invented electricity.

Taylor Swift's major contribution to twenty-first century

philosophy is the observation that, by and large, the players are gonna play, play, play, play, play, while, in counterpoint to this, the haters are more likely to hate, hate, hate, hate, hate. Her ingenious solution to this dichotomy at the heart of our culture is that she chooses to simply shake, shake, shake, shake, shake it off. These are words which have helped many of us, whether players or haters, through difficult times. But without electricity we wouldn't be able to hear her, which surely goes in Benjamin Franklin's favour?

WRITE YOUR WINNER IN BOX 11 ON THE WALLCHART

12 ROSA PARKS vs MADONNA

Rosa Parks is sometimes called 'the First Lady of Civil Rights'. On 1 December 1955 she refused to give up her seat in the 'coloured section' of a Montgomery bus to a white passenger, an act of bravery and defiance that became a powerful symbol of the burgeoning Civil Rights movement. She devoted her life to the fight for justice and equality, and on her death became the first woman in American history to lie in honour at the Capitol Rotunda in Washington DC.

I am glad she is drawn against Madonna, because I know

that Madonna would consider it a great privilege to be defeated by her in a way that, say, Charlie Sheen wouldn't.

WRITE YOUR WINNER IN BOX 12 ON THE WALLCHART

13 MICHAEL JORDAN vs MARTIN LUTHER KING

The official National Basketball Association website states that 'By acclamation Michael Jordan is the greatest basketball player of all time.' It is worth noting, however, that the NBA website also currently has the following genuine headlines on its home page.

'REVENGE! COUSINS OFF AS PELICANS RIP KINGS'

'GORDON SHOWS NO MERCY WITH ONE-HAND JAM'

'WIZARDS DESTROY JAZZ'

So frankly, who knows what to believe?

Martin Luther King Jr was one of the great heroes of the twentieth century, awarded the Nobel Peace Prize and the

Presidential Medal of Freedom for his lifelong activism and belief in the power of non-violent protest. He delivered possibly the greatest speech of the twentieth century, 'I Have a Dream'. Its words and its images remain powerful, and disappointingly relevant, to this very day.

WRITE YOUR WINNER IN BOX 13 ON THE WALLCHART

14 JFK vs MERYL STREEP

JFK had affairs with more than half of the other names on this list. He is also the only President in US history to have been named after an airport.

Meryl Streep is the most Oscar-nominated actor in the history of the Academy Awards. She has won three Oscars and been nominated an incredible twenty times. Or, to put it another way, she has lost seventeen Oscars, more than any other actor in history. Most of her acting work in recent years has come in the form of pretending to be delighted for Sandra Bullock or Jennifer Lawrence.

WRITE YOUR WINNER IN BOX 14 ON THE WALLCHART

15 GEORGE CLOONEY vs CHARLIE SHEEN

Charlie Sheen once accidentally shot one of his many ex-wives, and when asked if he was on drugs answered:

> **'I am on a drug. It's called Charlie Sheen. It is not available because if you try it once you will die. Your face will melt off and your children will weep over your exploded body.'**

He went on to add that he was able to survive because he had 'tiger blood' in his veins. George Clooney, meanwhile, does those incredibly irritating Nespresso adverts, so I don't envy you this decision.

WRITE YOUR WINNER IN BOX 15 ON THE WALLCHART

16 ______________ vs ______________

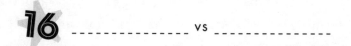

This is the wild-card vote. Who have I left off the list? William Shatner? Justin Bieber? Mike Myers? Jim Carrey? Ryan Gosling? Pamela Anderson? Keanu Reeves? The Rock? Every single one of them is Canadian I'm afraid, so think again. Even John Barrowman doesn't count; he's Scottish. Some candidates who would count include Henry Ford, Amelia Earhart, Bob Dylan, Jack Nicklaus and SpongeBob SquarePants.

WRITE YOUR WINNER IN BOX 16 ON THE WALLCHART

AMERICANS

THE WORLD CUP OF EVERYTHING

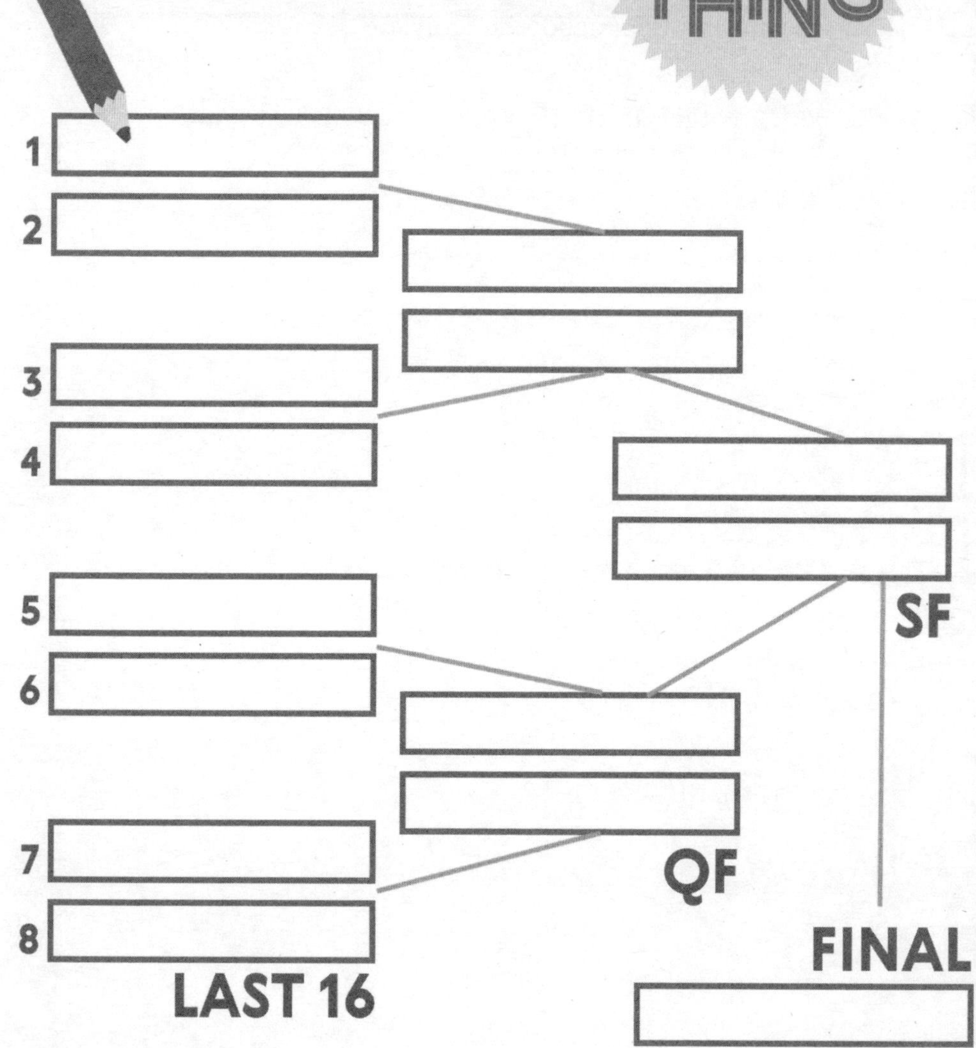

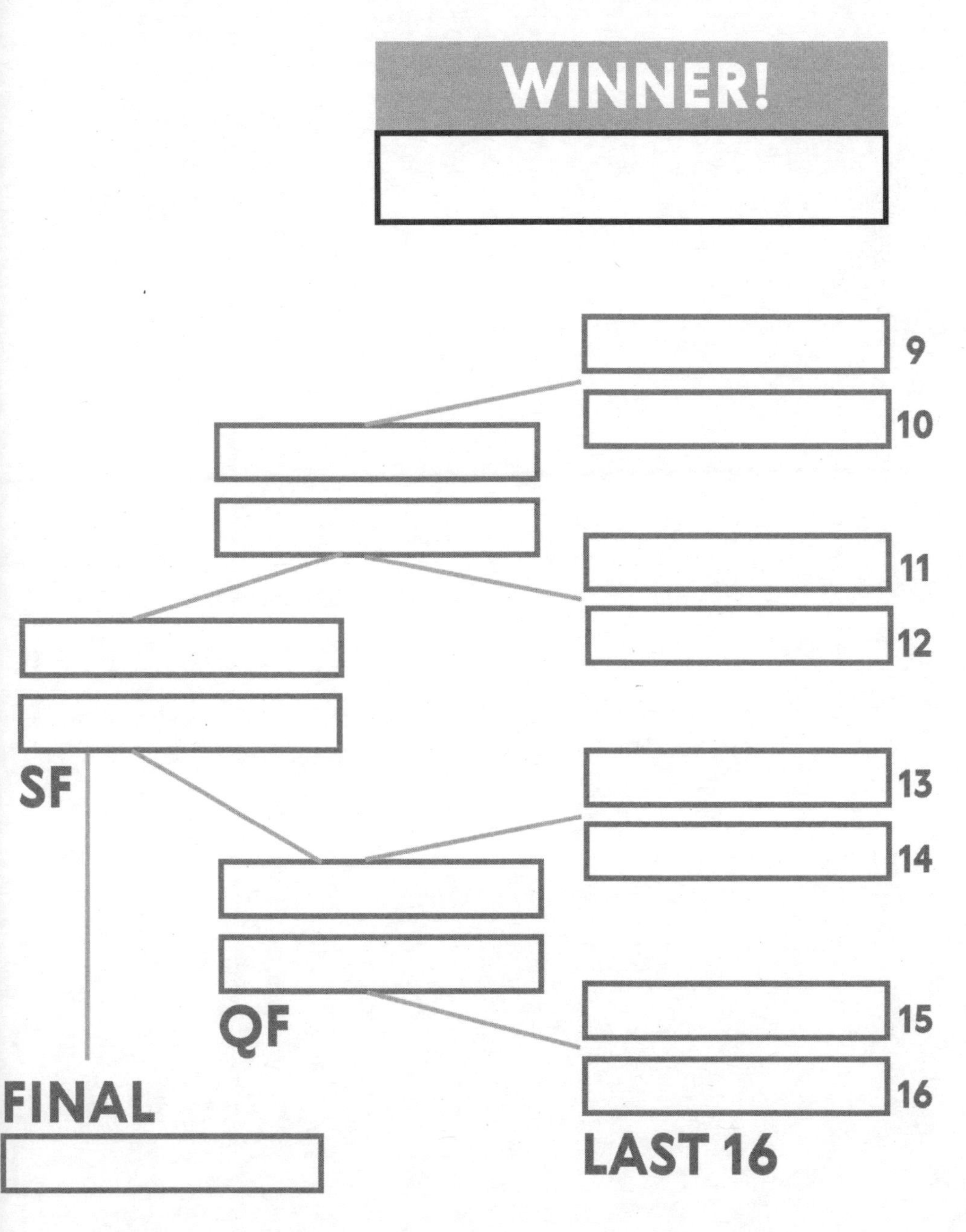
WINNER!
9
10
11
12
SF
13
14
QF
15
16
FINAL
LAST 16

WORLD CUP OF BRITISH SITCOMS

'Allo, 'Allo and welcome to the World Cup of British Sitcoms. Finish your Bread and Porridge (you eat weird stuff in your house). Call in your Father, Ted, and your mother, Miranda (theirs is A Fine Romance, an Absolutely Fabulous union; it is fair to say they both made Good Life choices). Who else is in the house to help with the vote? There are some Men Behaving Badly in the kitchen, real Likely Lads, I think they're Dad's Army mates, and it seems they're Not Going Out. But Mum isn't Outnumbered, she's got her Dinnerladies with her, Just Good Friends (Some Mothers Do 'Ave 'Em), all Birds of a Feather. George and Mildred from The Office are also there and have offered to Car Share with some of The Young Ones like Gavin and Stacey on the way home.

It's time for you all to start voting. The temperature is Rising, Damp patches appear under armpits in Ever Decreasing Circles (It Ain't Half Hot Mum). Everyone has Butterflies. Mrs Brown's Boys have just arrived with Steptoe and S . . .

Listen, you get the idea, we're talking about sitcoms. I can't keep writing this introduction as a series of puns on sitcom titles as there's literally no way to fit *Only Fools and Horses* in. Also, I know your time is precious and if you're anything like My Family you're probably having to do this World Cup on Christmas Day, and you may not have opened all your presents yet (we Open All Ours in the morning). You'll also be keeping an eye on Christmas dinner preparations, and I don't need to delay you any further when you have One Foot in the Gravy*.

So what is the greatest British sitcom of all time? Before we decide, here are a few little quizzes and arguments. Try to get to the Bottom of them.

* Sorry! (starring Ronnie Corbett)

★ CHALLENGE! ★

Name the sitcom! We all know the biggest-name stars in our sitcoms, from Ronnie Barker and David Jason to Victoria Wood and Dawn French, but can you identify these ten British sitcoms from the names of three actors slightly further down the cast list?

1. JOHN LAURIE, ARNOLD RIDLEY, JAMES BECK

----

2. HATTIE HAYRIDGE, NORMAN LOVETT, CLARE GROGAN

----

3. SAM KELLY, BRIAN WILDE, CHRISTOPHER BIGGINS

----

4. SAM KELLY, VICKI MICHELLE, ARTHUR BOSTRUM

----

5. PAULINE MCLYNN, FRANK KELLY, GRAHAM NORTON

----

6. BALLARD BERKELEY, GILLY FLOWER, RENEE ROBERTS

----

7. CHRISTOPHER RYAN, KATHY BURKE, LULU ____________

8. BUSTER MERRYFIELD, JOHN CHALLIS, TESSA PEAKE-JONES

____

9. MAXINE PEAKE, ANNE REID, SHOBNA GULATI

____

10. MELANIE HILL, JONATHON MORRIS, PETER HOWITT

____

Answers at the back of the book.

★ ARGUMENT! ★

As you know by now, I leave two wild-card places open in all of these tournaments so you can choose any particular favourites you think I've overlooked, either because I've forgotten them or because I don't like Topics. But a couple of our World Cups have such crowded fields that I have decided to leave four wild-card places open. The World Cup of British Sitcoms is one of those. Below are twenty-two sitcoms that were all fighting for a place in the line-up but just missed out for a variety of reasons. Why not take a vote on your favourites and select your four wild cards.

BIRDS OF A FEATHER
BLACK BOOKS
BOTTOM
BUTTERFLIES
CAR SHARE
DROP THE DEAD DONKEY
GAVIN & STACEY
THE INBETWEENERS
IT AIN'T HALF HOT MUM
JUST GOOD FRIENDS
KEEPING UP APPEARANCES
THE LEAGUE OF GENTLEMEN
THE LIKELY LADS
MEN BEHAVING BADLY
MIRANDA
NOT GOING OUT
OUTNUMBERED
PHOENIX NIGHTS
RISING DAMP
SPACED
STEPTOE & SON
TO THE MANOR BORN

You must, of course, feel free to add other names to this list. Perhaps your favourite sitcom of all time is Jim Davidson's *Up the Elephant and Round the Castle*?

★ CATCHPHRASE! ★

Below are the initials of ten famous catchphrases from UK sitcoms. Can you work out what they are and name the characters most famous for saying them? GLITQDFYCCBLTAUITBOTB!!! (That's my catchphrase, 'Good luck in this quiz, don't forget you can cheat by looking the answers up in the back of the book!!!')

1. IDBI! ____________
2. LJ! ____________
3. GOGOGOGOGOGOGO ____________
4. IF! ____________
5. IHACP ____________
6. LVC, ISSTOO ____________

7. NNNNNNNNNNY ____________

8. HYTTIOAOA? ____________

9. HDHC! HDH! ____________

10. WD! and DP! and SB ____________ and ____________ and ____________

Answers at the back of the book.

★ MUCH TOO ★ GEEKY CHALLENGE! ★

Here are fifteen cryptic clues to sitcoms, all of which appeared in the BBC top-ten British sitcoms list, but not necessarily in this competition. I say 'cryptic'; they are pretty much just bad puns, wordplays and anagrams. I promise you that unless you're the sort of person who enjoys this sort of thing, you definitely won't enjoy it. I would step away from this challenge and move straight to the voting. I particularly apologise for numbers 4, 7, 8, 9, 12 and 15.

1. EXPENSIVE TOILET
2. FOOTBALLER, AND WHEN FOOTBALLERS GO ON HOLIDAY
3. WHAT'S IN A ROBOT TOMATO?
4. DISTANT BEAR
5. AWFUL RABBIT SCENT
6. US SITCOM HIGHLIGHTS
7. 'MAY I RECOMMEND THE AMBROSIA?'
8. IT'S WHEN YOU GET A LOVELY HERBY SMELL
9. IT'S WHERE YOU PARK YOUR FOURTH CAR
10. GIVE ME CONTRACTIONS
11. LANCELOT & GUINEVERE
12. THE SINCLAIR EXECUTIVE 1972
13. I TOOK MY MILLS & BOON BACK LATE!
14. WHERE HAYES AND WINDSOR MEET
15. WHAT DID THE RACKET SAY TO THE TENNIS BALL?

Answers at the back of the book.

ARE WE READY THEN? Time for the World Cup of British Sitcoms. I think this is honestly one of the toughest competitions in the whole book. Enjoy your many arguments and remember that deep down you do love each other. In case of a draw in any of these battles, simply find yourself in a compromising position and wait for the vicar to pop round unexpectedly to cast the deciding vote.

DAD'S ARMY vs THE YOUNG ONES

The original script that eventually became *Dad's Army* was written by the brilliant Jimmy Perry. It was called 'The Fighting Tigers', was set not in Walmington-on-Sea but in Brightsea-on-Sea, and featured among its other characters, Privates Jim Duck and Joe Fish. The final cast were a truly extraordinary bunch. Arnold Ridley was over seventy when he began playing Private Godfrey (he was born in 1896; remember that when you're next watching those repeats on BBC2). He was a very successful playwright and was the great-uncle of Daisy Ridley, the heroine of the new *Star Wars* movies. Clive Dunn was only forty-eight when he started playing Corporal Jones, and indeed was just fifty-one when he had his number one single 'Grandad'. A lifelong socialist, he would have fierce political arguments with the archly conservative Arthur Lowe. John Laurie, forever associated with the role of Private Frazer, was one of the finest Shakespearean actors of his generation and also worked regularly for Alfred Hitchcock. The seven main cast members notched up fifteen marriages between them, an impressive 2.13 marriages each.

The Young Ones exploded like a comedy bomb across the playgrounds of Britain – mine included – when it first appeared in 1982. Now I think about it, I was eleven. Why on earth was my mum letting me watch *The Young Ones*? I'm going to ask her some stern questions about this. The Americans tried their own remake of *The Young Ones* called 'Oh, No! Not THEM!' which, despite Nigel Planer reprising his role as Neil, was never broadcast.

WRITE YOUR WINNER IN BOX 1 ON THE WALLCHART

Red Dwarf began life as a series of sketches on Radio 4 written by Rob Grant and Doug Naylor, entitled *Dave Hollins: Space Cadet*, in which Chris Barrie played the role of the ship's computer. For the TV series Chris Barrie switched to the lead role of Arnold Rimmer, after first choice Alfred Molina dropped out. Sixty-seven episodes later the show is still going strong and picking up a whole new generation of fans. As will become a common thread during The World Cup of British Sitcoms, they attempted to remake *Red Dwarf* in the USA, under the clever title 'Red Dwarf USA'. As will also become a common thread, the show was never broadcast, although it did feature Jane Leeves as the computer, just a year before she landed the role of Daphne Moon in *Frasier* at $250,000 per episode.

Su Pollard probably got less than that for playing Peggy Ollerenshaw in *Hi-De-Hi!*, but it was the 1980s, so you never know. The series was filmed in a real holiday camp on Hayling Island, but always had to be filmed off-season when the camp was empty. Because of that, eagle-eyed viewers will notice that the surrounding trees have no leaves, and Jeffrey Holland who played Spike was once treated for hypothermia, having been thrown in the camp pool one too many times in the depths of an English winter.

WRITE YOUR WINNER IN BOX 2 ON THE WALLCHART

3 ONLY FOOLS AND HORSES vs THE THICK OF IT

Before bringing the world Del Boy, Rodney, Grandad and Nelson Mandela House, writer John Sullivan had already had a huge hit on British TV with the sitcom *Citizen Smith*. Episode 2 of series 3 of *Citizen Smith* had a very familiar title; it was called 'Only Fools and Horses'.

Only Fools and Horses is possibly the most successful British sitcom of all time, and certainly the most watched. In 1996, 24.3 million people tuned in to the Christmas episode 'Time on Our Hands' – still a record for a British sitcom. Naturally the Americans tried a remake of the show, with the most notable cast member being Christopher Lloyd (Doc Brown, the mad scientist in *Back to the Future*) as Grandad. You will be surprised to learn that the pilot remains unbroadcast.

One show that sort of had a successful US remake was political satire *The Thick of It*, most famous for the mammoth swear-athons of Peter Capaldi's Malcolm Tucker, and for introducing the word 'omnishambles' to the British vocabulary. Despite the inevitable failed US pilot of *The Thick of It*, producer and writer Armando Iannucci then used *The Thick of It* as the basis for the US show *Veep*. Not only was *Veep* actually broadcast; to date it has run to six seasons and its star Julia Louis-Dreyfus has won five Emmys playing the lead role of Selina Meyer. At the time it was first broadcast it seemed a comically over-hysterical look at the craziness of running the USA. These days it looks pretty tame.

WRITE YOUR WINNER IN BOX 3 ON THE WALLCHART

 THE IT CROWD vs THE GOOD LIFE

The IT Crowd is one of two Graham Linehan-penned shows on the list, the other being *Father Ted*. It is my son's favourite sitcom of all time but don't let that sway your vote. You will be amazed to learn that the Americans made their own pilot of *The IT Crowd*, including Richard Ayoade reprising his role as Moss. You will also be amazed to hear that the pilot was never broadcast.

The Good Life is one of two John Esmonde- and Bob Larbey-penned shows on the list, alongside *Ever Decreasing Circles*. Of the stellar cast, only Richard Briers was a big star before the series, but Penelope Keith and Paul Eddington went on to make two more of Britain's most-loved sitcoms: *To the Manor Born* and *Yes Minister*. In fact Penelope Keith's co-star in *To the Manor Born*, Peter Bowles, was the original choice to play the role of her *Good Life* husband Jerry. If you fancy visiting the *Good Life* houses, they are in Kewferry Road, Northwood. It's about a ten-minute walk from Northwood tube. Don't tell them I sent you, just in case they don't like you gawping through their windows.

WRITE YOUR WINNER IN BOX 4 ON THE WALLCHART

5 ONE FOOT IN THE GRAVE vs THE ROYLE FAMILY

One Foot in the Grave writer David Renwick has a number of other notable TV successes to his name. After *One Foot in the Grave* he created and wrote every series of *Jonathan Creek*, but even more excitingly, before *One Foot in the Grave* he and his writing partner Andrew Marshall wrote the *Two Ronnies* sketch in which Ronnie Corbett goes on *Mastermind* with the specialist subject 'Answering the Question before Last'. It is almost impossible to imagine anyone but Richard Wilson playing Victor Meldrew, but after Wilson initially turned the role down, David Renwick briefly considered Les Dawson for the part. Wilson changed his mind and the rest is comedy history.

The peerless Caroline Aherne thought the initial episode of *The Royle Family* was so bad she tried to buy the rights to the show and ensure it was never broadcast. Fortunately for us all, the £250,000 price tag proved too much for her. Thank goodness she wasn't Jane Leeves. Was there a US remake you ask? Why yes, it was called 'The Kennedys' and featured Randy Quaid in the Ricky Tomlinson role. And was it ever broadcast, you ask? No.

WRITE YOUR WINNER IN BOX 5 ON THE WALLCHART

 PEEP SHOW vs OPEN ALL HOURS

Peep Show is the longest-running sitcom in the history of Channel 4, and sprung originally from the idea of having David Mitchell and Robert Webb's characters simply sitting around watching and commenting on TV shows. Channel 4 must have worked out that watching people watching and commenting on TV shows would never get ratings. It'd be like watching people competitively baking cakes or something. Yes, US pilot; no, never broadcast.

Open All Hours feels like a show that ran forever but, amazingly, until the recent *Still Open All Hours* reboot, only twenty-six episodes were made. If you want to visit Arkwright's shop, you still can; it is a hairdresser's in Lister Avenue, Balby, that shuts down for summer filming. Again, don't tell them I sent you. Unless you actually get your hair cut, in which case do tell them and I might get some sort of commission.

WRITE YOUR WINNER IN BOX 6 ON THE WALLCHART

 VICAR OF DIBLEY vs 'ALLO 'ALLO!

Another wildly successful sitcom, *Vicar of Dibley* is filmed in the beautiful Buckinghamshire village of Turville, which is also where they shoot *Midsomer Murders*. The inevitable US pilot, called 'The Minister Divine', was made by Jane Leeves' own production company and starred Kirstie Alley from *Cheers* in the Dawn French role. It was not broadcast.

'Allo 'Allo! is the answer to the question: 'Would it be okay to make a sitcom about the Nazis, based almost entirely on a painting of a naked woman, and including a character whose catchphrase was simply saying 'Heil Hitler' in a funny way?' The answer was a resounding 'yes'. Despite being set in the real French village of Nouvion, all of the external scenes in *'Allo 'Allo!* were shot in Norfolk. The interior scenes were shot at Elstree and if you Google it you can find an amazing photo of the cast of *'Allo 'Allo!* in an Elstree car park, mingling with the cast of *Doctor Who* during a fire alarm.

WRITE YOUR WINNER IN BOX 7 ON THE WALLCHART

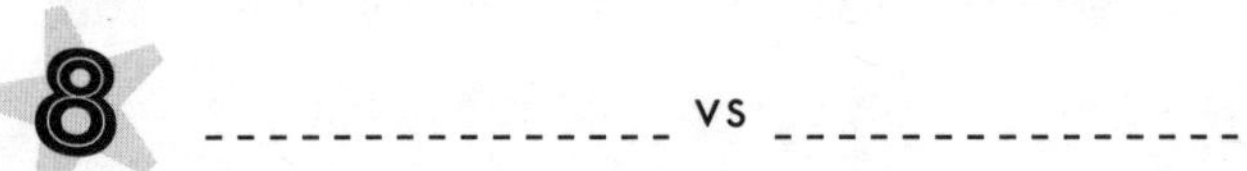

This is the first of your wild-card battles. If you're wondering why there are two wild-card battles instead of the usual one, that means you skipped over the challenges section in this chapter. I knew you would. I spend a lot of time thinking these things up, trying to make them fun but challenging, funny but informative. But for what? Just so you can blithely ignore me and get on with the voting. It's okay, I understand you are busy, and possibly by this time of the evening, fairly tipsy. Take a look back at the challenges and have a think about the shows you want to be represented here. I don't know exactly which shows you will choose, but I can confidently predict they will all have had an American remake which was never broadcast.

WRITE YOUR WINNER IN BOX 8 ON THE WALLCHART

 FAWLTY TOWERS vs ARE YOU BEING SERVED?

According to John Cleese, the response of the first BBC executive to read *Fawlty Towers* was: 'This is full of clichéd situations and stereotypical characters and I cannot see it as being anything other than a disaster.' Many of the critics were equally lukewarm about the first series, with the *Daily Mirror*'s review of the first episode headlined 'Long John Short on Jokes'. Honestly, if you can't trust BBC executives and TV critics then who can you trust? The only people I still have faith in are Russian oligarchs. It is a measure of the brilliance of *Fawlty Towers* that despite only twelve episodes having been made, it regularly tops British and world polls of best sitcom ever, and has not one but *four* unsuccessful US remakes.

Here is a full list of everything sold at Grace Brothers' department store, according to the theme song of *Are You Being Served?*

> GROUND FLOOR – Perfumery, stationery and leather goods, wigs and haberdashery, kitchenware and food (. . . going up)
>
> FIRST FLOOR – Telephones, gents ready-made suits, shirts, shoes, ties, hats, underwear and shoes (. . . going up)
>
> SECOND FLOOR – Carpets, travel goods and bedding, materials, soft furnishings, restaurants and ties (. . . going down)

Which begs the following questions. Why are they selling ties on two different floors? Why are soft furnishings not next to haberdashery? And surely there is extensive crossover between leather goods and travel goods; thus having them two floors apart was impractical at best? In my opinion Old Mr Grace had really taken his eye off the ball here, and Mr Rumbold lacked the authority to overrule him.

'Beane's of Boston' was the US remake and it didn't get made.

WRITE YOUR WINNER IN BOX 9 ON THE WALLCHART

10 ABSOLUTELY FABULOUS vs YES MINISTER

One of these series satirises a hollow, vacuous world full of fame-obsessed mediocrities, needlessly squandering absurd amounts of money in the desperate hope of courting some fleeting whisper of coolness and popularity. The other one is about the world of fashion.

WRITE YOUR WINNER IN BOX 10 ON THE WALLCHART

EVER DECREASING CIRCLES vs PORRIDGE

Two of my favourite sitcoms of all time matched against each other here. *Ever Decreasing Circles* is really a very beautiful, bittersweet look at a suburban England on its way out, played with elegance by Richard Briers, Penelope Wilton and Peter Egan. It is much more than that, of course – it is clever and funny and absurd and silly – but it has a melancholy that very few sitcoms can match. Do Howard and Hilda still exist somewhere in 2017 I wonder?

Porridge would be my winner in the World Cup of British Sitcoms. It originated from *Seven of One*, a series of seven one-off comedy pilots all starring Ronnie Barker in 1973. Barker's favourite of the seven shows featured him playing a Welsh gambling addict. That show didn't make it to series, but both *Porridge* and *Open All Hours* did.

Porridge was remade in the US as *On the Rocks*, featuring a Puerto Rican Fletcher in a Californian Slade Prison. It was unsuccessful.

WRITE YOUR WINNER IN BOX 11 ON THE WALLCHART

12 DINNERLADIES vs I'M ALAN PARTRIDGE

One of my favourite Twitter accounts is the wonderful @VictoriaQOTD, providing a daily dose of the extraordinary warmth and wit of Victoria Wood. I have just checked today's offering and it comes from *Dinnerladies*. A metropolitan-type is visiting the canteen and asks: 'Do you have sugar-free muesli?' to which Thelma Barlow witheringly replies: 'No. This is a canteen. Not a ground sheet at Glastonbury'. Victoria Wood wrote every word of every episode herself, and sadly the sixteen episodes are all we are ever going to see from this work of genius.

One of the most famous scenes in *I'm Alan Partridge* sees

him pitching increasingly outlandish new programmes to an indifferent BBC executive. Alongside 'Arm Wrestling with Chas & Dave' and 'Monkey Tennis' is the classic 'Youth Hostelling with Chris Eubank'. In 2015 Eubank was asked about the scene. Touchingly, he said he'd never heard of it, but was glad to have the mystery cleared up. People had been shouting jokes about youth hostelling at him for nearly twenty years, and he had never had any idea why.

WRITE YOUR WINNER IN BOX 12 ON THE WALLCHART

13 FATHER TED vs Mrs BROWN'S BOYS

Both of these shows were born in Ireland, but produced in Britain, so I think I'm allowed to count them. I expect inter-generational arguments over this battle. Two attempts have been made to create a US version of *Father Ted*. Both failed.

WRITE YOUR WINNER IN BOX 13 ON THE WALLCHART

 LAST OF THE SUMMER WINE vs BLACKADDER

Last of the Summer Wine is the longest-running comedy series in the UK, and is also the longest-running sitcom in the world. Incredibly, Peter Sallis appeared in all 295 episodes over thirty-seven years. He began his role as Clegg as a fifty-two-year-old, and left it as an eighty-nine-year-old. The writer, Roy Clarke, deliberately wanted a gentle end to his creation and gave Clegg the final line of the final episode; simply: 'Did I lock the door?' Considering that *The Young Ones* ended with Vyvyan driving a double-decker bus through a poster of Cliff Richard and over a cliff, whereupon it explodes, instantly killing every main cast member, you have to admire Roy Clarke's restraint.

Blackadder, of course, finished with possibly the greatest sitcom ending of all time. On being informed that Baldrick has the last in his long line of cunning plans, Captain Blackadder replies: 'Well I'm afraid it'll have to wait. Whatever it was, I'm sure it was better than my plan to get out of this by pretending to be mad. I mean who would have noticed another madman around here?' The whistle for the attack blows, Blackadder quietly adds 'Good luck everyone', and one by one the characters we had grown to love, run to their deaths, and the screen gently fades to the poppy fields of France.

WRITE YOUR WINNER IN BOX 14 ON THE WALLCHART

15 THE OFFICE vs BREAD

Was *The Office* remade for America? Yes it was! Was the show ever broadcast? No it wasn . . . wait a second, yes it was! Not only was it broadcast, it also starred Steve Carrell, it was a stonking huge hit running for nine seasons, it was brilliantly funny, and it provides the answer to the question 'How come Ricky Gervais has such an incredibly massive house?'

There is no way you could remake *Bread* for a US audience, because everyone in LA is on the Atkins.

WRITE YOUR WINNER IN BOX 15 ON THE WALLCHART

Your second wild-card battle. Finally Jim Davidson's *Up the Elephant and Round the Castle* gets its chance to shine.

WRITE YOUR WINNER IN BOX 16 ON THE WALLCHART

BRITISH SITCOMS

THE WORLD CUP OF EVERYTHING

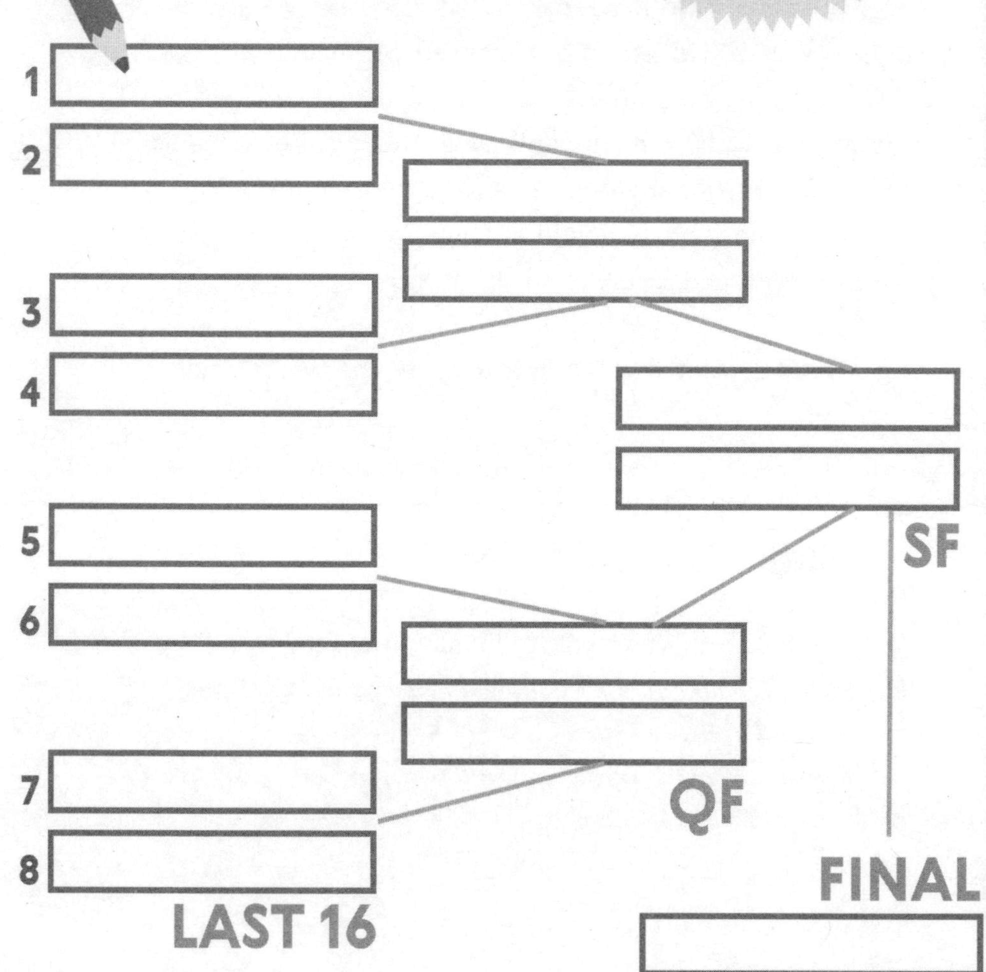

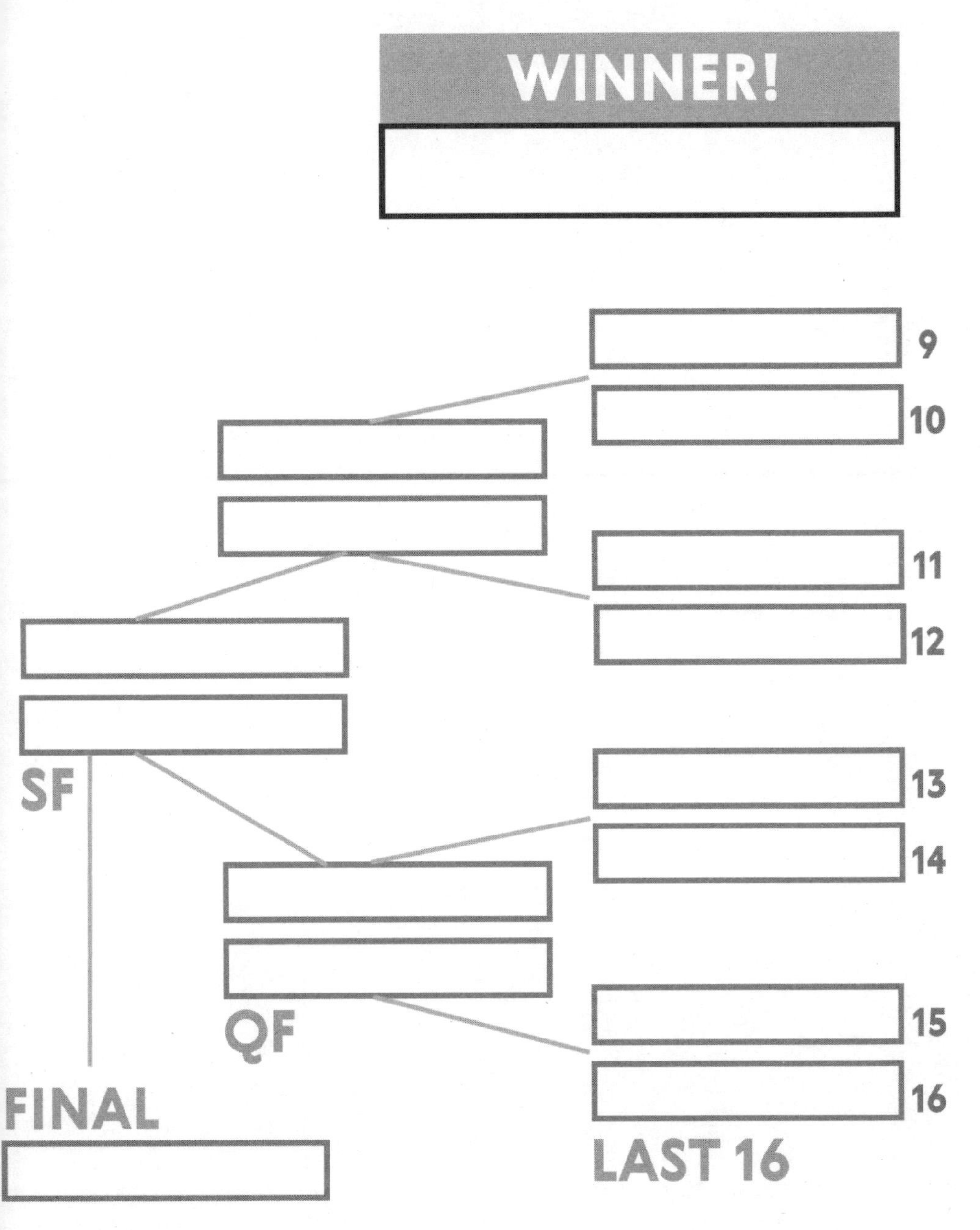
WINNER!
9
10
11
12
SF
13
14
QF
15
16
FINAL
LAST 16

WORLD CUP OF DISNEY

We all know that Disney is magical. A fantasy world of princesses and princes, of pirates and cowboys, of storybook beginnings and fairy-tale endings. It is hard to think of another company that has bought such unparalleled joy to children and adults alike over the last 100 years. Maybe SodaStream, or Fulham FC?

It all began in 1928 when Walt Disney and Ub Iwerks set up their own company, because they felt they weren't being paid enough to make a cartoon called *Oswald the Lucky Rabbit* for Universal. Turns out Oswald wasn't so lucky for Universal, because they missed out on the greatest entertainment empire the world has ever known. Walt and Ub immediately set to work on Mickey Mouse, with Walt even providing Mickey's voice in early cartoons. Mickey made them an unimaginable amount of money despite being, let's face it, probably the worst cartoon character in history. I mean, what is his thing? He's just a mouse with a high-pitched voice. Donald Duck I get, even Goofy has his moments, but Mickey Mouse is just Joe Pasquale with big ears.

For whatever reason though, Mickey Mouse caught on, and launched an empire that has spread happiness, laughter and stardust across the globe. In the World Cup of Disney you will have the chance to vote on some of the most-loved films in history, all the way from Disney's first feature-length cartoon *Snow White and the Seven Dwarfs*, to the run of extraordinary Pixar movies of the twenty-first century.

Before embarking on your quest, I just want to leave you with three quick points.

First, I want to thank the animation industry for experimenting with 3-D animation when my children were younger. It is literally impossible for your children to tell you've fallen asleep during *Wreck-It Ralph* when you are wearing dark glasses.

Second, don't you think Ub Iwerks is a cool name? If you are looking for a name for a forthcoming child, you could do a lot worse than Ub.

Finally, I wanted to relay the fact that the coldest I have ever been was on a visit to a largely deserted, windswept, Euro Disney in about 1994. In fact the whole experience felt very like visiting Chernobyl, but without the welcome warmth of background radiation. It is an urban myth that Walt Disney was cryogenically frozen after his death, but if he had wanted to be, then Euro Disney in 1994 would have been the perfect place.

★ CHALLENGE! ★

Can you name the top fifteen highest-grossing animated movies of all time from their initials alone? Between them these films have made over FOURTEEN *BILLION* DOLLARS. The list is skewed towards newer films because, in the olden days, you didn't have to remortgage your house to take two kids to the cinema. Or sell your house entirely to buy a bag of Revels.

1. F (2013)
2. M (2015)
3. TST (2010)

4. FD (2016)
5. Z (2016)
6. DMT (2013)
7. TLK (1994)
8. FN (2003)
9. ST (2004)
10. IA: DOTD (2009)
11. IA: CD (2012)
12. TSLOP (2016)
13. IO (2015)
14. STT (2007)
15. SFA (2010)

Answers at the back of the book.

★ INFORMATION ★ ★ AND CHALLENGE! ★

It took Disney a long time to settle on the final names of the seven dwarfs – Happy, Dopey, Sleepy, Sneezy, Grumpy, Bashful and Doc. Below are all genuine names circulated among Disney executives before the final choice was made. I have two challenges for you here. First, take a look through and work out which seven you would have gone for. Second, vote on the one which most suits whoever you are playing this with, and use that name for them throughout the World Cup of Disney.

AWFUL, BALDY, BIGGY-WIGGY, BLABBY, BURPY, CRABBY, CRANKY, CHESTY, DIPPY, DIRTY, DOLEFUL, DUMPY, FLABBY, GASPY, GLOOMY, GOOPY, GRACEFUL, HELPFUL, HOTSY, HUNGRY, JAZZY, JUMPY, LAZY, NEURTSY, NIFTY, PUFFY, SAPPY, SCRAPPY, SHIFTY, SHORTY, SILLY, SLUTTY, SNAPPY, SNIFFY, SNOOPY, SNURFLES, SOULFUL, TEARFUL, THRIFTY, TUBBY, WEEPY, WHEEZY, WISTFUL, WOEFUL.

★ CHALLENGE! ★

One of the most frustrating things about going to see a Disney movie at the cinema is recognising one of the voices and not being able to work out who it is. You can't even ask your kids, because they're like eight years old or something, and they are not capable of confidently whispering, 'I think it's Martin Sheen.' Can you tell me which actors voiced the following roles in Disney films?

1. WOODY in *TOY STORY* ____________
2. MUFASA in *THE LION KING* ____________
3. PRINCESS FIONA AND DONKEY in *SHREK* ____________ & ____________
4. DOC HUDSON in *CARS* ____________
5. ELSA in *FROZEN* ____________
6. KING LOUIE in *THE JUNGLE BOOK* (1967) ____________
7. DORY in *FINDING DORY* ____________
8. MIKE & SULLEY in *MONSTERS, INC.* ____________ & ____________
9. LUCIUS BEST in *THE INCREDIBLES* ____________
10. MAUI in *MOANA* ____________

Answers at the back of the book.

★ WILD CARD! ★

This is another World Cup where there are so many legitimate contenders, you might need a bit of extra help choosing your two wild-card options. Below are twenty-four films, all of which have not been included in the World Cup of Disney, but certainly could have been. Which two will you choose?

A BUG'S LIFE – ALICE IN WONDERLAND – BASIL THE GREAT MOUSE DETECTIVE – BRAVE – BROTHER BEAR – BOLT – CARS 2 – DINOSAUR – FANTASIA – HERCULES – LILO & STITCH – MONSTERS UNIVERSITY – OLIVER AND COMPANY – ROBIN HOOD – SLEEPING BEAUTY – TARZAN – THE ARISTOCATS – THE FOX AND THE HOUND – THE GOOD DINOSAUR – THE HUNCHBACK OF NOTRE DAME – THE PRINCESS AND THE FROG – THE RESCUERS – TOY STORY 2 – WRECK-IT RALPH

ALL RIGHT, FOLKS, I THINK WE'RE ABOUT READY TO VOTE. In case of a tie, get one of the children to sing 'Let

It Go' over and over again until somebody submits. Good luck, and try not to get too animated.

FINDING NEMO VS THE LION KING

Finding Nemo was the highest-grossing animated film of all time upon its release, but has since been overtaken and is struggling to stay in the top ten. However, it was also the highest-selling DVD of all time, and given that DVD sales are now falling rapidly, that is a title it may hold for the rest of time.

The Lion King was also the highest-grossing animated movie of all time when it was released in 1994. When you next watch the film, take a listen to the very beginning of 'Circle of Life'. It begins very clearly with the words 'Arsène Wenger'. Wenger first arrived at Arsenal in 1996, so the song was clearly some sort of prophecy. The 'Circle of Life' indeed.

WRITE YOUR WINNER IN BOX 1 ON THE WALLCHART

2 BAMBI vs ZOOTOPIA

Bambi remains one of the saddest films of all time, and the best episode of *The Young Ones* ever. The film revolves around the relationship between Bambi and his mother. In real life the voice actors who played the mother and son were actually married to each other. Move along, nothing to see here.

Zootopia is a film I am unfamiliar with, as it was released in 2016, and my children are all grown up. I now no longer have to take weekly Saturday-morning trips to the cinema to watch something called 'Ernest The Troubled Toaster', 'Monkey Jockeys 4', or 'Meerkat Werewolf', just to buy me ninety minutes' snoozing time. However, I feel a bit sad to have missed *Zootopia,* as I read that it concerns a European rabbit police officer who teams up with a con-artist fox, and also includes a grizzled police chief voiced by Idris Elba, and a gazelle played by Shakira.

WRITE YOUR WINNER IN BOX 2 ON THE WALLCHART

3 TOY STORY vs ALADDIN

It is easy to forget that, back in 1995, *Toy Story* was an enormous risk for Disney, as the first ever feature-length computer-animated film. In the original scripts for *Toy Story* our two heroes, Woody the cowboy and Buzz Lightyear, were supposed to be a ventriloquist's dummy and a tiny tin soldier called Tinny. By the way, if you have a talking Woody doll at home, then I regret to inform you that his voice, although it does sound like Tom Hanks, was actually recorded by Tom's brother, Jim Hanks.

Toy Story, and much of Pixar's subsequent output, was in some way inspired by Disney's *Aladdin*. The creative brains at Pixar felt that Disney's regular animated films featured heroes and heroines who were too perfect. They cited *Aladdin* as a prime example of a great movie with a dull hero. As Andrew Stanton, the genius behind *Finding Nemo*, said 'Why do they name these movies after the most boring characters in the film?'

WRITE YOUR WINNER IN BOX 3 ON THE WALLCHART

 PETER PAN vs THE LITTLE MERMAID

Walt Disney had planned to make *Peter Pan* in 1935, as the follow-up to his first feature film *Snow White and the Seven Dwarfs*. However, it took him four years to get the rights, eventually coming to an arrangement with Great Ormond Street Hospital to whom J.M. Barrie has bequeathed the work. Animation began in earnest in 1939, to be ready for a 1941 release. However, the US then joined the Second World War, and the US military immediately took control of Disney's studio to make propaganda films. Once war had ended, the Disney studio was now in debt and couldn't afford to produce the film. So it wasn't until 1953, fully eighteen years after Disney had started trying, that *Peter Pan* was released.

The Little Mermaid, released in 1989, marked the start of the era known as the 'Disney Renaissance'. After a string of backroom squabbles and box-office flops during the 1980s, a reinvigorated Disney released *The Little Mermaid, Beauty and the Beast, Aladdin, The Lion King, Pocahontas, The Hunchback of Notre Dame, Hercules, Mulan* and *Tarzan* all within the space of ten years. Between them those films earned Disney $3.78 billion at the box office. A nice renaissance to have.

WRITE YOUR WINNER IN BOX 4 ON THE WALLCHART

 THE INCREDIBLES vs RATATOUILLE

At the end of *The Incredibles,* a new villain named The Underminer appears. The Underminer is voiced by John Ratzenberger, best known to UK audiences as Cliff in *Cheers.* Ratzenberger is Pixar's lucky charm, and to date he has appeared in all of the following: *Toy Story, A Bug's Life, Toy Story 2, Monsters, Inc., Finding Nemo, The Incredibles, Cars, Ratatouille, WALL-E, Up, Toy Story 3, Cars 2, Brave, Monsters University, Inside Out, The Good Dinosaur, Finding Dory* and *Cars 3*.

In *Ratatouille* Ratzenberger plays another small role: Mustafa the Waiter. It is not the only similarity between the two films. Both were directed by Brad Bird, both won Oscars for Best Animated Feature, and the technique of 'sub-surface light scattering' used in *Ratatouille* to make fruit and veg look real, had been developed for *The Incredibles* to make the human faces look real. The *New York Times* described *Ratatouille* as 'a nearly flawless piece of popular art, as well as one of the most persuasive portraits of an artist ever committed to film'.

WRITE YOUR WINNER IN BOX 5 ON THE WALLCHART

 DUMBO vs INSIDE OUT

Dumbo and *Inside Out* are essentially the same film. They both feature child heroes who feels alone and displaced, but who eventually overcome the odds and find happiness and self-acceptance. I mean, sure, one of them is an elephant with big ears forced to join the circus, and the other is an eleven-year-old girl forced to move to San Francisco, and made to endure broccoli on her pizza. And, yes, one is helped by an anthropomorphic mouse named Timothy, while the other is helped by a series of five multicoloured neuropsychological 'emotions' living inside her head. And one reaches self-acceptance by using his large ears to fly, despite the absence of a magic feather given to him by the mouse, and the other one reaches self-acceptance by allowing sadness and joy to work together, after a lengthy metaphor about a 'train of thought'. But apart from that, they are exactly the same film.

WRITE YOUR WINNER IN BOX 6 ON THE WALLCHART

BEAUTY AND THE BEAST vs BRAVE

Beauty and the Beast was the first animated film in history to be nominated for a Best Film Academy Award. Belle, the 'Beauty', was modelled on Judy Garland while the Prince, the 'Beast', was slightly more complicated, being modelled on the head and horns of an American bison, the arms and body of a bear, the ears of a deer, the eyebrows of a gorilla, the jaws, teeth and mane of a lion, the tusks of a wild boar and the legs and tail of a wolf. If he was real, you can bet that Heston Blumenthal would cook him.

Brave is another I haven't seen, forgive me, but I'm aware it is Scottish and much loved, exactly like one of its stars, Billy Connolly. It was the first Pixar film to feature a female protagonist. Merida, voiced by Kelly Macdonald, was originally supposed to be voiced by Reese Witherspoon, but Witherspoon admitted she had to leave the project due to her inability to master a Scottish accent. Not a problem for Billy Connolly.

WRITE YOUR WINNER IN BOX 7 ON THE WALLCHART

WALL-E vs LADY AND THE TRAMP

Brad Bird had already bagged two Oscars for *The Incredibles* and *Ratatouille,* and Andrew Stanton matched his feat with *Wall-E,* adding to the Oscar he had won for *Finding Nemo.* It contains almost no dialogue for long stretches of the film, but despite that, John Ratzenberger still manages to be in it.

Lady and the Tramp is best remembered for the scene in which Lady and Tramp share a plate of spaghetti. I have a number of issues with this. In real life, you really shouldn't encourage dogs to eat pasta, as canine stomachs don't process starch as effectively as humans. Also, for food hygiene reasons, the two dogs should not have been served in the first place, particularly as they are at a table with a naked flame, which is a further health and safety breach. Perhaps most importantly of all, pure-bred American Cocker spaniel pups sell for around £800 each, and it is therefore very unlikely that Lady's owners would let her anywhere near Tramp, let alone go to a restaurant with him. He's called Tramp for a reason, and we can also see by how they eat their spaghetti that she's totally into him. This single date could cost Lady's owners a windfall of somewhere around £6,400.

WRITE YOUR WINNER IN BOX 8 ON THE WALLCHART

TANGLED vs FINDING DORY

Tangled, loosely based on the story of Rapunzel, is, by some reports, the most expensive animated film ever produced, with an eventual budget of $260 million. It ended up making over $590 million at the box office though, so I don't want you to be up all night worrying about Disney.

In 2016 *Finding Dory* became the fourth film on this list to make over a billion dollars at the box office (the first three were *Toy Story 3, Frozen* and *Zootopia*). I do hope Disney have invested this money wisely, perhaps in a couple of buy-to-let properties, and maybe a cash ISA.

WRITE YOUR WINNER IN BOX 9 ON THE WALLCHART

10 FROZEN vs MULAN

I don't need to tell you anything about *Frozen*; it has been on a loop in your house for nearly five years now, and the lyrics to 'Let It Go' are more familiar to you than your own PIN number. Good luck in your efforts to stop this winning the World Cup of Disney. *Frozen* was directed by Jennifer Lee, the first woman to direct a Walt Disney Animation Studios feature film, and also the first woman in history to direct a billion-dollar-grossing movie. 'Let It Go' was written by Robert Lopez and Kristen Anderson-Lopez. Robert Lopez was also the co-writer of the musical *Book of Mormon,* and is the youngest person in history to win an Emmy, a Grammy, an Oscar and a Tony.

Mulan is a lovely film, was nominated for an Oscar, contributed to the successful 'Disney Renaissance' and made over $300 million, but it's up against *Frozen,* so what are you going to do?

WRITE YOUR WINNER IN BOX 10 ON THE WALLCHART

11 PINOCCHIO vs UP

The most famous voice actor of all time, Mel Blanc, receives a credit on *Pinocchio.* Blanc, who would later go on to become the voice of Bugs Bunny, Daffy Duck, Woody Woodpecker, Barney Rubble, Porky Pig, Tweety Pie, Sylvester the Cat, Foghorn Leghorn, Pepé le Pew, Wile E. Coyote, Road Runner, Yosemite Sam and Speedy Gonzales, plays the part of Gideon in *Pinocchio.* If you know the film well, then you will know that Gideon is mute throughout, a decision Disney made very late in the process. Blanc still received a credit, however, for recording a solitary hiccup, which is repeated three times in the finished film. Mel Blanc died in 1989, and his gravestone, in Hollywood, reads 'That's All Folks'.

Next time you need to stump that guy at work who knows all about films, ask him this question. What has the shortest title of any film ever nominated for a Best Picture Oscar? He will think for a while and say *Up*, which was nominated in 2009. But he would be wrong, as the obscure French-Algerian film *Z* was nominated in 1969. He won't like getting this wrong. Three three-letter films, *JFK*, *Her* and *Ray*, have been nominated, but the shortest title to win the Best Picture Oscar is shared between *Gigi* and *Argo*. I know this is only tangentially related to the World Cup of Disney, but I really enjoyed working it all out.

WRITE YOUR WINNER IN BOX 11 ON THE WALLCHART

12 TOY STORY 3 vs 101 DALMATIONS

Andy's mum has a new car in *Toy Story 3*, but she keeps her old number plate, which reads 'A113'. There is a good reason for this. 'A113' was a classroom number at the California

Institute of Arts, where Pixar's founder John Lasseter studied character animation, alongside both Brad Bird, Andrew Stanton and many others. You will see 'A113' somewhere in every single Pixar film. Sometimes it is obvious; it is the code forbidding humans to return to earth in *Wall-E* for example. Sometimes it is very obscure; it is the make of the scuba divers' camera in *Finding Nemo*, and even turns up in *Brave* as 'ACXIII' carved above the doorway in a witch's hut. But it is always there. A113 is still in use at CalArts and is currently the first-year Graphic Design classroom. In the UK the A113 runs between Leytonstone and Chipping Ongar. Via Chigwell.

After *Sleeping Beauty* had been an expensive flop for Disney in 1959, there had been genuine talk about having to close down the animation studios for good. Animation had simply become too expensive. Fortunately our old friend Ub Iwerks had been hard at work inventing new animation techniques involving Xerox cameras. *One Hundred and One Dalmations* was the first feature film on which Ub's new techniques were used, and it was estimated to have halved the cost of the animation process. By a neat stroke of luck it was particularly effective at animating the spots on the Dalmatians. The finished film contains a mind-boggling 6,469,952 spots, so it is fair to say this saved them a bit of time. The film was a huge box-office hit, exactly when one was needed. So, money was saved, time was saved, the puppies were saved, and ultimately Disney was saved too.

WRITE YOUR WINNER IN BOX 12 ON THE WALLCHART

13 POCAHONTAS vs THE JUNGLE BOOK

The real Pocahontas had an extraordinary, if all too brief, life. Having travelled to England with her husband, a tobacco planter named John Rolfe, Pocahontas died before ever returning to her homeland. She is buried in St George's Church in Gravesend, but the exact location of her grave is unknown. Her son, Thomas Rolfe, did return to the US, and among the direct descendants of Pocahontas are two First Ladies, Edith Wilson and Nancy Reagan, and the astronomer Percy Lowell, who discovered Pluto.

Most of the character names in *The Jungle Book* are pleasingly literal. 'Baloo' is a Hindi word for bear, 'Bagheera' is a Hindi word for panther, 'Hathi' is a Hindi word for elephant, and 'Shere' is a Hindi word for tiger. Kipling made up 'Mowgli' and 'Kaa' all by himself. The vultures in the film were modelled on The Beatles, but John Lennon vetoed the idea of The Beatles themselves providing the voices. Ringo Starr would have to wait another seventeen years to get his big break with *Thomas the Tank Engine. The Jungle Book* was the last film to feature Walt Disney as producer, as he passed away during its production. This lovely, funny, happy, sad, smart and joyful film is a fitting legacy.

WRITE YOUR WINNER IN BOX 13 ON THE WALLCHART

14 MONSTERS, INC. vs CINDERELLA

Another of John Lasseter's classmates in room A113 at CalArts was Pete Docter. Just like Brad Bird and Andrew Stanton, Pete Docter has also bagged himself two Oscars, as director of *Up* and *Inside Out*. The second win must have been a relief to him – imagine going to a school reunion and being the only person in the room without two Oscars? *Monsters, Inc.* was Docter's directorial debut and, I think, the funniest Pixar film of all.

Back in the days of *Cinderella*, released in 1950, there were no Oscars for Best Animated Film, but it still managed to bag the Best Original Song Oscar for 'Bibbidi-Bobbidi-Boo'. I'm not surprised at all, it is very hard to argue with either salagadoola or mechika boola, and impossible to dispute bibbidi-bobbidi-boo.

**'Salagadoola, mechika boola,
Bibbiddi-bobbidi-boo'**

Wise words indeed.

WRITE YOUR WINNER IN BOX 14 ON THE WALLCHART

15 MOANA vs SNOW WHITE AND THE SEVEN DWARFS

One of Disney's most recent classics, released in 2016, against the first Disney feature film ever released, in 1937. Eighty years, over fifty Oscar wins, over one hundred Oscar nominations, twenty-two Oscars for Walt Disney himself, more than any other individual in history. Not to mention the singing, the dancing, the laughter, the tears, the endless skill, the invention, the attention to detail, and the flights of fancy beyond normal imagination. You have to wonder what Oswald the Lucky Rabbit would have made of it all.

WRITE YOUR WINNER IN BOX 15 ON THE WALLCHART

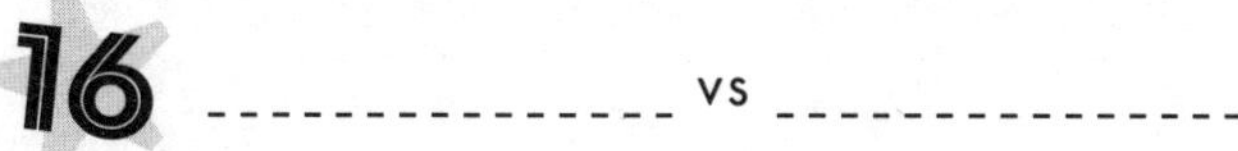

We've done the wild-card choice already, remember? It was in the 'Wild Card!' section, just after the bit where you decided you were going to call your family Burpy, Baldy and Woeful all evening? *Toy Story 2* and *Monsters University* would be my choices!

WRITE YOUR WINNER IN BOX 16 ON THE WALLCHART

DISNEY

THE WORLD CUP OF EVERYTHING

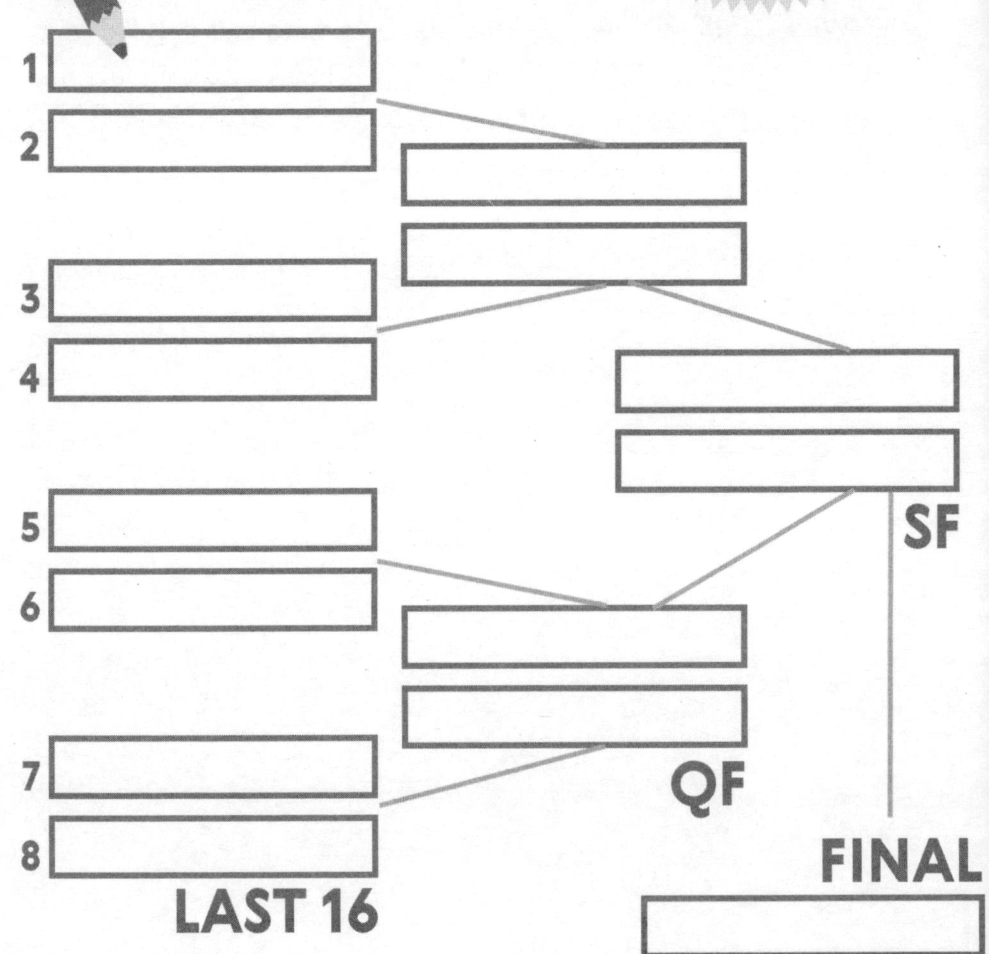

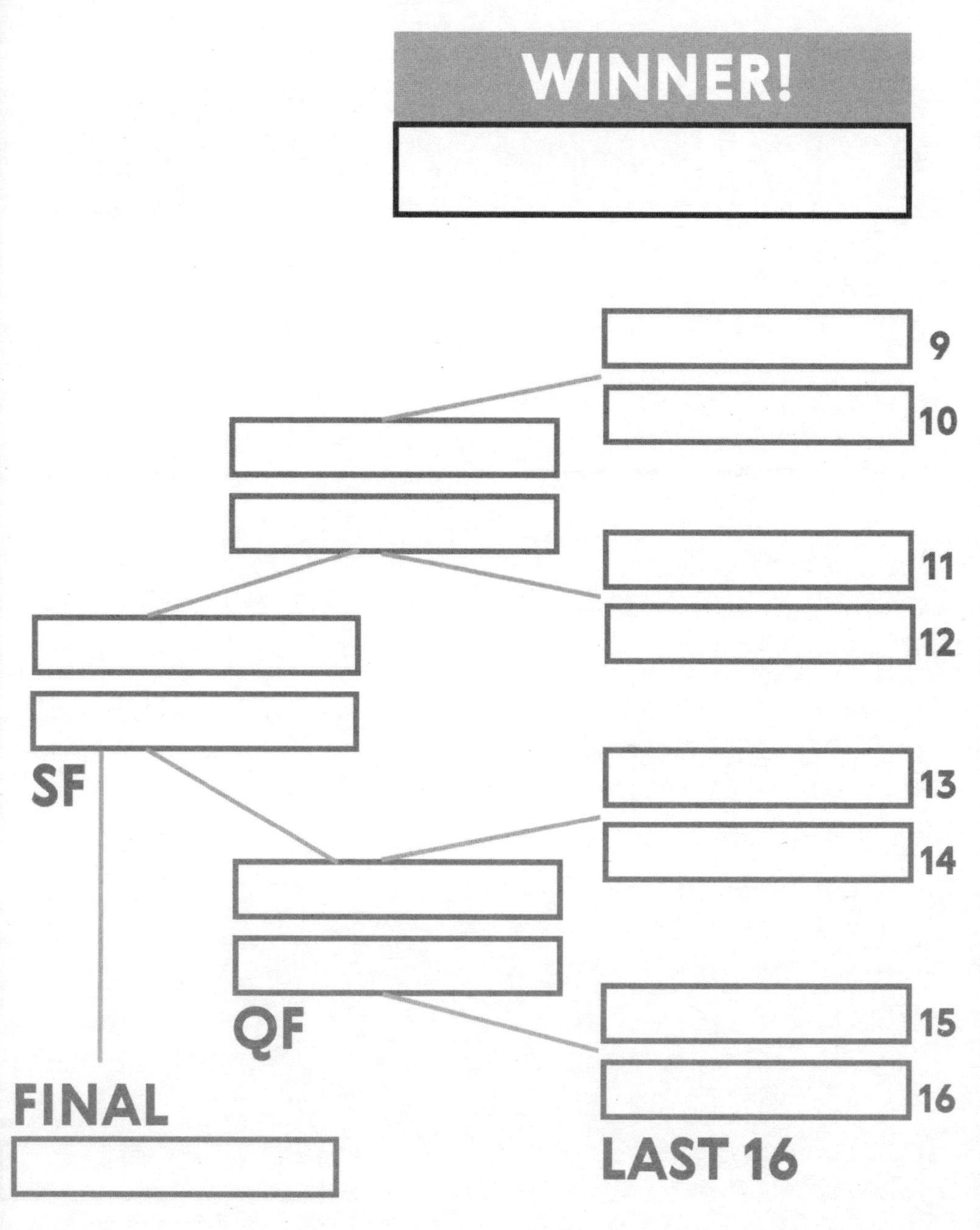
WINNER!
9
10
11
12
SF
13
14
QF
15
16
FINAL
LAST 16

WORLD CUP OF DRINKS

Strictly speaking, the winner of the World Cup of Drinks should be water. Each and every one of us is made up of around 60 per cent water. We are more water than anything else. We are like Manchester. Essentially for tax purposes we are all offshore. There are some exceptions to this rule. Your uncle Keith is, for instance, 60 per cent vodka.

You can last up to thirty days without food, but you can only last around four days without water. This is why Nando's is legally obliged to give you free drink refills but not free chicken refills.

All the water on earth arrived on comets and asteroids sometime over four billion years ago. Except for organic coconut water, which arrived on an Ocado delivery van.

In most places where humans live you will find abundant sources of water, but you can still choose to spend an awful lot of money on it if you wish. The most common trend among the very expensive water brands is to either draw their water from glaciers, or high mountain streams, or from deep underwater. Aqua Amore is harvested from icebergs off the coast of Newfoundland, yours for just £35 a bottle. Aquadeco claims its water is over 18,000 years old, though for some reason it still comes with a best before date, VEEN comes from the Konisaajo spring in Finnish Lapland, and will cost you £20 a bottle. It is so expensive it makes me wonder if Finnish Lapland is actually a pole-dancing club.

You could even pay $60,000 for a bottle of Acqua di Cristallo – Tributo a Modigliani, which is a blend of Fijian and French spring water and glacier water from Iceland. To be fair, they do then add 5mg of actual 23-carat gold dust, so in some ways you're not really paying for the water.

Coconut water was the latest way to make us pay exorbitant amounts of money for something which comes out of a tap in our own house, but it now has a series of rivals on the scene. I visited Whole Foods Market in Piccadilly, and these are, genuinely, some of the products on offer in the water fridge. I promise I have made none of these up. You can buy Bamboo Water, Pure Birch Water, Black Birch Water, Coconut Tapped Birch Water, Bilberry and Lingonberry Birch Water, Beetroot Water, Cucumber

Water, Cucumber & Lime Water, Watermelon Water, Ginger Water, Icelandic Glacier Water, Artesian Well Water, Sodium Free Aqua Water, Everyday Value Electrolyte Water, and Lemonade Flavoured Zero Calorie Nutrient Enhanced Water.

So, let's disqualify water from the World Cup of Drinks, as all drinks are water really. It would be a bit like a potato winning the World Cup of Crisps or a camera winning the World Cup of Christmas Films. Let's also disqualify coconut water, Birch Water and Lemonade Flavoured Zero Calorie Nutrient Enhanced Water, on the grounds that we all have taps, and if we wanted to add something with spurious health benefits to our water we could just have a Lemsip.

I have included booze and soft drinks. In fact, every first-round battle here is booze v non-booze. Careful with the voting though, as it is worth noting that it is impossible to say the sentence 'Oh look, all sixteen of the alcoholic drinks have made it through to the second round', without saying 'alcoholic'.

★ CHALLENGE! ★

Drink is clearly the inspiration for almost all great art ever made. Below is a list of titles of all sorts of things – books, films, plays, songs – all of which have a type of drink in their title. I have missed the drinks out of the titles. Can you fill in the blanks please in this quiz that I'm calling 'Pintless', hosted by Jeremy Vino and Shandy Toksvig.

1. ____________ WITH ROSIE (NOVEL)

2. ____________ & TV (BLUR SINGLE)

3. LAST ____________ IN PARIS (FILM)

4. ____________ & JUICE (SNOOP DOGG SONG)

5. ____________ (LONG-RUNNING ITV DOCUMENTARY SERIES)

6. ____________ (SEAN PENN FILM)

7. ____________ (BEYONCÉ ALBUM)

8. THE ____________ SONG (RUPERT HOLMES)

9. ____________ (FILM)

10. EUGENE ONE ____________ (TCHAIKOVSKY OPERA)

11. ____________ (KELIS SONG)

12. ____________ MOCKINGBIRD (NOVEL. Forgive me, I couldn't resist it)

Answers at the back of the book.

★ INFORMATION! ★

Below is a list of the top ten countries that drink the most beer per capita. There is no way in a thousand years that anyone will get all ten, but do feel free to test people. The findings were compiled, by the way, by the Kirin Beer Company, and given that they operate the world's only Beer University, I think we should trust them.

1. CZECH REPUBLIC
2. THE SEYCHELLES (Whaaaa?)
3. AUSTRIA
4. GERMANY (There they are look)
5. NAMIBIA
6. POLAND
7. IRELAND (Good showing)
8. LITHUANIA
9. BELIZE
10. ESTONIA

The United Kingdom came a very disappointing twenty-eighth, behind such legendary drinkers as Gabon, Panama and Venezuela.

★ PUB CRAWL CHALLENGE! ★

Can you guess the names of these pubs from the initials below. They are all on the list of the top thirty most common British pub names. The first five on the list are the most common pub names in Britain in that order.

1. TRL
2. TC
3. TRO
4. TWH
5. TS
6. TWH (a different one, obvz)
7. TKA
8. TQH
9. TCAH
10. TBH
11. TRAC
12. TPOW
13. TFAH
14. TKH
15. TW

Answers at the back of the book.

★ INFORMATION! ★

These are the top ten best-selling soft drinks brands in the world, according to the most recent figures from *Beverage Digest*.

1. COCA-COLA
2. DIET COKE
3. PEPSI
4. MOUNTAIN DEW
5. DR PEPPER
6. SPRITE
7. DIET PEPSI
8. DIET MOUNTAIN DEW
9. FANTA
10. DIET DR PEPPER

OKAY, SHALL WE BEGIN? Here comes the World Cup of Drinks. Beer? Coke? Coffee? Hydrogenated Birch Water? You decide. In case of a tie, make two people down a can of Diet Coke and the first one to burp loses.

WHISKY vs MILK

After the levying of the English Malt Tax in 1723, the booming Scottish whisky distillation industry was forced underground almost overnight. In order to stop the dreaded government excise men from spotting the smoke from illegal stills, the Scots began operating homemade stills at night. For this reason, whisky was the origin of the name 'moonshine'. Conversely, in the US, a government crackdown was very, very good for the whiskey trade. During the Prohibition era from 1920–33, the only alcohol legally available was whiskey prescribed through a doctor and sold through a licensed pharmacy. Coincidentally, I'm sure, the tiny Walgreens pharmacy chain in the US grew from twenty outlets to over four hundred during this period. It has never looked back and is now one of the world's largest and most profitable pharmacy chains.

By 'milk' we traditionally mean milk from cows, or sometimes milk from semi-skimmed cows, but there are many, many other examples. We're familiar with goat's milk and sheep's milk. Reindeer milk is popular in Lapland and has six times the fat content of cow's milk, so Rudolph's red nose possibly came from poor circulation caused by constricted arteries. Half of all milk consumed in India is water-buffalo milk. Camel milk can last for seven days at temperatures of 86 degrees, and can keep for three months when refrigerated. I think that's the stuff they use in motorway service stations. The Mongolians drink horse milk, while one of Serbia's greatest delicacies is donkey cheese. Quite apart from all of these, you can now buy soy milk, almond milk, cashew milk, hazelnut milk, rice milk, hemp milk, flax milk, coconut milk and human milk.

WRITE YOUR WINNER IN BOX 1 ON THE WALLCHART

2 TEQUILA vs DIET COKE

Tequila can only be made from the blue agave plant in the area around the city of Tequila in central Mexico. For many years it was illegal to import tequila into China, but this ban was lifted after President Xi Jinping's visit to Mexico in 2013. Blimey, he must have had a good time.

Diet Coke, the second biggest-selling soft drink in the world, was only launched in 1982. Since it launched, the world obesity crisis has been cured (citation needed). They now also make Coke Zero with a sleek red and black design, marketed at men. Every time I reach for a Coke Zero instead of a Diet Coke, I realise what a powerlessly deluded pawn of the advertising industry I am. I still do it though.

WRITE YOUR WINNER IN BOX 2 ON THE WALLCHART

3 BEER vs RED BULL

At any given time, 0.7 per cent of the population are drunk. That means that roughly 49 million people are drunk as you read this. Look around you; can you spot one? Someone not among their number is former world darts champion Andy 'The Viking' Fordham. He drank twenty-four bottles of beer before winning the 2004 World Darts final and has subsequently admitted he can't remember winning it. He says his drinking record was sixty bottles of beer on a night out with his wife. He doesn't say if he had to finish on a double though. Andy is happily sober now, and on the comeback trail.

One of the two men who set up Red Bull, Dietrich Mateschitz, is the richest person in Austria, while the son of the other founder, Chalerm Yoovidhya, is the fourth-richest person in Thailand. Rather neatly, one of the people ahead of him on that list made his money in beer. Charoen Sirivadhanabhakdi, the son of a Bangkok street vendor, is head of Thailand's largest brewery and is worth a neat $16.9 billion.

WRITE YOUR WINNER IN BOX 3 ON THE WALLCHART

BAILEYS vs TANGO

If you found the first battle, Whisky vs Milk, too difficult to decide, then Baileys is the drink for you! I love Baileys. I once got a bottle of Baileys for Christmas which came with its own cup, but the cup was made of chocolate and you got to eat it afterwards. I truly love Santa sometimes. Baileys Irish Cream was first introduced in 1974 but no one called Bailey was involved. It was launched by the Gilbey family, and named after a restaurant owned by a man named Chesterman. The 'R A Bailey' signature on the bottle was 'inspired by' the Bailey's hotel in London. Although there is no real Bailey in Bailey's Irish Cream there is certainly plenty of real Irish. The whiskey comes from Irish distilleries and the cream comes from a dairy in County Cavan, though at busier times of the year (I'm guessing Christmas right?) another dairy in County Kilkenny helps out too.

The first three battles actually mix quite nicely – whisky and milk make Baileys, a Don Julio Blanco is a great tequila and Diet Coke cocktail, and, of course, there would be no Jägerbomb these days without beer and Red Bull. With this is mind I have just mixed, then tried on your behalf, a Baileys and Orange Tango cocktail. I have called it 'You Know When You've Been Blotto-ed' and it is awful beyond words. I love the fact that even though you know I'm telling you the truth, some of you will now try it too. Good luck: it is a lot less like an alcoholic Chocolate Orange than you are hoping.

WRITE YOUR WINNER IN BOX 4 ON THE WALLCHART

5 RUM vs COFFEE

Rum has been associated with the Royal Navy since they landed on the island of Jamaica in 1655. Before that date, sailors' 'daily rations' were French brandy, but rum very soon became ubiquitous. This daily ration or 'tot' of rum continued all the way up until 1970, and is still served on special occasions. Legend has it that when Nelson's body was transported back to England following his death at the Battle of Trafalgar, it was preserved in a cask of rum. However, when the cask was opened upon arrival in England, the rum had disappeared. Enterprising sailors had drilled a hole in the bottom of the cask and slowly drunk the lot during the voyage.

Coffee was discovered by Ethiopian shepherds roughly 1,200 years ago. The story goes, two shepherds were wandering through the high and desolate mountains of Northern Ethiopia, hundreds of miles from the nearest civilisation. One of the shepherds spotted an unfamiliar bush on a trail, never before used by humankind, sprouting unusual bright red berries. As he bent to inspect the berries, someone opened a Starbucks right next to it, and the shepherds had a venti soy latte and a grande caramel macchiato. The last section of that story was not true. Not just the very last bit about what they ordered, but the whole Starbucks bit. In fact Ethiopian shepherds had noticed their goats 'dancing' after having chewed on coffee berries, so they picked them and began to experiment. Strictly speaking, then, goats invented coffee.

WRITE YOUR WINNER IN BOX 5 ON THE WALLCHART

6 WHITE WINE vs IRN-BRU

One's taste in white wine changes significantly as one ages, and as one's taste buds develop. For example, a student would favour a wine such as a '£3.99 from the newsagent', while someone in their twenties begins to develop a taste for a slightly more complex '£5.99 from the newsagent'. On entering the thirties we begin to experiment with the new world, say an '£8.99 from Oddbins' and then into our forties an '£11.99 thing from Sainsbury's that they were talking about on *Sunday Brunch*'. Of course some people are real wine experts and are able to talk at length about 'Just anything French from Waitrose' or 'Something with a picture of a castle on it'. You can take courses where you learn all of this stuff. It is made from grapes for example!

Irn-Bru remains the most popular soft drink in Scotland, narrowly outselling Coke. (Peru with Inca Kola and India with Thums Up are the only other two countries in the world where a local soft drink outsells Coke.) It was originally called 'Iron Brew', but a change in the law in 1946 meant they had to change the word 'Brew' as it wasn't actually brewed. They had the smart idea of changing both names and Irn-Bru was born. Its famous advertising claim, 'Made in Scotland, from girders!', has some truth in it. It is made in Cumbernauld and it contains 0.002 per cent ammonium ferric citrate.

WRITE YOUR WINNER IN BOX 6 ON THE WALLCHART

7 ALCOPOPS vs MILKSHAKES

Everyone got very worried about Alcopops a few years ago, but they seem to have calmed down now. Alcopops remain indispensable to teenagers who don't yet enjoy the taste of alcohol, but desperately need to be slightly drunk in order to ask someone out. It also means that when their parents have to deal with their vomiting, it can often be an alarming colour, but at least has the faint hint of lemon or peach.

The term 'milkshake' can first be traced back to 1885, when it referred to a wildly alcoholic drink, made with eggs and whisky, though it quickly seems to have been co-opted into the form we know today. The two big milkshake advances that really brought all the boys to the yard were the invention of the electric blender, and the experimental addition of malted milk powder to the mix, by our old friends at Walgreens. The new taste proved a sensation. Malted milk powder was originally intended as a restorative health product for young children, and was the invention of a man with a justly familiar surname: William Horlick.

WRITE YOUR WINNER IN BOX 7 ON THE WALLCHART

8 VODKA vs ORANGE JUICE

Vodka famously comes from the Slavic word for water, while whisky comes from classical Gaelic and means 'water of life'. However, neither should be used to rehydrate in the gym.

When I was a child and we would have our once-yearly

carvery restaurant visits, 'Orange Juice' was genuinely a starter.

Vodka and orange juice together is a screwdriver, mainly because the next morning it leaves you with a cross head.

WRITE YOUR WINNER IN BOX 8 ON THE WALLCHART

BACARDI vs SLUSH PUPPIE

In the mid-nineteenth century a young man left Spain for Cuba. The son of bricklayers, he found work in a general store in Santiago de Cuba, before, in 1844, opening a shop of his own. With a friend he began to experiment with distilling rum as a sideline. It went pretty well. That man was Facundo Bacardi, and today the Bacardi company is the largest, privately held, family-owned spirits company in the world. It has sales of nearly $5 billion a year, and it is run by Facundo's great-great-grandson, Facundo J.

Slush Puppies, which are famously only ever sold in cinemas, bowling alleys, weird newsagents and by the seaside, are the single best way in existence to give yourself a brain-freeze headache. They were invented in Cincinnati, by Will Radcliff, his sister Phyllis and his mum Thelma. They came up with the name 'Slush

Puppies' while sitting on their front porch. They eventually sold the company to Cadbury Schweppes for $16 million, which is not exactly Bacardi, but not bad for a bit of ice and syrup.

WRITE YOUR WINNER IN BOX 9 ON THE WALLCHART

10 RED WINE vs LILT

Here is something else I have learnt about wine. European wine varieties tend to be named after where they are made (e.g. Bordeaux) while non-European wines are named after types of grape (Pinot Noir, Malbec). That fact leads me to believe that Jacob's Creek might not be a real place. The big downside of red wine is that it can stain your teeth, so while your drunk brain is telling you that you look like George Clooney as Batman, your teeth mean you actually look like Jack Nicholson as the Joker. However, there are things you can do to fix it. First, brush your teeth before going out (you probably should anyway, to be fair), as red wine clings to plaque; drink sparkling water, as the bubbles loosen up the stains; and finally, don't drink white wine before red, as it basically acts as an undercoat for the red wine to cling to. I hope that helps.

Lilt contains real grapefruit and pineapple juice and is made by Coca-Cola. It is only available in Great Britain and Ireland, and that's now making me think that the 'Lilt man' and the 'Lilt float' from the adverts might not be real either.

WRITE YOUR WINNER IN BOX 10 ON THE WALLCHART

11 GIN vs ORANGE SQUASH

The very first British cocktail, published in the very first British cocktail book, William Terrington's *Cooling Cups and Dainty Drinks,* was a gin cocktail with ginger syrup, orange curaçao and bitters. Gin remains the basis of some of the greatest cocktails of all time, though James Bond's famous instruction to serve his Martini 'shaken, not stirred' is vigorously opposed by most modern bartenders. They believe it dilutes the taste too much. To make up for this gaffe, Ian Fleming invented the Vesper cocktail, gin, vodka and vermouth, with a lemon twist. The most popular cocktail of all time is one we never think of as a cocktail, the simple gin and tonic.

What actually is orange squash, when you really think about it? Technically it is a 'non-alcoholic concentrated syrup used in beverage preparation'. Here is the ingredient list from Tesco's Double Strength, No Added Sugar Orange Squash:

Water, Comminuted Orange from Concentrate, Citric Acid, Flavourings, Acidity Regulator (Sodium Citrate), Sucralose, Acesulfame K, Potassium Sorbate, Sodium Metabisulphite, Carboxymethylcellulose, Beta-Carotene.

Brits often find to their incomprehension and horror that they don't have orange squash in America. They must be getting their carboxymethylcellulose fix from elsewhere.

WRITE YOUR WINNER IN BOX 11 ON THE WALLCHART

12 CIDER vs TEA

The Wurzels are The Beatles of the West Country, and the greatest ever cider ambassadors. The Wurzels are to cider what Chas & Dave are to rabbit. Among their songs you will find 'I Am a Cider Drinker', 'Drink Up Thy Zider', 'Drink, Drink Yer Zider Up' (different song), 'I'll Never Get a Scrumpy Here', and 'I'd Love to Swim in the Zider Zee'. However, they have also done a couple of albums of their own unique takes on songs such as 'Common People' by Pulp, 'Don't Look Back in Anger' by Oasis and 'It Wasn't Me' by Shaggy. I recommend you seek these out.

Tea bags were invented by accident. In 1908, US tea merchant Thomas Sullivan created small silk bags to give samples to his customers. One of his customers thought the bag was supposed to be placed directly into the teapot rather than emptied out, and an entire new industry was born. The rectangular tea bag was not invented until 1944 for some reason, and these days it is believed that the optimum shape for tea bags is the tetrahedron. Whatever that might be.

WRITE YOUR WINNER IN BOX 12 ON THE WALLCHART

13 CHAMPAGNE vs COCA-COLA

I think we've all basically agreed that Prosecco is just as nice as champagne, haven't we? And much cheaper. I've included champagne, though, in the World Cup of Drinks, as it would seem rude not to. The most expensive champagne ever sold was 200 bottles of 1907 Heidsieck, salvaged from a Second World War shipwreck in 1997. Those 200 bottles sold for $275,000 *each*. The most expensive Prosecco ever sold was £14.99 from Tesco, but it was 'Taste the Difference' so it was worth it.

Coca-Cola was invented by Confederate colonel John

Pemberton, who developed a morphine addiction after being wounded in the American Civil War, and was looking for a cure. His first attempt was his 'French Wine Coca' nerve tonic, in 1885. When Atlanta passed prohibition legislation in 1886, he launched a non-alcoholic version of this wine, and he called it Coca-Cola. John Pemberton died two years later and never saw this non-alcoholic nerve tonic – which he claimed could cure morphine addiction, indigestion, nerve disorders, headaches and impotence – go on to sell over 1.8 billion servings *every single day* around the planet.

WRITE YOUR WINNER IN BOX 13 ON THE WALLCHART

14 BRANDY vs RIBENA

Brandy is a much stronger, much more expensive, and much worse version of wine. You would only ever have a brandy if . . .

- **a)** You have never had one before, so you don't yet know that it is pretty grim.
- **b)** There is literally no other booze available. You might be at a brandy sales conference for example, or in France.
- **c)** You want to set fire to a Christmas pudding, even though

we never set fire to any other puddings. We are not a nation of crumble arsonists, for example.

Ribena was invented in 1933 by Vernon Charley, a scientist at the University of Bristol. He was involved with development work into fruit syrups, and discovered that blackcurrant syrup was unusually high in vitamin C. The manufacture of Ribena, by Bristol-based H.W. Carter, didn't begin until 1938. During the war, other fruits rich in vitamin C, such as oranges, became increasingly hard to obtain, so the cultivation of blackcurrants was enthusiastically encouraged by the government. From 1942, almost the entire crop of British blackcurrants was used to make Ribena, and it was distributed free to the nation's children. Production output kept on escalating until, in 1947, H.W. Carter moved it to the Royal Forest Factory in the Forest of Dean. Over seventy years later that is exactly where Ribena is still made.

WRITE YOUR WINNER IN BOX 14 ON THE WALLCHART

15 SHANDY vs HOT CHOCOLATE

Shandy is what we had to drink as teenagers in the 1980s because no one had invented Alcopops yet.

Studies by Cornell University show that hot chocolate is richer in antioxidants that both tea and wine. From this we conclude two things. First, chocolate proves once again that it is the greatest substance on earth. Second, it must be fun to work at Cornell University.

WRITE YOUR WINNER IN BOX 15 ON THE WALLCHART

Plenty of choice for the wild-card battle. Tizer? Special Brew? A Tizer and Special Brew cocktail? By all means choose Pepsi, or Diet Pepsi, or, if you're an idiot like me, a Pepsi Max. There's no Sprite or 7-Up on the list, but feel free to remedy that. Then I will have an excuse to use the old Tom O'Connor joke about the bloke looking at someone else's crossword and saying, 'Just so you know, seven up is lemonade'.

WRITE YOUR WINNER IN BOX 16 ON THE WALLCHART

DRINKS

THE WORLD CUP OF EVERYTHING

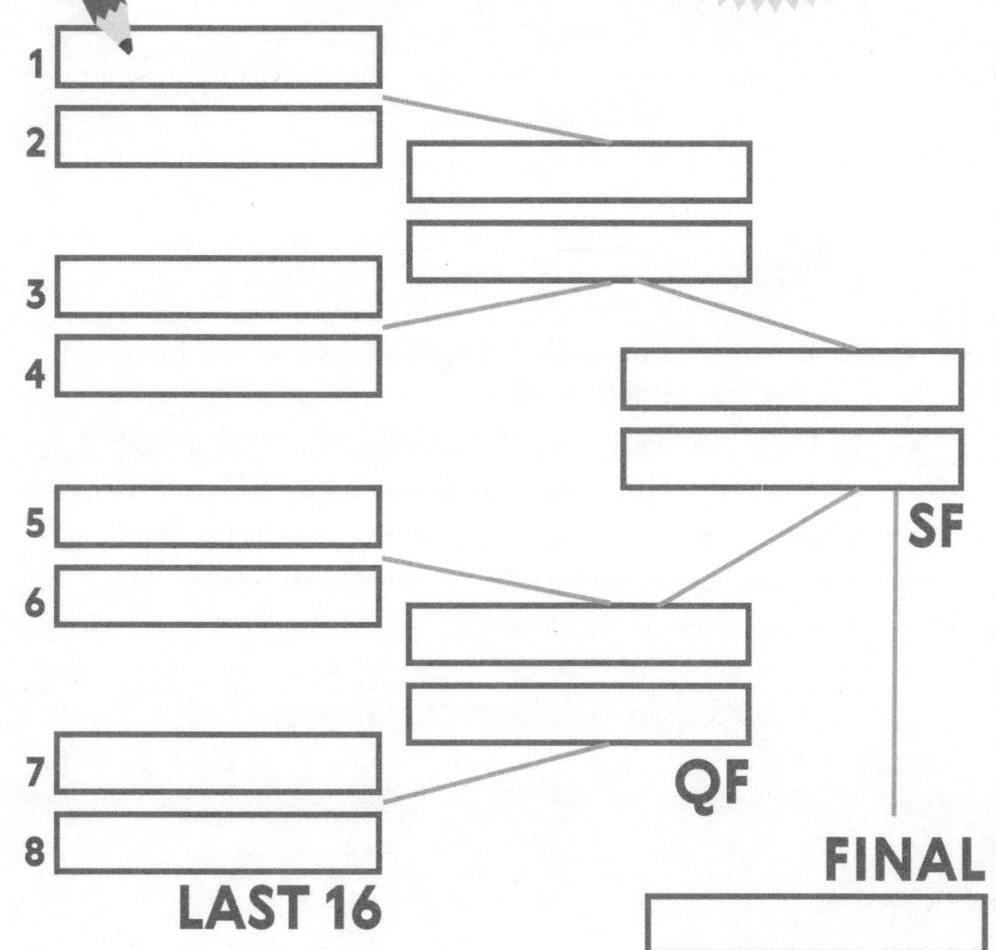

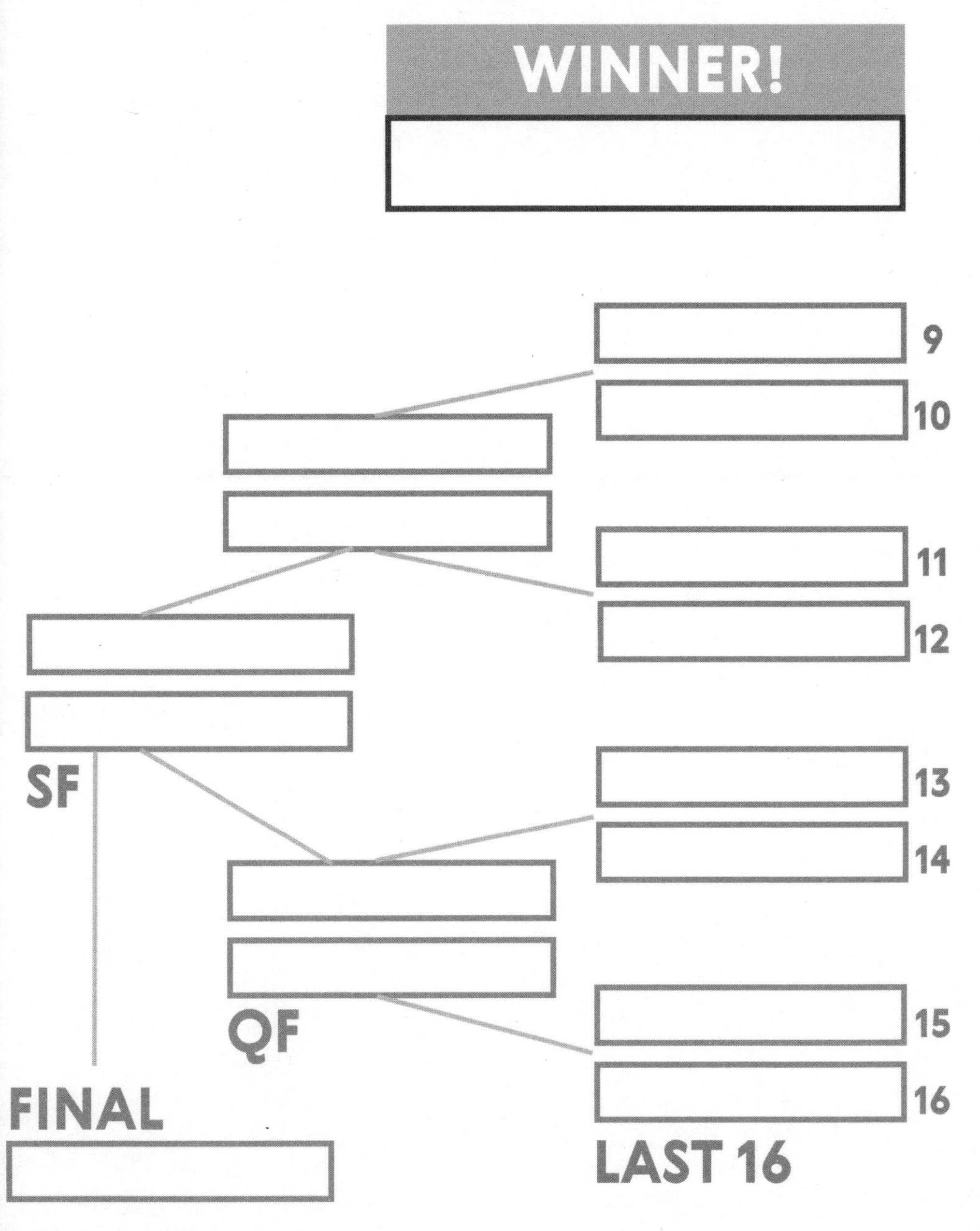
WINNER!
9
10
11
12
SF
13
14
QF
15
FINAL
16
LAST 16

WORLD CUP OF CHRISTMAS FILMS

There's money in Christmas films. And not just chocolate money: actual money. *Home Alone* has made nearly half a billion dollars, and its big star was an eight-year-old boy so they only had to pay him the same rate he would get for a paper round. *Love Actually* made $250 million, though they had to spend a lot of that money on reshoots as Liam Neeson originally spent every single scene killing everyone until they told him where his daughter was.

On an entirely unconnected note I have decided to write a Christmas movie. I haven't done this for cynical reasons, you understand? I have done it to spread Christmas joy and happiness. If the film should go on to gross over $500 million worldwide, and I end up with a mansion in Malibu, a golden helicopter, and another helicopter that gives my golden helicopter a lift so its rotor-blades don't get dusty, then so be it. Please just think of it as my Christmas present to you.

I have tried to come up with a plot that will please everyone. You might notice the occasional similarity to other Christmas films, but I assure you that those similarities are coincidental.

It's Christmas Eve, a light snow begins to fall, tree lights sparkle as we hear Bing Crosby start to sing 'I'm dreaming of a white Christmas'. But not everyone is wrapped up safe and warm. Bruce Willis is wearing a vest. He is a maverick cop who is supposed to be looking after Macaulay Culkin, but has to leave because Alan Rickman is blowing up a building, and is also cheating on Emma Thompson, whose brother is the Prime Minister. The Prime Minister, Hugh Grant, has made a lot of money because his dad once wrote a Christmas song, and is also looking after a twelve-year-old boy, for reasons I forget, but something to do with Rachel Weisz's character. After saving the building and Emma Thompson's marriage, Bruce hitches a ride home on a magical Christmas train driven by Tom Hanks. On the way he discovers that a Grinch, played by Jim Carrey, is trying to ruin Christmas by buying

the last Christmas toy before a harassed dad played by Arnold Schwarzenegger can buy it for his son. Fortunately Rowan Atkinson takes so long wrapping the toy that Mel Gibson and Danny Glover (who is sitting on a toilet) manage to intercept it. This miracle helps to convince Jimmy Stewart (who is in black and white) that Father Christmas, played by Sir Richard Attenborough, is real. It also helps Will Ferrell and the Muppets convince Sir Michael Caine that he must mend his ways, and also that The Italian Job *is not actually a Christmas film, despite often being shown at Christmas.*

Arnie manages to deliver the toy to his son, but unfortunately the toy is a gremlin and the boy feeds it after midnight, thus beginning a nightmare before Christmas. Also everyone has forgotten about Macaulay Culkin, who has now flown off with an animated snowman, and so they have to do the same thing again next year. Colin Firth walks through the snow with Clarence the angel, while the skaters glide around Central Park ice rink. They look up to see Keira Knightley flying through the night sky on her sleigh as 'Stay Another Day' by East 17 starts to play. Fade to black, and now you can go to the toilet.

I hope you like it. I wanted a title that has the simplicity and impact of two of my favourite Christmas films, *Home Alone* and *Die Hard*, so I have called it 'Die Alone'. Merry Christmas everyone!

Are you ready for the World Cup of Christmas Films? A whole host of seasonal classics all vying for your festive attention. But before the full roast dinner that is the voting, why not start with the glass of Baileys that is my selection of challenges?

★ CHALLENGE! ★

Can you identify the five genuine Christmas films on this list, hidden among five I have just made up?

1. THE SATAN CLAUSE
2. SANTA WITH MUSCLES
3. JACK FROST 2 – REVENGE OF THE MUTANT KILLER SNOWMAN
4. THE TURKEY THAT ATE CHRISTMAS
5. RUDOLPH'S RABID RAMPAGE
6. A SLAY IN A MANGER
7. WHAT WOULD JESUS BUY?
8. SANTA CLAUS CONQUERS THE MARTIANS

9. NATIVITY 3 - DUDE, WHERE'S MY DONKEY?
10. IT'S CHRISTMAS EVE AND I CAN'T FIND THE END OF THE SELLOTAPE

Answers at the back of the book.

★ INFORMATION! ★

Of course Christmas Day is not just about films. It is also about deeper, more meaningful things, such as television. Below is a list of the five most-watched programmes ever broadcast on Christmas Day in the UK. You'll notice there is one big family entertainment show, but it isn't *Morecambe & Wise*, and there is also one film, but it's not *The Great Escape*.

1. EASTENDERS (1986 – Den leaves Ange): 30.15m
2. CORONATION STREET (1987 – Hilda leaves the Street): 26.65m
3. CROCODILE DUNDEE (1989): 21.74m
4. THE MIKE YARWOOD SHOW (1977): 21.4m
5. ONLY FOOLS AND HORSES (2001): 21.31m

Only Fool and Horses also finished sixth on the list, followed by *The Morecambe & Wise Show* from 1977, beaten by Mike Yarwood. How about *Crocodile Dundee* eh? I didn't see that coming.

★ CHALLENGE! ★

Can you guess some of the greatest Christmas films of all time simply from the names of three cast members? Some of these may have been the biggest stars in these films, but others have been taken from a long way further down the cast list.

1. WILL FERRELL, ZOOEY DESCHANEL, JAMES CAAN
2. MICHAEL CAINE, FRANK OZ, ROBIN WEAVER
3. CHERYL BAKER, DANNY GLOVER, MEL GIBSON
4. JOE PESCI, CATHERINE O'HARA, DONALD TRUMP
5. CAMERON DIAZ, KATE WINSLET, JUDE LAW
6. PAUL GLEASON, BONNIE BEDELIA, ALAN RICKMAN
7. ROBERT MITCHUM, BILL MURRAY, BOBCAT GOLDTHWAIT
8. BING CROSBY, DANNY KAYE, ROSEMARY CLOONEY
9. ANTHONY McPARTLIN, DECLAN DONNELLY, HUGH GRANT
10. DAN AYKROYD, DENHOLM ELLIOTT, JAMIE LEE CURTIS

11. JAMES McAVOY, JANE HORROCKS, HUGH LAURIE
12. ALASTAIR SIM, GEORGE COLE, HATTIE JACQUES

If it helps, I don't think the actor in question 3 is Cheryl Baker out of Bucks Fizz.

Answers at the back of the book.

★ CHALLENGE ★ ★ AND ARGUMENT! ★

I ran a Twitter poll to see which one word people associated with Christmas. Below are the ten highest-scoring answers. Can you guess what they are, and once you have, do you agree with them?

1. P _ _ _ _ _ _ _
2. T _ _ _ _ _
3. S _ _ _ _
4. T _ _ _
5. F _ _ _ _ _

6. **B _ _ _ _ /A _ _ _ _ _ _ _ /D _ _ _ _**
7. **S _ _ _**
8. **J _ _ _ _**
9. **E _ _**
10. **C _ _ _ _ _**

I bet number 8 will be gutted to lose to number 6. Answers which were suggested, but which failed to make the top ten, include ‘Baileys’, ‘Flatulence’, ‘Roses’ and ‘Receipt’.

Answers at the back of the book.

OKAY FOLKS, LET’S PLAY the World Cup of Christmas Films. In case of a draw in any of these votes, the person who got the worst Christmas present this year can have the casting vote.

1 THE MUPPET CHRISTMAS CAROL vs LETHAL WEAPON

Overshadowed on its initial release by *Home Alone 2*, *The Muppet Christmas Carol* has gone on to become one of the most-loved Christmas films of all time. Michael Caine agreed to play Ebenezer Scrooge on the proviso that he would be allowed to perform the role as if he was 'working with the Royal Shakespeare Company' rather than the Muppets. Caine thought the film would be funnier the more seriously he took it, and he was absolutely right. Gonzo had pretty much the same demands when he was asked to play Charles Dickens.

Is *Lethal Weapon* a Christmas movie? I am willing to let it in to this competition because it does work towards a Christmas denouement, where Mel Gibson gives Danny Glover a bullet as a Christmas present. Glover gives Gibson a John Lewis voucher.

WRITE YOUR WINNER IN BOX 1 ON THE WALLCHART

2 BATMAN RETURNS vs THE POLAR EXPRESS

Batman Returns is certainly a Christmas movie, particularly if you are Michael Keaton, who was paid $10 million to reprise the role. Annette Bening was originally due to play Catwoman before she dropped out due to pregnancy, and Michelle Pfeiffer won the role against competition from Cher and Madonna.

When *The Polar Express* was released in 2004 it was the most expensive animated film ever made, but the animation style put off many critics. *Rolling Stone* described it as 'a failed and lifeless experiment in which everything goes wrong', the *Toronto Star* said: 'If I were a child I would have nightmares' and CNN commented that the film was 'at best disconcerting, and at worst a wee bit horrifying'. However, you can't beat the combination of Tom Hanks and the North Pole and *The Polar Express* became the fifth-highest-grossing Christmas film in history, making $307 million.

WRITE YOUR WINNER IN BOX 2 ON THE WALLCHART

Gremlins was released on the same weekend in 1984 as *Ghostbusters*. The gremlins themselves were originally to be played by monkeys, but the first monkey to be given a gremlin mask panicked and puppets were made instead. The three rules of looking after gremlins are:

1) No bright lights – much easier these days with those energy-saving light bulbs we have to buy.

2) Don't get them wet – just like suede shoes and electricity substations.

3) Never feed them after midnight – I have always worried about rule 3 because I don't know when it stops being after midnight? If I feed a gremlin at 7 a.m. am I still contravening the law?

In *About a Boy*, Hugh Grant's character lives off the royalties of a Christmas song written by his father. In reality the song 'Santa's Super Sleigh' was written by Pete Brewis, writer of countless TV comedy songs including *Spitting Image*'s 'I've Never Met a Nice South African'.

WRITE YOUR WINNER IN BOX 3 ON THE WALLCHART

THE SANTA CLAUSE vs HOME ALONE 2

Both *The Santa Clause* and *The Santa Clause 2* are among the ten highest-grossing Christmas movies of all time. In the first one, Santa falls from Tim Allen's roof and Tim Allen becomes contractually obliged to replace him. Tim Allen is a huge star in the US, but we don't really know him very well in the UK.

We do, however, know his voice, as he plays Buzz Lightyear in the *Toy Story* movies.

Only one Christmas film has ever made more money than *Home Alone 2*, and that is *Home Alone*. After *Home Alone 2* Macaulay Culkin became the first child star ever to be paid $1 million for a film (*My Girl*). He announced his retirement at the age of fourteen, exactly the same age that Red Rum retired. Culkin went on to form a band called 'The Pizza Underground', which wrote and performed Velvet Underground songs with the lyrics replaced by pizza references. They were last heard of in 2014 when they were booed off stage in Nottingham during a Macaulay Culkin kazoo solo. Amazingly this is all true.

WRITE YOUR WINNER IN BOX 4 ON THE WALLCHART

5 THE NIGHTMARE BEFORE CHRISTMAS vs THE SNOWMAN

In *The Nightmare Before Christmas*, Jack Skellington's puppet had over 400 different heads, each conveying a subtly different emotion. This is also how Adam Woodyatt now insists on playing Ian Beale on *EastEnders*.

The Snowman is only twenty-seven minutes long, but we

have to have it on the list, surely? *The Snowman* practically *is* Christmas in the UK. In the book and the script for the film, the boy has no name, but Joanna Harrison, one of the animators, decided to write a name on a gift tag of one of the presents under the tree. She was dating a guy called James, so used his name. You will be delighted to know they were soon, and are still, man and wife, and the name James has been used in every updated version of the film. Whenever we watched *The Snowman* growing up, we would always spot the beautiful crossroads with white picket fences that the boy and the snowman flew over. It was just outside Ditchling, near where we lived, and near where Raymond Briggs lived too. A proper piece of old England. About fifteen years ago they put in a roundabout and dumped the white picket fencing to widen the roads. Another snowman melted forever.

WRITE YOUR WINNER IN BOX 5 ON THE WALLCHART

IT'S A WONDERFUL LIFE vs THE HOLIDAY

It's A Wonderful Life, that beautiful Christmas fairy-tale, had an unusual genesis. It is based on the short story 'The Greatest Gift', written in 1943 by the Civil War historian Philip Van

Doren Stern. Van Doren Stern couldn't find a publisher for his story and so decided to have it printed himself, and sent it out as a Christmas card to 200 friends. One of the friends showed the Christmas card to a film producer, who in turn showed it to Cary Grant, who persuaded RKO to buy the rights. Dorothy Parker wrote on an early draft of the script.

The Holiday was written, produced and directed by Nancy Meyers, who is one of the coolest women in Hollywood for three reasons. First, she started her career as a production assistant on *The Price is Right.* Second, she wrote *Private Benjamin,* and was nominated for a screenplay Oscar after being told for years that no one wanted a film without a bankable male star in it. And third, she wrote, produced and directed *What Women Want,* which became, at the time, the most successful film in history to be directed by a woman.

WRITE YOUR WINNER IN BOX 6 ON THE WALLCHART

WHITE CHRISTMAS vs BAD SANTA

How likely is a white Christmas in the UK? In the fifty-six years since 1960, this is how many times snowflakes have fallen on Christmas Day itself:

SCOTLAND - 37
NORTH OF ENGLAND - 26
NORTHERN IRELAND - 16
WALES -16
SOUTHERN ENGLAND - 10

In 2006 Australia had a white Christmas as a rare summer snowstorm hit the Snowy Mountains in New South Wales and Victoria.

Bill Murray and Jack Nicholson were both keen to play the lead role that was eventually given to Billy Bob Thornton in *Bad Santa*. Jack Nicholson had to turn it down because he had the immense good fortune to be working with Nancy Meyers at the time, on the huge hit *Something's Gotta Give*. Bill Murray had to turn it down as he was filming *Lost in Translation* at the time, a role for which he was Oscar-nominated. So pretty much everyone ended up happy.

WRITE YOUR WINNER IN BOX 7 ON THE WALLCHART

8 NATIVITY! vs ELF

Debbie Isitt has now made three enormously successful 'Nativity' films, starring everyone from Martin Freeman and David Tennant to Celia Imrie and Alan Carr. Now my children are eighteen and sixteen I am happily free of having to watch nativity plays. However, I do accept that as the father of an eighteen-year-old you are only ever three bottles of WKD away from becoming a grandfather, so I suppose I shouldn't get too complacent.

There is a scene in *Elf* where Will Ferrell's character, Buddy, belches for a full twelve seconds. This belch was not computer generated; it was performed, in real time, by voice actor Maurice LaMarche. To my mind this is one of the greatest feats in cinema history.

WRITE YOUR WINNER IN BOX 8 ON THE WALLCHART

DIE HARD vs DIE HARD 2

Die Hard and *Die Hard 2* are definitely Christmas films, and I can prove it. First, they both take place on Christmas Eve. In one, John McClane is visiting his estranged wife in Los Angeles, and in the other he is waiting for her in Washington. Now, not only is his wife called Holly, but also, she is played by Bonnie Bedelia. And Bonnie Bedelia's Christmas connection? She's Macaulay Culkin's aunt!

WRITE YOUR WINNER IN BOX 9 ON THE WALLCHART

10 A CHRISTMAS CAROL vs HOW THE GRINCH STOLE CHRISTMAS

Okay, you can go a number of ways with *A Christmas Carol*, sort of like a 'Choose Your Own Adventure' book. You could choose the 1908 silent film, the 1938 American film, the 1951 British film, the 1969 animated film, the 1971 UK animated film, the 1977 Michael Hordern remake, the 1982 Australian film, the 1984 American film, the 1997 Whoopi Goldberg animated film, the 1999 Patrick Stewart film, the 2000 Ross Kemp adaptation, the 2004 musical or the 2009 Jim Carrey vehicle. My choices would be either the 1951 British version with Alastair Sim, or the 2009 Jim Carrey version, which is the fourth-highest-grossing Christmas movie in history.

Whichever one you choose will have to go up against the third-highest-grossing Christmas movie in history. *How the Grinch Stole Christmas*, also starring Jim Carrey. There is no Alastair Sim version to compare this film with, and, unbelievably, not even a Ross Kemp adaptation.

WRITE YOUR WINNER IN BOX 10 ON THE WALLCHART

11 GHOSTBUSTERS II vs SCROOGED

It's the battle of Bill Murray. Do you prefer the Bill Murray who clearly doesn't want to be in the sequel to his most famous film, or the Bill Murray appearing in yet *another* cinematic adaptation of *A Christmas Carol*? I think that if *Caddyshack* had been set at Christmas it would have got my vote here.

WRITE YOUR WINNER IN BOX 11 ON THE WALLCHART

12 MEET ME IN ST. LOUIS vs HOME ALONE

Lovely film though it is, I should point out that it would be rather inconvenient to meet me in St. Louis, as no airlines currently fly directly there from the UK. We would have to change in Paris or Frankfurt. I can't help thinking it might be more convenient to meet me in Chicago or New York, both of which are well served by flights from Gatwick, Heathrow and Manchester. Thinking it through in even more depth, it might just be best if we meet in Wolverhampton, or anywhere else that is central with good rail links? Perhaps Rugby or Crewe? If you do still want to meet me in St. Louis, however, it is worth noting that, according to foodie websites, the two greatest culinary creations of the city are Gooey Butter Pudding and Toasted Ravioli.

When I ran the World Cup of Christmas Films on Twitter, *Home Alone* ran out as the eventual winner, beating *Elf* in a hotly contested final. But will it win your World Cup? *Home Alone* is notable for many reasons, particularly that it is the only film in history which rhymes with 'Jo Malone'.

WRITE YOUR WINNER IN BOX 12 ON THE WALLCHART

13 TRADING PLACES vs ARTHUR CHRISTMAS

In the film *Trading Places* the villainous Duke brothers plan to profit from frozen concentrated orange juice futures cont acts after coming into possession of an unpublished Department of Agriculture report into the orange harvest. This form of insider trading was the exact subject of the following legislation passed by Congress in 2010.

Dodd-Frank Wall Street Reform and Consumer Protection Act, Section 746; Wall Street Transparency and Accountability Act, Section 136; Recommendation

To Ban Use of Misappropriated Government Information To Trade In The Commodity Markets.

This is quite a mouthful, and so this piece of legislation is genuinely known in Wall Street and in legal circles as 'The Eddie Murphy Rule'.

Arthur Christmas is one of the newer entries in this competition, and is destined to become yet another Christmas classic. Made with the traditional wit and charm of Aardman Animations, it is so good it even makes up for using Justin Bieber's version of 'Santa Claus is Coming to Town' over the closing credits.

WRITE YOUR WINNER IN BOX 13 ON THE WALLCHART

14 MIRACLE ON 34TH STREET vs JINGLE ALL THE WAY

I'm going for the Sir Richard Attenborough 1994 version of *Miracle.* Reviews at the time compared it unfavourably with the 1947 original, with *The Washington Post* confidently stating that unlike the earlier film, the 1994 version 'will not be found on television half a century from now'. Well, nearly twenty-five years later it is still going strong, and pulls in huge audiences on British TV every year. If there's one thing we know in the UK it's that you don't mess with the Attenboroughs.

Jingle All the Way was produced by Chris Columbus, the director of the first two *Home Alone* movies. He was drawn to the idea after seeing parents fighting over a Buzz Lightyear doll in the run-up to Christmas 1995. The sequel *Jingle All the Way 2* has a virtually identical plot, but an entirely different cast. For some weird reason it went straight to video.

WRITE YOUR WINNER IN BOX 14 ON THE WALLCHART

15 THE APARTMENT vs THE BISHOP'S WIFE

This is my real Christmas gift to you. If you have seen neither of these films then you have a treat in store. Seek them out, crack open the Baileys and enjoy. There are no car chases, helicopter crashes, exploding buildings, super-villains, CGI or Mel Gibson. But there is warmth, heart, snappy dialogue and Christmas cheer. *The Apartment* was writer and director Billy Wilder's Christmas follow-up to *Some Like It Hot*, and *The Bishop's Wife* was the Christmas film that Cary Grant made instead of *It's a Wonderful Life*. If you have kids though, do warn them they're in black and white.

WRITE YOUR WINNER IN BOX 15 ON THE WALLCHART

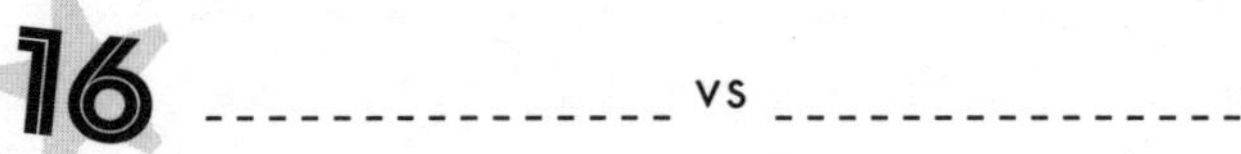

And finally, the wild-card battle. I thought long and hard about whether to put *The Great Escape* in this competition, because it is so associated with Christmas TV. I decided not to in the end, but I would have no argument if you decided to. Please tell your dad to stop saying *Planes, Trains and Automobiles*. I know it was snowy, but I'm afraid it's a Thanksgiving film, not a Christmas one. You could also go for *Jingle All the Way 2*, or *Home Alone 3*, but that would mean you would have to watch them, and I wouldn't wish that on anybody, especially at Christmas.

WRITE YOUR WINNER IN BOX 16 ON THE WALLCHART

CHRISTMAS FILMS

THE WORLD CUP OF EVERYTHING

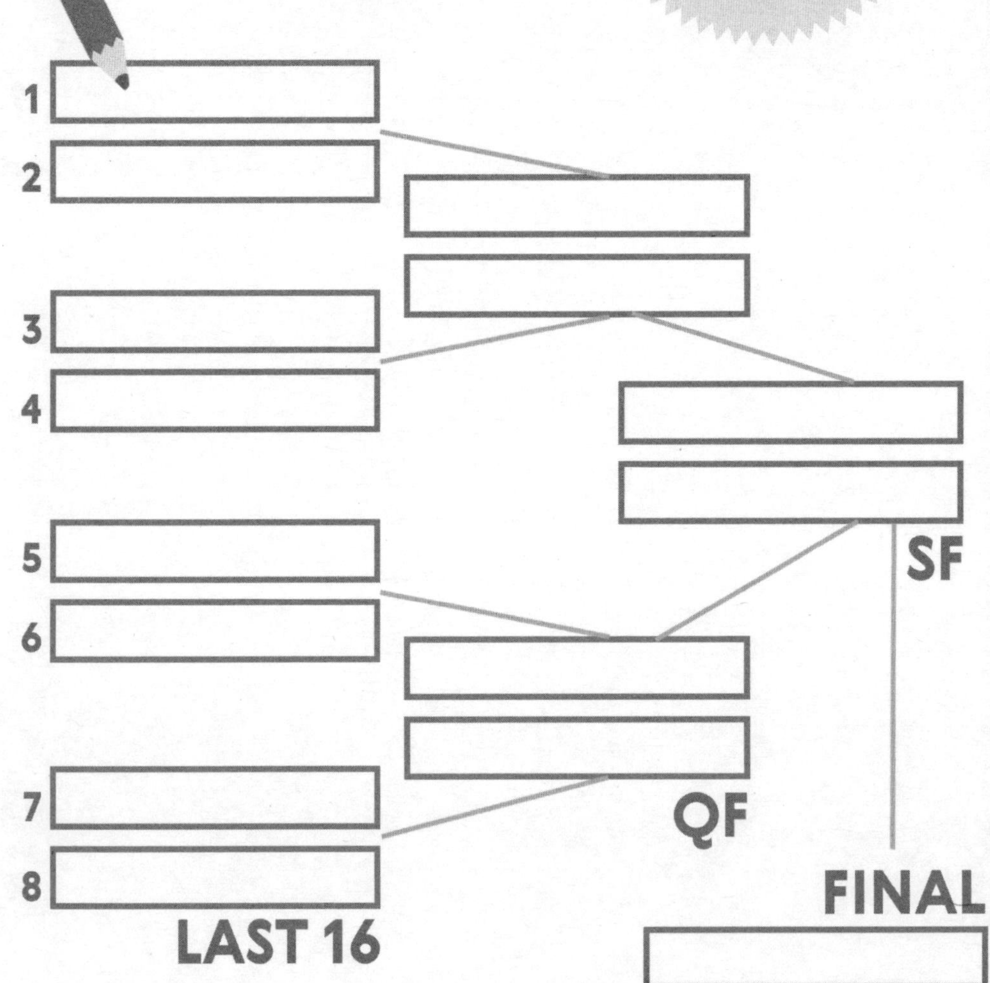

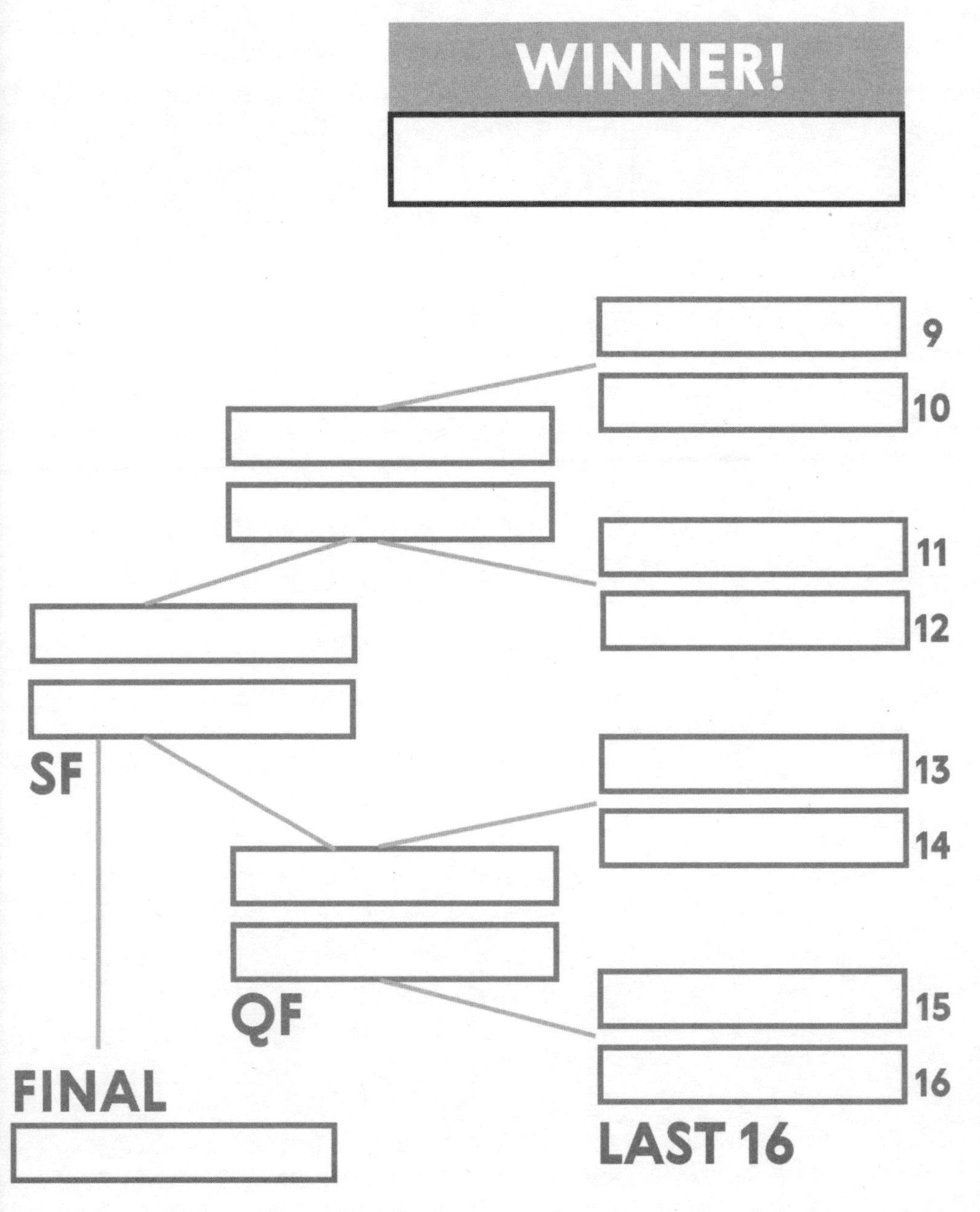
WINNER!
9
10
11
12
SF
13
14
QF
15
16
FINAL
LAST 16

WORLD CUP OF BISCUITS

What actually is a biscuit? No one really knows. What are biscuits made from? Again, scientists are unclear on this question, but we believe they are probably a mixture of flour and sugar, or maybe oats, and they sometimes have chocolate on the top or jam in the middle. Biscuits do not grow organically on trees or bushes, so at some point they must have been invented by someone. Probably by monks, as they always seem to have had a lot of time on their hands. But we simply don't know.

Biscuits – whatever they are – were popularised on ships, as they were nutritious and easy to store, and if they were kept airtight they would last for years without going stale. Anyone who had a nan in the 1970s will know the truth of this. To make them long-lasting, ship's biscuits were baked as hard as possible (they were sometimes called 'hard tack'), so in order to eat them they would have to be dunked in liquid to soften them. This is where the habit of dunking biscuits comes from, although these days you could probably just about manage to chew your way through a shortbread finger without softening it with boiling water first. The word 'biscuit' comes from the Latin *bis* (twice) and *coquere* (cooked), though some believe it comes from the Greek *bysk* (I'm afraid I have just eaten) and *quoit* (a whole packet in one go).

This World Cup is only for sweet biscuits of course, not for savoury biscuits or crackers. Savoury biscuits are not biscuits at all in my opinion. I wouldn't have cheese chocolate, cheese ice cream or cheese Fruit Pastilles, so I'm not going to have cheese biscuits. I would have cheesecake, but that is where I draw my line. The first sweet biscuits were ginger biscuits, and they were made with the offcuts of gingerbread, baked in the cooling ovens. Historical records show that Swedish nuns were baking gingerbread to aid digestion as far back as 1444. I told you monks or nuns would be involved. They always are.

Typically the Americans don't call biscuits biscuits. They call biscuits 'cookies'. This comes from the Dutch word '*koekje*', which is a type of cake. So we can say with certainty that the Americans have got this one wrong as usual. To make matters worse, the Americans do have biscuits but their biscuits are what we would call scones. Though they would probably pronounce it 'scones'. They really are a contrary bunch.

The modern history of biscuits is far better known, thanks to the work of biscuit pioneers such as Steve McVitie's, Sir Reginald Hobnob and Elaine Custard-Cream.

I have gathered together thirty-two giants of the biscuit world to do battle. Your job is to choose the very best. When we ran this competition on Twitter there were over 2 million votes. The Chocolate Digestive beat Chocolate Fingers in the final, with Custard Creams and Chocolate Hobnobs defeated in the semi-finals. But does that sound right to you? There was an enormous amount of controversy during the World Cup of Biscuits as to whether the Jaffa Cake should count as a biscuit, or whether it is really a cake. You will be delighted to hear that my full legal ruling as to why it is a biscuit is published below.

★ BROKEN BISCUITS! ★

Here is a challenge that 62 per cent of you will hate, but 38 per cent of you will love. But fortunately it is not compulsory. Below are twelve biscuits in anagram form. Can you name these broken biscuits?

1. BOOB RUN
2. ITCH EAR
3. WIFE PRANK
4. GIVE DIETS
5. ILL FROG
6. URGENT GIN
7. I CLINCH BOOZE
8. NEW AGE HOWL
9. GENETIC ARCHFOOL
10. CURSED TARMAC
11. ANGRY TRIP
12. ABHORRENT FRIDGES

Answers at the back of the book.

★ INFORMATION! ★

McVitie's are the delicious, crumbly overlords of the British biscuit world. Below is a list of their ten best-selling brands in the UK.

1. CHOCOLATE DIGESTIVES
2. DIGESTIVES

3. JAFFA CAKES (You see, even McVitie's think they're biscuits)
4. RICH TEA
5. GINGER NUTS (Ginger Nuts more popular than Chocolate Hobnobs! Whaaa?)
6. CHOCOLATE HOBNOBS
7. HOBNOBS
8. CARAMEL DIGESTIVES
9. FRUIT SHORTCAKE (Not even in the World Cup. Real strength in depth)
10. MINI JAFFAS (Still biscuits)

★ CHALLENGE! ★

One country that you can genuinely trust with biscuits is Australia. They don't just copy us, they come up with new and original products and they are delicious. It is worth visiting Australia just for the biscuits. In fact most brands are available at the airport supermarkets, so you could be there and back within forty-eight hours. Below I've listed ten popular Australian biscuit brands. Five are real, and five are biscuits I've just made up but would like to try.

1. PASSIONFRUIT CREAMIES
2. COCONUT JIMJAMS
3. KANGAROOTS
4. HONEY JUMBLES
5. ICED VOVOS
6. BOOM-MERINGUES
7. TIC TOCS
8. CARAMEL CROWNS
9. RASPBERRY LASSITERS
10. KYLIES

Answers at the back of the book.

★ JAFFA CAKE RULING! ★

When I included Jaffa Cakes in the World Cup of Biscuits it caused quite the storm. I even ran a Twitter poll asking if Jaffa Cakes were cakes or biscuits, and fully 55 per cent of the 100,000 respondents said they were cakes. Clearly they are wrong, and this is why. Below is the final legal ruling explaining exactly why Jaffa Cakes are biscuits and not cakes.

It is the finding of this court that in regards to the case

'Osman v Some People on the Internet Who Disagreed with Osman 2017' we find in favour of the plaintiff, Mr Osman, for the following reasons.

1) *It was often stated in argument that biscuits go soft when stale, while cakes go hard. As Jaffa Cakes go hard when stale, it was argued that this was definitive proof that Jaffa Cakes are cakes. However, it is the finding of this court that anyone who would ever be able to leave a packet of Jaffa Cakes lying around for long enough for them to go stale is not to be trusted. This court finds in favour of Mr Osman.*

2) *It was also stated in argument that Jaffa Cakes literally have cake in their name and therefore must be a cake. Mr Osman argued that Bonnie Tyler has literally got Tyler in her name but he wouldn't hire her to regrout his bathroom. The court finds for Mr Osman.*

3) *No one has ever offered you 'a lovely slice of Jaffa Cake'. No one has ever stuck a candle in a Jaffa Cake and got their child to blow it out on their birthday, before slicing it into tiny slivers, wrapping them in Peppa Pig serviettes and putting them in everyone's party bags.*

4) *They look like biscuits, they're wrapped like biscuits, they sell them with the biscuits in the biscuit aisle.*

5) *No one has ever won the* Great British Bake-Off *with a Jaffa Cake as their showstopper.*
6) *THEY ARE BISCUITS. The court finds for Mr Osman and awards him £40 million in damages for emotional harm. Case dismissed.*

Not my words there, but the words of an independent court. I am glad that has finally been cleared up once and for all.

OKAY, MAKE A POT OF TEA, AND LET'S START VOTING. Argue in a civilised fashion please. In the case of a tie in any of these battles, simply hold a competition to see who can dunk a Rich Tea the longest, and the winner gets to choose.

1 CUSTARD CREAM vs GARIBALDI

There is one very unusual thing about biscuits, and that is that very few of them have trademarked names. You or I couldn't go out tomorrow and start manufacturing and selling 'Dairy Milk', 'Frazzles' or 'Coca-Cola', but we could legally make and sell 'Digestives', 'Bourbons' or 'Custard Creams'. No one owns the names. If you did want to change the name of Custard Creams, I would recommend 'Cuzztrd Creemz', 'Custard Dreams', 'My Tiny Sandwich' or 'I Can't Believe It's Not Custard'.

The same is true of Garibaldis, which have been made in various forms in the UK for over 150 years. The biscuit was first created in 1851 by Jonathan Carr, working for the Bermondsey biscuit company Peek Freans. In 1854 the Italian general Giuseppe Garibaldi had made a high-profile visit to South Shields, and the biscuit was named in his honour. Please don't tell him that generations of schoolchildren have called them 'squashed fly biscuits' ever since.

WRITE YOUR WINNER IN BOX 1 ON THE WALLCHART

2 CHOCO LEIBNIZ vs MINT VISCOUNT

Choco Leibniz were also named after a random dignitary, in this case the eighteenth-century German philosopher and mathematician Gottfried Leibniz. Leibniz had been one of the most famous inhabitants of Hanover where the Bahlsen company started producing Leibniz biscuits in 1891. They have lots of tiny indentations, or 'teeth', around their edges, and if you've never counted them I have done it for you. There are fifty-two. In other news, I am currently waiting in for British Gas to arrive and I have too much time on my hands.

Mint Viscounts were one of the great lunchbox staples. This was back in the 1970s when we didn't have to bring little Tupperware pots of carrot batons into school, and we could eat Monster Munch instead of couscous. I have sad news though. Burton's biscuits have confirmed that while the Mint Viscount is still going strong, the Orange Viscount is no longer with us. My thoughts are with you at this difficult time.

WRITE YOUR WINNER IN BOX 2 ON THE WALLCHART

 FIG ROLL vs TUNNOCK'S CARAMEL WAFER

The Fig Roll might be the oldest biscuit of them all, as it dates back to Egyptian times. In 1892 Charles Roser of Philadelphia was awarded a patent for inserting fig crème into cake-like dough and the modern Fig Roll was born. I don't think the Dragon's Den would have much time for a machine that inserted fig crème into cake-like dough, but it made Charles Roser his fortune and his biscuits, Fig Newtons, are still a bestseller in the US today. Despite what you would think by now, they weren't named after Isaac Newton; merely after a town called Newton. Which also wasn't named after Isaac Newton. However, you won't be surprised to learn that nobody owns the name 'Fig Roll', so McVitie's, and Jacobs, and all the major supermarkets all make their own versions, and you could too.

Tunnock's, or Thomas Tunnock & Co., are one of Scotland's oldest surviving family firms, having been founded as a bakery in Uddingston in 1890. The actual official name for Tunnock's Caramel Wafer is Tunnock's Milk Chocolate Coated Caramel Wafer Biscuit.

WRITE YOUR WINNER IN BOX 3 ON THE WALLCHART

NICE vs CHOCOLATE DIGESTIVE

Nice is a coconut biscuit which lots of different people claim to have invented, including the Australian company Arnott's Biscuits. Certainly Britain's Huntley & Palmers were selling them as early as 1904, and the Dutch 'Nizza' is branded as the Netherlands 'most beloved cookie'. Again no one owns the name, but if you decide to start making them yourself you will probably want to know whether they are pronounced Nice or Nice. I can confirm they are pronounced Nice.

McVitie's caused uproar in 2017 when they stated for the record that the chocolate in a Chocolate Digestive is technically on the bottom of the biscuit and not the top. So we've been holding them the wrong way up for years.

WRITE YOUR WINNER IN BOX 4 ON THE WALLCHART

5 CHOCOLATE CHIP COOKIE vs GINGER NUT

The Maryland Chocolate Chip Cookie is the only cookie we're allowing in this World Cup, and that's because they were brought over from the US in 1956, and so have now qualified for a British passport. Also, language changes. In 1956, if someone had said 'Cookies are enabled on your desktop' it would just mean that you were allowed to eat biscuits in your office.

While you're voting in this World Cup, try a dunking competition too. I'll bet the Ginger Nut wins.

WRITE YOUR WINNER IN BOX 5 ON THE WALLCHART

WAGON WHEEL vs HOBNOB

The Wagon Wheel was invented in 1968 by Garry Weston, son of one-time British MP W. Garfield Weston. Fans of Wagon Wheels have long protested that Wagon Wheels have got smaller over the years, but their UK manufacturer, Burton's, have always denied this. It is worth noting though that the UK Wagon Wheel is 18mm smaller in diameter than the Australian Wagon Wheel, though it is 4mm thicker.

Now, as Wagon Wheel and Hobnob are both more modern inventions, they are both trademarked, so don't start selling them and telling everyone I said it was okay. Hobnobs were created in Scotland by McVitie's in 1985. The word 'hobnob' was first used by Sir Toby Belch in Shakespeare's *Twelfth Night*. Other biscuit names invented by Shakespeare include Orange Club and Tunnock's Milk Chocolate Coated Caramel Wafer Biscuit.

WRITE YOUR WINNER IN BOX 6 ON THE WALLCHART

FOX'S VIENNESE vs JAFFA CAKE

The World Cup of Biscuits on Twitter made me realise that Fox's make great biscuits, but with almost zero name recognition. Fox's were a family business launched in 1853 from a terraced house in Batley (the house is still there) and Viennese biscuits are one of their premium sellers. For many years Fox's Production Director was Colin Montgomerie's dad, James.

Every single McVitie's Jaffa Cake is made in their Stockport factory. The production area covers more than an acre, and the production line alone is over a mile long. Again, McVitie's didn't trademark the name when they launched Jaffa Cakes in 1927, so feel free to launch your own. I am going to launch 'Jaffa Biscuits' just to wind people up on Twitter.

WRITE YOUR WINNER IN BOX 7 ON THE WALLCHART

8 PENGUIN vs MALTED MILK

Now Penguin *is* a trademark, and Asda once tried to get around it by producing an almost identical biscuit called a 'Puffin'. Penguin took them to court and won a case of 'passing off', so let that be a lesson for you. The Australian biscuit Tim Tam is also pretty much identical, but they didn't call it 'Pelican' so I think they've got away with it.

The Malted Milk is a biscuit first produced by Elkes Biscuits of Uttoxeter in 1924. It contains both milk and malt. The biscuits are known for the folksy designs printed on them, the main three of which are a cow and a calf, a cow and a gate and two milk churns and a cow. If you have any other designs then immediately take them along to *Antiques Roadshow*; you are sitting on a goldmine.

WRITE YOUR WINNER IN BOX 8 ON THE WALLCHART

Rich Tea biscuits were invented in Yorkshire in the seventeenth century, and are particularly known for their dunking qualities. One of Prince William's favourite treats as a child was a cake made with Rich Tea biscuits and dark chocolate, set in a freezer rather than baked in the oven. He loved the cake so much that on his marriage to Kate Middleton he chose it as his wedding cake. The Palace sent the recipe to McVitie's, and they supersized it for the wedding, making a cake with 40lb of chocolate and 1,700 Rich Tea biscuits.

And talking of royal connections, the Bourbon was named after the Royal House of Bourbon when introduced by Peek Freans in 1910. Just like the Garibaldi, though, they failed to trademark the name. So if you want to sell biscuits or become a minor Italian royal then your path is clear.

WRITE YOUR WINNER IN BOX 9 ON THE WALLCHART

10 ORANGE CLUB vs PARTY RING

'If you like a lot of chocolate on your biscuit, join our club.' If you are over forty then you will now be singing this for the rest of the day. In 2012 it was voted the seventh-catchiest jingle of all time. Can you guess the winner of that poll? I'll let you know when we get on to Mint Clubs later.

Party Rings were introduced by Fox's in 1983, in direct response to advances in the chemical food-dye industry. I am aware that this means it has a slightly less romantic story than some of the other biscuits.

WRITE YOUR WINNER IN BOX 10 ON THE WALLCHART

JAMMIE DODGER vs FOX'S CHOCOLATEY

Jammie Dodgers were originally named after the *Beano* character Roger the Dodger, which certainly makes a change from being named after eighteenth-century German philosophers and mathematicians. Burton's, who created the Jammie Dodger over fifty years ago, have factories across Britain making Jammie Dodgers, Maryland Chocolate Chip Cookies, Wagon Wheels, Lyons' Biscuits and all sorts of supermarket-own brands of biscuit. The first ever Burton's biscuits were baked by George Burton in the nineteenth century on Corporation Street in Blackpool. From those beginnings, it is an interesting insight into the world of global food brands that, since the year 2000, Burton's Biscuits has been owned in succession by Associated British Foods; Hicks, Muse, Tate & Furst Private Equity of Dallas; Duke Street Capital (UK); the Canadian Imperial Bank of Commerce and Apollo Global Management, and finally, after 2013 by The Ontario Teachers' Pension Plan.

The Fox's Chocolatey, or 'Extremely Chocolatey', is well named, as in extensive laboratory-controlled taste experiments conducted by leading scientists in 2017, it was confirmed that they were the most chocolatey of all the chocolate biscuits. For clarification, by leading scientists I mean me and my son, and by laboratory-controlled, I mean 'sitting at home watching *Top Gear* repeats on Dave.

WRITE YOUR WINNER IN BOX 11 ON THE WALLCHART

12 PINK WAFER vs OREO

Pink wafers are wafers coloured pink. The pink colouring comes from different sources depending on the brand, but it is sometimes provided by beetroot. I am not a qualified nutritionist but I'm fairly sure this means it counts as one of your five-a-day.

The first Oreo was produced in 1912 by the National Biscuit Company (now Nabisco) on 9th Avenue in New York City. Because it was made by Americans they immediately trademarked the name, I'm afraid. They were only officially introduced to the UK in May 2008, but are now made here too, in the Sheffield Cadbury factory. By some estimates they are the best-selling biscuit of all time. It is believed that since 1912 over 450 billion have been sold. When I was visiting China recently, they had Strawberry Oreos, Blueberry Oreos and Lemon Oreos. I recommend them to you.

WRITE YOUR WINNER IN BOX 12 ON THE WALLCHART

13 CHOCOLATE FINGER vs CRUNCH CREAM

How many different Fingers are there? Rather wonderfully there are ten. Cadbury Fingers, Cadbury Finger Toffee Crunch, Cadbury Fingers Double Chocolate, Cadbury Dream Fingers, Cadbury Bournville Fingers, Cadbury Fabulous Fingers, Cadbury Honeycomb Fabulous Fingers, Cadbury Praline Fabulous Fingers, Cadbury Mini-Fingers and Cadbury Toffee Crunch Mini-Fingers. I'm afraid that the name is trademarked, so you're going to have to try and market Chocolate Toes instead.

Crunch Creams are another one of Fox's biscuits that you've never heard of but would quite like.

WRITE YOUR WINNER IN BOX 13 ON THE WALLCHART

14 DIGESTIVE vs MINT CLUB

Digestive biscuits were originally so named for their supposed healing qualities, and were first created by two Scottish doctors. With an ingredients list of brown wheat flour, sugar, malt extract, vegetable oil, sodium bicarbonate, tartaric acid, malic acid and salt, they do certainly sound pretty healthy. It is fair to say that if you combined the Digestive with the Pink Wafer, you would have created a superfood.

I have included the Mint and Orange Clubs in this competition, but if you felt that I have unfairly overlooked the excellent Fruit variety, or the new kid on the block Honeycomb version, then you will know what to do with your wild-card battle. I promised to let you know what beat the Club jingle to be voted the catchiest jingle of all time. Final guesses? It was 'Just One Cornetto!'

WRITE YOUR WINNER IN BOX 14 ON THE WALLCHART

15 SHORTBREAD FINGER vs CHOCOLATE HOBNOB

Of course to everyone telling me that Jaffa Cakes shouldn't be allowed in the World Cup of Biscuits because they have 'cake' in their name, I'm assuming you'll be telling us next that Shortbread Fingers are bread? One of the many prides of Scotland, the Shortbread Finger is delicious – chunky but crumbly, sugary but wholesome – and utterly un-trademarked.

In 1987, two years after McVitie's introduced the Hobnob, came this brainwave from top biscuit scientists. 'People seem to really like Hobnobs. Do you think they would like them even more if we put chocolate on the top?' This was immediately countered with: 'Surely you mean put chocolate on the bottom?' and a new biscuit sensation was born. Interestingly the official name for biscuit science in the UK is Hobnology, while in the US it is Oreology.

WRITE YOUR WINNER IN BOX 15 ON THE WALLCHART

As always this one is up to you. You might feel that if I have allowed Jaffa Cakes into the tournament then Tunnock's Tea Cakes might also be acceptable. Maybe you like a Chocolate Malted Milk or a Lemon Puff. I love Lemon Puffs and included them in the original competition, but they got the lowest votes of any competitor so I have reluctantly had to relegate them. If you enjoy the combination of incredibly tiny yet still difficult to eat, then do think about including the Iced Gem.

WRITE YOUR WINNER IN BOX 16 ON THE WALLCHART

BISCUITS

THE WORLD CUP OF EVERYTHING

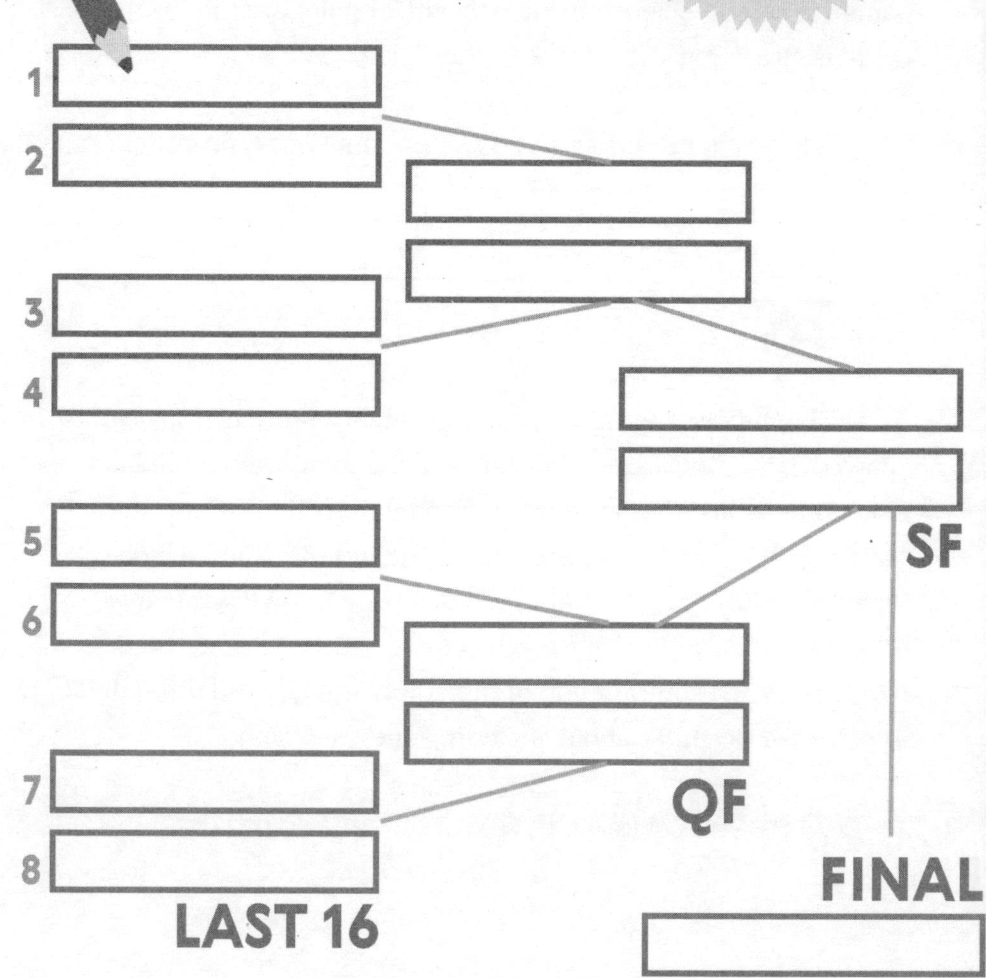

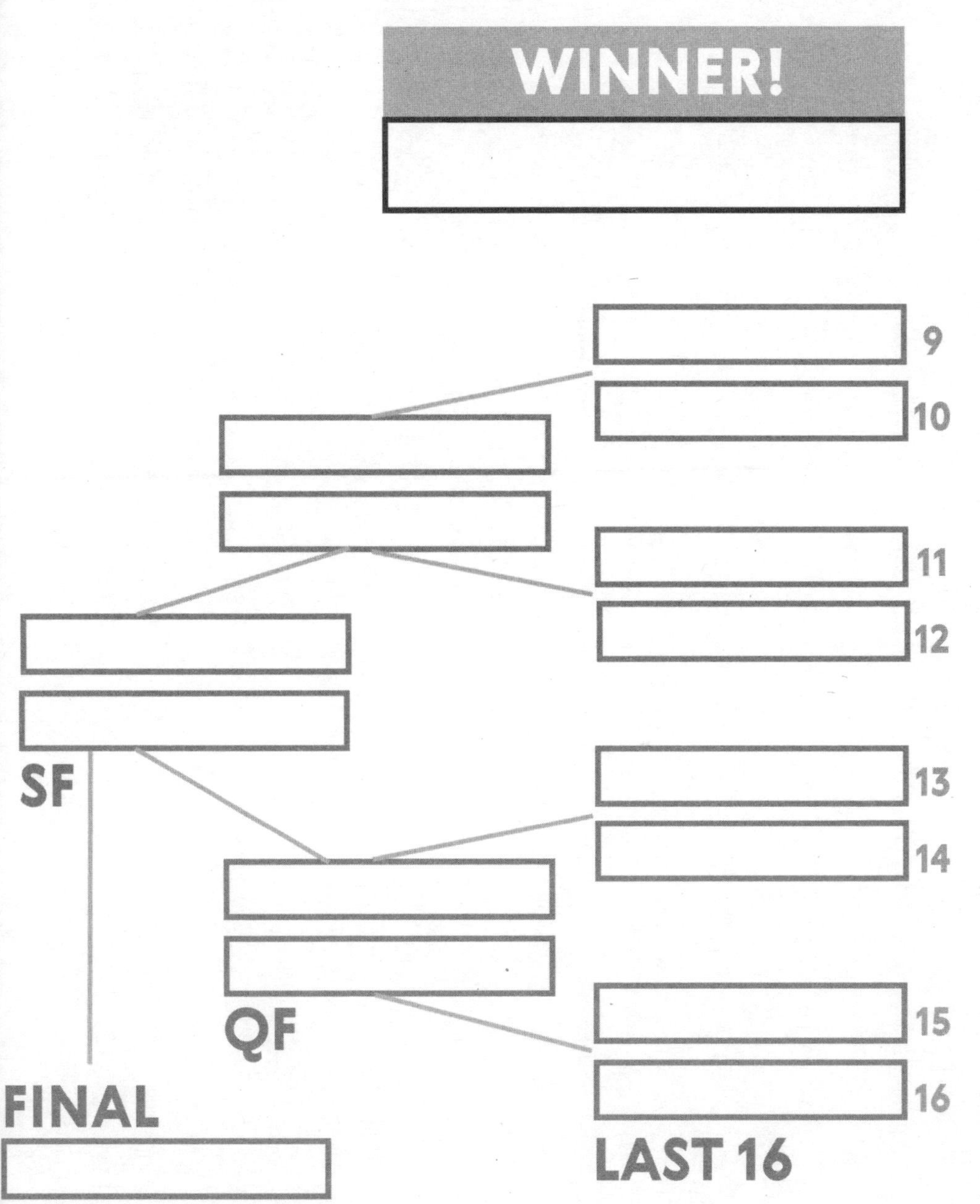
WINNER!
9
10
11
12
SF
13
14
QF
15
16
FINAL
LAST 16

WORLD CUP OF GAME SHOWS

My entire career has been spent working on game shows and quiz shows. For many years I was a creator and producer, and then, by one of those twists you never see coming, as some sort of latter-day Bob Holness. Over twenty-five years I've created a few blockbusters, but also more than my fair share of blanks (or blankety blanks). Ironically, the failure-to-success rate for new quiz shows is roughly fifteen to one.

Perhaps the biggest hit I had as a producer was *Deal or No Deal*, and the moment you have a big hit as a producer, the pressure is on from everyone to produce some lucrative spin-offs. That's why you get *Celebrity Deal or No Deal* and *Deal or*

No Deal-Live, not to mention *Deal or No Deal* quiz machines, online games, mugs, duvets, fondue sets, his and her bathrobes, canteens of cutlery and a cuddly toy. In fact the entire Brexit referendum was simply a 'Deal or No Deal' spin-off, which got out of hand.

You can also take advantage of a hit show by selling other shows that are very similar to it. In this spirit I thought I would share with you some of the rip-offs of *Deal or No Deal* we came up with in order to cash in on its success. Do feel free to think of some of your own, but if you sell them I get 50 per cent. Deal?

SQUEAL OR NO SQUEAL – The game show that asks 'Are you ticklish?'

BEALE OR NO BEALE – Contestants have to work out if they want to watch *EastEnders* or not.

SEAL OR NO SEAL – The quiz in which all you have to do is 'Spot the Walrus'.

PEAL OR NO PEAL – The search for Britain's best bell ringers.

PEEL OR NO PEEL – Could *you* find the satsuma in a ball-pool full of mandarins?

HEEL OR NO HEEL – Dog-obedience game show.

TEAL OR NO TEAL – Are you colour-blind?

KEEL OR NO KEEL – Hovercrafts race against yachts.

WHEEL OR NO WHEEL – Hovercrafts race against cars.

EEL OR NO EEL – Hovercrafts race against fish.

VEAL OR NO VEAL – Advice for people about to go on first dates with vegetarians.

HE'LL OR NO HE'LL – The first show ever to combine ideas about the afterlife with the dangers of autocorrect.

STEEL OR NO STEEL – Questions about the decline of Britain's manufacturing industries.

FEEL OR NO FEEL – What's the best way to judge a mango?

LILLE OR NO LILLE – Should we move to France?

DEAL OR NO DEAL – Should we move to Kent?

I swear that every single one of those shows is real.* Sadly we only managed to sell seven of them.

⋆ CHALLENGE! ⋆

Lots of hit TV shows sell their format all around the world. Can you guess which hit shows were remade under the following titles, in the following countries?

* (or no real)

1. HALUATKO MILJONAARIKSI (Finland) ____________
2. EL PRECIO ES CORRECTO (Colombia) ____________
3. DESAFIO FAMILIAR (Chile) ____________
4. DES CHIFFRES ET DES LETTRES (France) ____________
5. TOPA OU NAO TOPA (Brazil) ____________
6. EL RIVAL MAS DEBIL (Mexico) ____________
7. SELEBRITIS INDONESIA (Indonesia) ____________
8. SALVEN EL MILLON (Uruguay) ____________
9. ABC PROGRAM (Saudi Arabia) ____________
10. NULL GEWINNT (Germany) ____________

Answers at the back of the book.

★ CHALLENGE! ★

Lots of successful game shows go through more than one presenter in their lifetime. Personally I think this is shortsighted and dangerous, and I honestly think Alexander and I do a better job than Jedward would. Can you name the British game shows which have been presented by these groups of people? Some of these groups don't list every presenter who has ever hosted the show.

1. BOB MONKHOUSE, LES DENNIS, VERNON KAY

----

2. ROY WALKER, NICK WEIR, MARK CURRY, STEPHEN MULHERN ------------

3. BOB MONKHOUSE, WARWICK DAVIS

----

4. MICHAEL ASPEL, LIZA TARBUCK, SIMON MAYO

----

5. WILLIAM G. STEWART, ADAM HILLS, SANDI TOKSVIG

----

6. DES O'CONNOR, DES LYNAM ------------

7. BRUCE FORSYTH, MATTHEW KELLY, DARREN DAY

----

8. LESLIE CROWTHER, JOE PASQUALE

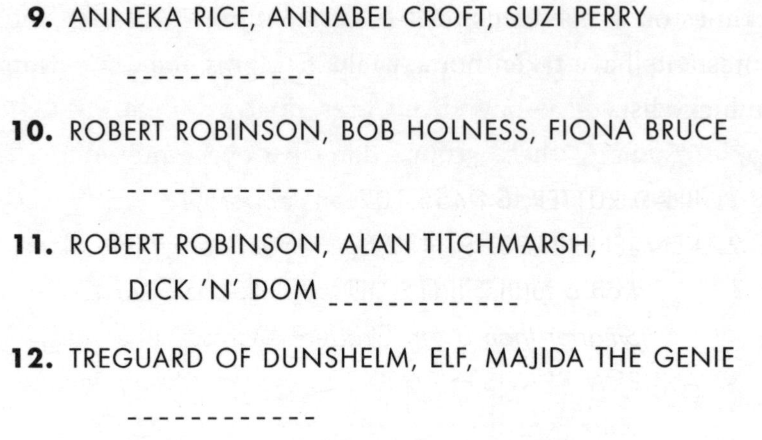

9. ANNEKA RICE, ANNABEL CROFT, SUZI PERRY

_ _ _ _ _ _ _ _ _ _ _ _

10. ROBERT ROBINSON, BOB HOLNESS, FIONA BRUCE

_ _ _ _ _ _ _ _ _ _ _ _

11. ROBERT ROBINSON, ALAN TITCHMARSH,
DICK 'N' DOM _ _ _ _ _ _ _ _ _ _ _ _

12. TREGUARD OF DUNSHELM, ELF, MAJIDA THE GENIE

_ _ _ _ _ _ _ _ _ _ _ _

The most extraordinary entry we might include on this list would surely be *University Challenge.* It has now been on the air for fifty years, and in all that time has had only two presenters, Bambi and Paxo.

Answers at the back of the book.

★ JACKPOT ANSWERS! ★

The most that a quiz show contestant has ever won on British TV is a million pounds, most famously, of course, a number of times on *Who Wants to Be a Millionaire?* In the US, eight contestants have taken home jackpots higher than this. Here's the lucky list.

1. BRAD RUTTER, $4,455,102 on *Jeopardy!*
2. KEN JENNINGS, $3,422,700 on *Jeopardy!* (He also won a further half a million dollars on *Are You Smarter than a 5th Grader?* It turns out he was.)
3. ANDREW KRAVIS, $2,600,000 on *The Million Second Quiz* (Kravis had previously been on *Who Wants to Be a Millionaire?*, where he crashed out with $1,000.)
4. KEVIN OLMSTEAD, $2,180,000 on *Who Wants to Be a Millionaire?* (In the States they did a few 'specials' of the show, with bigger prizes.)
5. ED TOUTANT, $1,860,000 on *Who Wants to Be a Millionaire?*
6. ASHLEE REGISTER, $1,795,000 on *Duel.* (I'm guessing that her middle name is 'Cash'.)
7. DAVID LEGLER, $1,765,000 on *Twenty One.*
8. CURTIS WARREN, $1,400,000 on *Greed.*

★ WHAT DO CHALLENGES ★ ★ MAKE? PRIZES! ★

Every game-show host needs a catchphrase. Mine is 'And by country I mean a sovereign state that is a member of the UN in its own right', but I don't make any money out of it, because it is too long to fit on a mug. Can you guess the game-show catchphrases below from just the initials of the phrase and the initials of who said it?

1. NTSYTSYN - BF
2. ITYFA? - CT
3. QON? - WGS
4. COD! - LC
5. YATWL, G - AR
6. NITGFTIAB - JB
7. HOL? - BF
8. ISSIF - MM
9. IGBINR - RW
10. OSS! - BM
11. PAMBAYC - JV
12. IHAPPB - Contestants to BH

VWDIYGTAH. (Very well done if you got those at home.)

Answers at the back of the book.

OKAY, LET'S GET VOTING IN THE WORLD CUP OF GAME SHOWS. Thirty great shows on display here, all quizzes and challenge shows, no comedy shows, celebrity shows or talent shows. I have left out *Pointless*, purely because I couldn't bear the thought of being knocked out by *3-2-1* in the first round. Enjoy the arguing, and if there's a tie, then the person who comes up with the best *Deal or No Deal* pun can have the casting vote.

1 BULLSEYE vs FIFTEEN TO ONE

If you ever see a house in the north of England with a rusting 1980s speedboat in the driveway, you know that someone has been on *Bullseye*. A huge hit for ITV from 1981–95, *Bullseye* was co-created by northern comic, Norman Vaughan, the man who took over from Bob Monkhouse on *The Golden Shot*. At this point your dad is almost certainly saying 'They should bring back *Bullseye.*' You can tell him that it was brought back, by Challenge TV in 2006, with Dave Spikey as host. If your dad didn't watch it then he only has himself to blame.

Fifteen to One was hosted by William G. Stewart, a television producer turned quiz-show host. This is the sort of career move I disapprove of strongly. William G. Stewart had produced game shows of his own, including the UK version of *The Price is Right*, but was also a renowned sitcom producer, numbering *Love Thy Neighbour* and *Bless This House* among his many credits. William G. Stewart clearly has a very time-efficient attitude towards dating. His second wife, Sally Gleeson, played Sid James's daughter on *Bless This House*, and his third wife, Laura Calland, was the authoritative female voice on *Fifteen to One*.

WRITE YOUR WINNER IN BOX 1 ON THE WALLCHART

2 WHO WANTS TO BE A MILLIONAIRE? vs TELLY ADDICTS

Who Wants to Be a Millionaire? was created by David Briggs, Chris Tarrant's Capital Radio producer, with Steven Knight and Mike Whitehill, who, at the time, were writers for Jasper Carrott. All three men are now millionaires themselves many, many times over, as *Who Wants to Be a Millionaire?* became one of the most profitable quiz shows in the history of television. Steven Knight has gone on to another enormously successful career as a film director and writer. Among the many others who made millions from the show was one of the co-owners of Celador, the production company behind the show. His name? Jasper Carrott.

Telly Addicts was on BBC1 from 1985 until 1998. It was originally played as 'winning family stays on', but a single family, the Paynes, lasted for almost the entire first series, and so it became a knockout tournament from then on. In 1998 it was decided that viewers didn't want to just watch families sitting on sofas watching TV clips, and so a huge revamp took place, involving lots of physical games and celebrity cameos. The show never returned.

WRITE YOUR WINNER IN BOX 2 ON THE WALLCHART

3 GOING FOR GOLD vs THE CRYSTAL MAZE

Going for Gold will forever be fondly remembered by certain generations. It was scheduled directly after the lunchtime showing of *Neighbours,* which was then a huge hit. I was a student when

Going for Gold was in its pomp, and so for me it was breakfast television. Its host was the very wonderful Henry Kelly. The show largely involved British contestants losing to Ukrainians and Finns, even though all the questions were in English, and were usually about Anne of Cleves or Tottenham Hotspur.

The Crystal Maze was invented pretty much accidentally. Channel 4 had wanted to make a UK version of the French challenge show *Fort Boyard*, set on a huge offshore military fort off the coast of France. However, when they discovered that the *Fort Boyard* set wasn't available for the filming dates they wanted, producers approached the creator of *Fort Boyard*, Jacques Antoine, and asked if he could create them something similar. He knocked together *The Crystal Maze* in just two days, and Channel 4 agreed to make that instead. Seems to have worked out okay.

WRITE YOUR WINNER IN BOX 3 ON THE WALLCHART

MASTERMIND vs THE GENERATION GAME

It is commonly suggested that the specialised subjects on *Mastermind* have got easier over the years. I couldn't possibly comment, but in its first ten years the specialised subjects of

Mastermind champions included 'The History of Music 1550–1900', 'Athens 500–400 BC' and 'The Vikings in Scotland and Ireland, AD 800–1150', while in more recent years champions' subjects have included *Blackadder*, *Father Ted* and *Thunderbirds*.

Such is the way of television, *The Generation Game* came about as a remake of a Dutch game show and chat format called *Één Van De Aacht* – 'One of the Eight'. The BBC dropped the chat element, and then also dropped most of the game-show element too, keeping only the iconic conveyor-belt round from the Dutch show. But that bit of the show had come from the Dutch host Mies Bouwman, who had herself taken it from a show she had seen on German TV. So quite what the BBC thought they were remaking is unclear. Again, it seemed to work out okay though. The show was unsuccessfully piloted in the US as *A Piece of Cake*, with Brucie as host.

WRITE YOUR WINNER IN BOX 4 ON THE WALLCHART

5 EGGHEADS vs TREASURE HUNT

Eggheads is the quiz where you take on 'perhaps the best quiz team in Britain'. That is something of an understatement. Here are the quizzing achievements of some of the regular Eggheads:

KEVIN ASHMAN – *Mastermind* champion 1995. Record-holder for highest ever score on *Mastermind. Brain of Britain* champion 1996. Record-holder for highest ever score on *Brain of Britain.* Five-time World Quiz champion, and world-ranked number one quizzer in the world. Even better, Kevin also once won on *Sale of the Century.*

CHRIS HUGHES – *Mastermind* champion 1983, with the specialised subject 'British Steam Locomotives 1900–63'. International *Mastermind* champion 1983. *Brain of Britain* champion 2005.

JUDITH KEPPEL – First ever British winner of £1,000,000 on *Who Wants to Be a Millionaire?*

DAPHNE FOWLER – Now retired and greatly missed, Daphne won *Brain of Britain* in 1997, won two series of *Fifteen to One*, and even managed to win *Going for Gold*, even though she is not Ukrainian or Finnish.

PAT GIBSON – And finally the guy who has done it all. *Mastermind* champion 2005, *Brain of Britain* champion 2006, four-time World Quiz champion, *Mastermind* 'Champion of Champions' 2010, and to add to all this, he also won £1,000,000 on *Who Wants to Be a Millionaire?* in 2004. I love Pat even more because he's the *Mastermind* champion with the specialist subject of *Father Ted.*

Treasure Hunt was another invention of that canny Frenchman Jacques Antoine, though this one probably took longer than two days to come up with. The voice of original presenter, Kenneth Kendall, can be heard as a BBC announcer in Stanley Kubrick's *2001: A Space Odyssey*. In the 2002 reboot of *Treasure Hunt*, the host's role was taken by Dermot Murnaghan. Twelve months later, with the *Treasure Hunt* reboot unsuccessful and not returning, Murnaghan took another TV job instead, host of a brand-new TV quiz, *Eggheads*.

WRITE YOUR WINNER IN BOX 5 ON THE WALLCHART

BLANKETY BLANK vs THE CHASE

Blankety Blank will forever be associated with Sir Terry Wogan, though he actually presented fewer episodes than Les Dawson. His famous stick microphone was just a prop, made out of an old car aerial with a ball of foam stuck on the end. Kenny Everett always delighted in coming up with new and ingenious ways of attacking it. It feels like Kenny Everett was always on *Blankety Blank*, though he actually appeared only fourteen times, way behind the twenty-nine appearances of the most regular guest. I'll give you a moment to guess who the most regular *Blankety Blank* guest was.

The Chase is one of the most successful quiz shows in ITV history, and a perennial but friendly rival of the BBC quiz show *Pointless,* which I hear good things about. Over 1,000 episodes in and *The Chase* is still regularly in ITV's ten highest-rated shows every week. In addition to the UK *Chase,* there is an American *Chase,* an Australian *Chase,* a German *Chase,* a Russian *Chase* and a Chinese *Chase.*

Have you guessed the most regular guest on *Blankety Blank* yet? I've just been trying to help you out by mentioning her name eight times. It was Lorraine Chase.

WRITE YOUR WINNER IN BOX 6 ON THE WALLCHART

7 FAMILY FORTUNES vs KNIGHTMARE

These are just a few genuine answers given over the years on *Family Fortunes*:

NAME A YELLOW FRUIT – 'Orange'
NAME SOMETHING MADE OF WOOL – 'A sheep'
NAME A BODY PART WITH FOUR LETTERS – 'Arms'
NAME SOMETHING YOU DO IN THE BATHROOM – 'Decorate'

NAME A BIRD WITH A LONG NECK – 'Naomi Campbell'
NAME A JOB FOR WHICH YOU WOULD NEED A TORCH – 'Burglar'
NAME A GAME YOU CAN PLAY IN BED – 'Hide & Seek'
NAME SOMETHING RED – 'My cardigan'

Knightmare ran on CITV for seven years, and was a sort of junior version of *The Crystal Maze*. I have to confess that I have never seen it, but I have to include it on the list because everyone younger than me loves it, and I'll be in trouble on Twitter if I don't mention it.

WRITE YOUR WINNER IN BOX 7 ON THE WALLCHART

8 YOU BET! vs DEAL OR NO DEAL

You Bet! was based on the German show *Wetten, daas . . .?*, a show created by its German host, Frank Elstner. For a while in the 1980s it was the most successful game-show format in the world. In 2008 Ant and Dec hosted a version of the show for ABC in the States, called *Wanna Bet?*

Deal or No Deal ran for over 3,000 episodes on British TV, giving away a total of over £40 million in prize money. Just

£10 of that money went to a contestant who would become a great deal more famous a few years later: Olly Murs. Olly attempted to gain revenge on the Banker by coming back for a celebrity version of the show in 2012. This time round it went even worse and Olly won just 50p.

WRITE YOUR WINNER IN BOX 8 ON THE WALLCHART

9 3-2-1 vs THE WEAKEST LINK

3-2-1 was absolutely bonkers in every way. Try to watch an old episode on YouTube (other video-sharing websites are available). It will always be remembered for Ted Rogers' lightning-fast 3-2-1 hand gesture, which would be copied endlessly in school playgrounds with mixed, and often offensive, results. It will also be remembered for the cryptically impossible riddles describing the prizes. Finally, it will always be remembered for the greatest booby prize in TV history, Dusty Bin. Dusty Bin was designed by John Sutherland, who went on to design, among many other things, the Jorvik Viking Centre in York.

The off-screen voice on *The Weakest Link* belongs to Jon Briggs, who many people already have a very personal relationship with. He is the male voice of Siri. Paul Farrer, who composed *The Weakest Link* theme music, once revealed in an interview that he receives £980 every time an episode is transmitted. Given that they made well over 1,000 episodes in the UK alone, and there were further series in nearly fifty other countries, his catchphrase for many years now must have been 'bank'.

WRITE YOUR WINNER IN BOX 9 ON THE WALLCHART

10 ONLY CONNECT vs PLAY YOUR CARDS RIGHT

Only Connect started life as an obscure quiz on BBC4. Its questions were written by obscure quizzers, to be answered by obscure quizzers. Its obscure category choices were hidden behind obscure Egyptian hieroglyphs, and each obscure answer was followed by an obscure explanation. Now, because this is Britain, ratings started creeping up, series after series, until this obscure quiz was promoted onto BBC2, and it is now regularly the second-most-watched show on the entire channel. The most watched? Well, that's *University Challenge.* You can point this fact out next time someone tells you TV is dumbing down.

Back in the days before TV had 'dumbed down' came *Play*

Your Cards Right. TV legend always used to have it that Brucie would spend most of the year living in the Caribbean, fly in to the UK for two weeks, record two series of *Play Your Cards Right* and two series of *The Price is Right*, thus completing his entire year's TV work in a fortnight, then fly straight back again. I like to think that this is true.

WRITE YOUR WINNER IN BOX 10 ON THE WALLCHART

11 BIG BREAK vs THE KRYPTON FACTOR

Big Break did for snooker what *Bullseye* did for darts, except that it was on the BBC so there were no speedboats. The theme to *Big Break* was called 'The Snooker Song'. It was sung by Captain Sensible and written by Mike Batt. As well as writing all the Wombles songs, and later selling millions of records with Katie Melua, Mike Batt also wrote the theme music to *Wetten, daas . . .?* The BBC attempted to follow up *Big Break* with a golf-based game-show format called *Jimmy Tarbuck's Full Swing*. It is well worth hunting down clips of this show.

The Krypton Factor was a UK-created show where, if memory serves me right, to win you would answer some general knowledge questions, watch a short video and try to remember what colour hats everyone was wearing, assemble a polystyrene 3-D model of the Arc De Triomphe, and then jump over some cargo nets in a coloured tracksuit.

WRITE YOUR WINNER IN BOX 11 ON THE WALLCHART

12 TIPPING POINT vs CATCHPHRASE

They brought *The Krypton Factor* back a few years ago, with Ben Shephard as host. But Ben Shephard was due to have his very own hit game show, with an even more unlikely format, *Tipping Point*. It's a quiz with a format relying on an enormous version of one of those coin-pusher machines you find in seaside arcades. This led to it being derided by initial critics, but it is actually a deceptively brilliant format. Many, many shows are launched in daytime, but vanishingly few succeed. *Tipping Point* was an almost immediate ratings success, and continues to go from strength to strength.

On 16 September 1985 the original *Catchphrase* launched in the US, before being taken off air due to poor ratings just four months later. Two days after it was taken off air in the US, ITV launched the British version, now rather worried that they had an expensive flop on their hands. Thirty years later it seems they needn't have worried. If there's one thing that the story of many of these game shows should teach you, it's that it's almost impossible to predict what will turn into a hit and what won't.

WRITE YOUR WINNER IN BOX 12 ON THE WALLCHART

13 UNIVERSITY CHALLENGE vs BOB'S FULL HOUSE

University Challenge has been on TV for over fifty years now. In all that time it only had a brief, three-year spell off air. That break coincided with the three years I was at university, and so I never had the chance to appear on the show. I definitely think I could be the team member on the end. You know, the one who nods at everyone else's answers as if he actually knew that Napoleon defeated Tsar Alexander I at the Battle of Austerlitz, and then buzzes in once during the whole game, when there's a question about obscure 1990s indie bands. When I watch *University Challenge* at home and there is a maths question, I always answer '-1'. It is right a surprising amount of the time.

I recently watched an old episode of *Bob's Full House* for a

BBC iPlayer collection of classic quiz shows (you can still find the collection there; it's properly fascinating). As a producer, one of the oldest rules of quiz shows is 'get to the questions as quickly as possible'. In the half-hour episode I watched, Bob asks the first question at seventeen minutes and three seconds in. Though if anybody could bend the rules of quiz shows it was Bob Monkhouse, the greatest quiz show host of them all. Except maybe Alexander Armstrong.

WRITE YOUR WINNER IN BOX 13 ON THE WALLCHART

BLOCKBUSTERS vs **THE MILLION POUND DROP**

Bob Holness had two daughters, and at one point, in September 1982, both of them had UK hit singles at the same time. His daughter Carol, known by the stage name Nancy Nova, was in the UK charts with 'No No No', at the same time as his other daughter, Ros, was in the top ten with 'I Eat Cannibals', as part of the band Toto Coelo.

The Million Pound Drop is one of the most profitable formats of the twenty-first century, made in over sixty countries worldwide. The money on-screen is all real, and it has the greatest security presence of any TV show. If you ever want to stage an elaborate heist on a TV show, this is the one to choose. Unless you really, really want a speedboat, in which case go for *Bullseye*. If you want to steal Maltesers then try *Pointless*, as I always have a packet under my desk.

WRITE YOUR WINNER IN BOX 14 ON THE WALLCHART

15 STRIKE IT LUCKY vs COUNTDOWN

It probably tells you everything you need to know about the different attitudes towards success in the UK and US that in the UK we call this show *Strike it Lucky*, while the Americans call it *Strike it Rich*. I'm guessing if there were a German version it would be called 'Strike it Efficiently', and a French version would simply be called 'Strike'.

To me, *Countdown* represents everything I love about game shows, and everything I love about television in general. It launched in 1982 and has run for over 6,000 episodes already. It provides a very concrete link to the past for so many people. In the 1980s, every time *Countdown* started I would see my grandad take out his pen and his notebook, cup of tea by his side, and happily play along. A while ago I had the opportunity to play *Countdown* and, before filming, I had a little cry in my dressing room, thinking of how much it would have made him smile to see me there, and how proud that made me feel. These programmes are a shared experience. They become part of who we are as a nation, and who we are as families, and that is very special. Add to this the fact that I have a huge crush on Susie Dent and it was a very emotional day all round.

WRITE YOUR WINNER IN BOX 15 ON THE WALLCHART

Your wild-card battle. This is where you could put *Pointless* if you really wanted to. Don't forget though that *Pointless* only wins if it gets the fewest votes. You might think about *Celebrity Squares, Every Second Counts* or *Ask the Family*. But if you're like me then you definitely won't want to leave out *Turnabout* with Rob Curling. I say bring it back!

WRITE YOUR WINNER IN BOX 16 ON THE WALLCHART

GAME SHOWS

THE WORLD CUP OF EVERYTHING

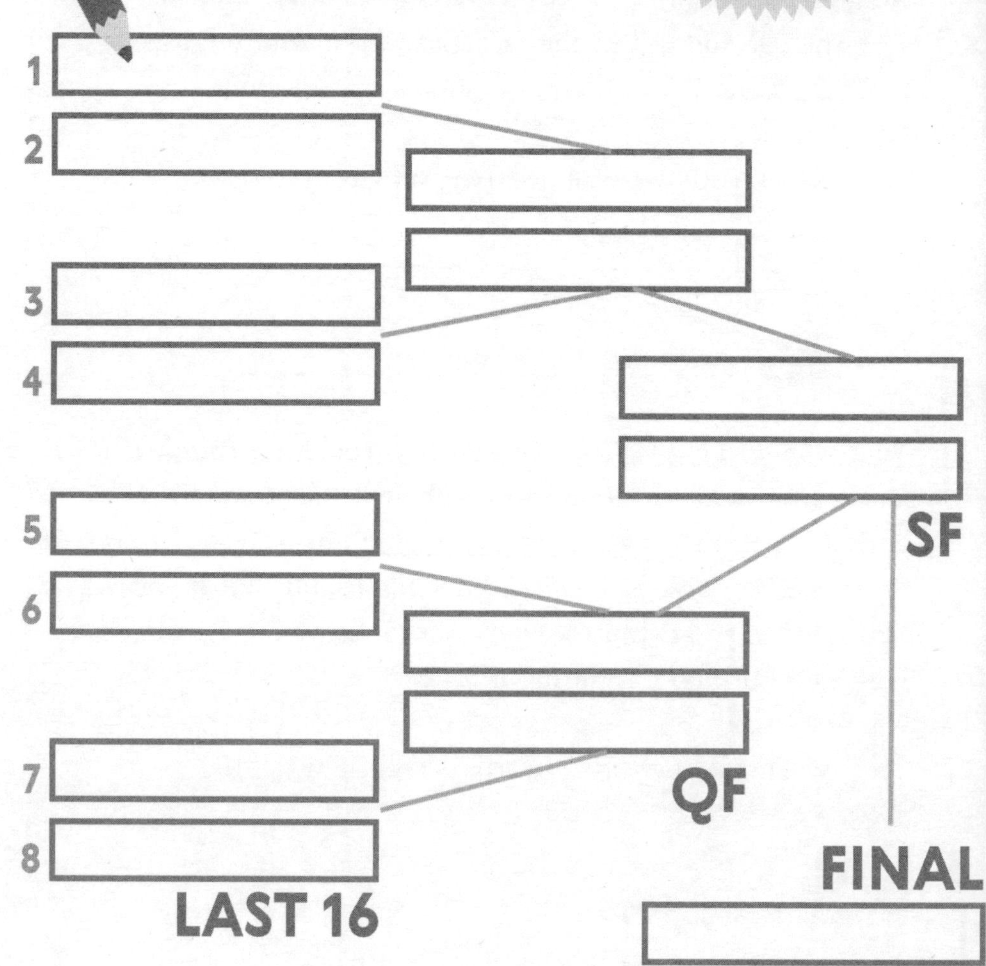

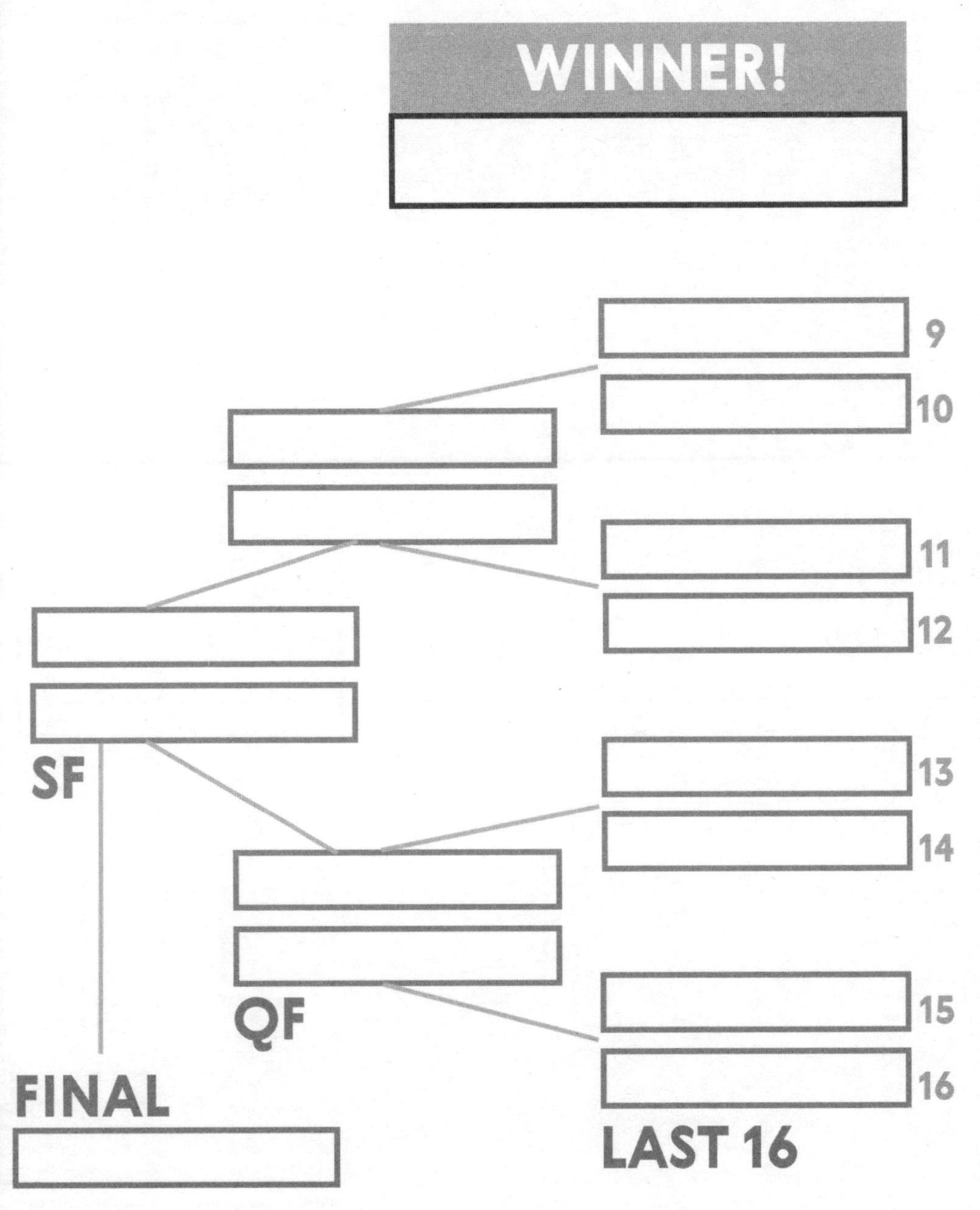
WINNER!
9
10
11
12
SF
13
14
QF
15
16
FINAL
LAST 16

WORLD CUP OF CHRISTMAS SONGS

Defining a Christmas song is almost as difficult as defining a Jaffa Cake, but much less delicious. In the end I have decided that if a song falls into any of the following four categories then it can be included.

1. CAROLS – The most boring of all the Christmas songs. A 'carol' in pagan times was a dance, but good luck dancing to 'Away in a Manger'. Carols tend to be about Jesus, God, angels, or a combination of the three. They can be very beautiful when sung by a full choir in a cathedral on

Christmas Eve, but less beautiful when sung by four members of your local Rotary Club who have knocked on your door when you're in the middle of watching the *Top Gear* Christmas special. The irony of having your evening constantly interrupted by people singing 'Silent Night' should not go unremarked.

2. SANTA SONGS! – At some point in the nineteenth century people got bored of trying to dance to 'Away in a Manger' and started writing Christmas songs that weren't about God and Jesus and angels. Instead they wrote about Santa, snowmen, reindeer, sleigh rides and jingling bells. How you vote in the World Cup of Christmas Songs may have a lot to do with where you stand on the whole Jesus vs Santa debate. For the record I like both of them.

3. CHRISTMAS HITS – From Bing Crosby singing 'White Christmas' to George Michael singing 'Last Christmas', from Nat King Cole singing 'The Christmas Song' to Wizzard singing 'I Wish It Could Be Christmas Everyday', from Dean Martin singing 'Winter Wonderland' to Michael Bublé singing a pretty much identical version of

'Winter Wonderland', we have now had over sixty years of Christmas hits. These are the songs we sing in karaoke booths rather than cathedrals. Though in a lot of ways, when you really think about it, isn't a karaoke booth just like a modern-day cathedral?*

4. NON-CHRISTMAS CHRISTMAS SONGS – These are the songs that don't mention Christmas at all, but are still somehow Christmas songs. 'Stay Another Day' by East 17 doesn't mention God or Jesus or angels. It doesn't mention Santa, Rudolph, snow, snowmen or snowballs. It fails to mention roasting chestnuts, Parson Brown, treetops glistening, children listening, Jack Frost, presents, Baileys, turkey, mistletoe, wine, one-horse open sleighs, parties for hosting, marshmallows for toasting, stockings, open fires, good cheer or facing unafraid the plans that we made. However, it does have a couple of jingling bells at the end and, for whatever reason, it will always make us think of Christmas. We have come a long way from the first Latin carols of the twelfth century,

* No, it isn't.

to Brian Harvey wearing a big, furry hat on *Top Of The Pops,* but isn't the whole point of Christmas that everyone is invited?

★ CHALLENGE! ★

So we've had over sixty years of Christmas number one singles, but only nine of them have really been 'Christmas' songs. The rest have been an extraordinary combination of genuinely awful novelty songs, genuinely awful winners of TV talent shows and, very occasionally, the Pet Shop Boys. Below are the initials of twelve songs and their artists, all of which were UK Christmas number one singles. Can you name them all?

1. IWTHYH – TB (1963) ____________
2. GGGOH – TJ (1966) ____________
3. E(TFMITW) – BH (1971) ____________
4. MXE – S (1973) ____________
5. TNQLG – SWSC (1980) ____________

6. SYL - RAR (1982) ____________

7. MAW - CR (1988) ____________

8. MB - MB (1993) ____________

9. 2B1 -SG (1996) ____________

10. CWFI - BTB (2000) ____________

11. MW - MA & GJ (2003) ____________

12. KITN - RATM (2009) ____________

Answers at the back of the book.

★ CHRISTMAS ★ ★ TURKEYS! ★

Only six Christmas number one singles actually have the word 'Christmas' in their title. However, this doesn't stop scores of acts desperately shoehorning the word into a song every year to try and have a hit. Below are ten genuine songs with 'Christmas' in their titles, which somehow managed to avoid the number one spot.

1. WHITE CHRISTMAS
   by Freddie Starr (1975)
2. MAKE A DAFT NOISE FOR CHRISTMAS
   by The Goodies (1975)
3. CHRISTMAS IN SMURFLAND
   by Father Abraham & The Smurfs (1978)
4. OH BLIMEY, IT'S CHRISTMAS!
   by Frank Sidebottom (1987)
5. I WANT AN ALIEN FOR CHRISTMAS
   by Fountains of Wayne (1997)
6. MR HANKEY THE CHRISTMAS POO
   by Mr Hankey (1999)
7. HAVE A CHEEKY CHRISTMAS
   by The Cheeky Girls (2003)
8. LAST CHRISTMAS
   by The Cast of *The Only Way is Essex* (2011)
9. MINECRAFT CHRISTMAS
   by Area 11 (2012)
10. 12 DAYS OF CHRISTMAS
    by The Eddie Stobart Truckers (2012)

★ CHALLENGE! ★

Well we've just done it for Christmas number one singles, so it's only polite to do it for carols too. In 2016 Classic FM ran a poll to find Britain's favourite Christmas carol of all. Below is the top ten. Can you guess them from their initials?

1. OHN
2. SN
3. ITBM (Holst Version)
4. HTHAS
5. OCAYF (The answer to this one looks like it is written in text-speak).
6. ITBM (Darke Version) – I'm assuming that Holst vs Darke is the Blur vs Oasis of the carolling world.
7. OLTOB
8. OIRDC
9. COTB
10. JTTW

Some big names missing out on the top ten there. 'Away in a Manger' was number 12 ('Away in a Manger – Dance Megamix' wasn't even in the top thirty), 'God Rest Ye Merry Gentlemen' was 13, and the actual best carol, 'Ding Dong Merrily On High' was only number 16. Gutted.

Answers at the back of the book.

★ CHRISTMAS PLAYLIST! ★

As a gift from me to you, here are ten great alternative Christmas songs that you might not know. I guarantee that you will hate some of them, but you might just find some that you like too! They're all on Spotify, so try mixing these up with some of the classics you'll be voting on below. Who knows, you might even find something for your wild card battle?

JUST LIKE CHRISTMAS
by Low
BABY, IT'S COLD OUTSIDE
by Rufus Wainwright & Sharon Van Etten
AIN'T NO CHIMNEYS IN THE PROJECTS
by Sharon Jones & The Dap Kings

WHITE WINE IN THE SUN
by Tim Minchin
CHRISTMAS (BABY PLEASE COME HOME)
by Slow Club
FELIZ NAVIDAD by El Vez
WE WISH YOU A MERRY CHRISTMAS by Shonen Knife
HAVE YOURSELF A MERRY LITTLE CHRISTMAS
by Tracey Thorn
DON'T SHOOT ME SANTA
by The Killers
CHRISTMAS WRAPPING
by The Waitresses
SILENT NIGHT
by Sinead O'Connor
WHEN THE THAMES FROZE
by Smith & Burrows

HERE WE GO THEN, I'VE MADE A LIST, I've checked it twice, it's beginning to look a lot like the World Cup of Christmas Songs. If there is a tie in any of these battles then put 'Away in a Manger' on the stereo, crank the volume up loud and stage a dance-off. Best dancer gets to choose the winner.

MERRY CHRISTMAS EVERYONE vs JINGLE BELLS

'Merry Christmas Everyone' was Christmas number one in 1985 for the Welsh Elvis, Shakin' Stevens. It was written by Bob Heatlie, who also co-wrote the theme tune to Pat Sharp's *Fun House*. 'Merry Christmas Everyone' was produced by Dave Edmunds, completing a neat double, as he'd sung his way to his very own Christmas number one in 1970 with 'I Hear You Knocking'.

'Jingle Bells' was written in 1857, by James Lord Pierpont, who, as far as I know, was not the other co-writer of the theme tune to Pat Sharp's *Fun House*. It was originally titled 'One Horse Open Sleigh'. The phrase 'jingle bells' is usually understood to mean a type of bell, but it is actually an instruction to the driver of a sleigh. 'Jingle bells' essentially means the same as 'Beep horn' or 'Flick V-signs at the Uber driver who just cut you up at the lights'.

WRITE YOUR WINNER IN BOX 1 ON THE WALLCHART

O COME ALL YE FAITHFUL vs I WISH IT COULD BE CHRISTMAS EVERYDAY

No one knows for certain who wrote 'O Come All Ye Faithful', though one theory is that it was written by King John IV of Portugal, which I bet is not true. It is the only proper carol that schoolchildren enjoy singing because you get to do the 'O come let us adore him' bit louder and louder.

If it really was Christmas every day then you would spend just over £1,000 a year on Quality Street, £2,950 a year on Christmas crackers, £3,650 a year on Alexander Armstrong CDs for your nan, £8,760 a year on Baileys, £21,550 a year on turkey, and £367,920 on guilty-joining a gym online late on Christmas night that you will never visit. In fact the only person who could afford Christmas every day would be Roy Wood of Wizzard, who would make even more in royalties than he already does.

WRITE YOUR WINNER IN BOX 2 ON THE WALLCHART

RUDOLPH THE RED-NOSED REINDEER vs FAIRYTALE OF NEW YORK

'Rudolph the Red-Nosed Reindeer' was a US Christmas number one in 1949 for Gene Autry, and eventually sold over 12 million copies. It was written by Johnny Marks who, despite being Jewish, specialised in Christmas songs. He also wrote 'Rockin' Around the Christmas Tree' for Brenda Lee and 'Run Rudolph Run' for Chuck Berry.

Is there a single more evocative and beautiful line in any Christmas song than the Pogues' description of the boys of the NYPD choir and the bells ringing for Christmas day?

Every year pedants point out that the NYPD doesn't have a choir, but even they can't spoil the magic of this most beautiful song. It was, such is the way of these things, recorded in London on a sweltering July day. 'Fairytale of New York' has never been number one, having been kept off that slot on its original release by 'Always On My Mind' by the Pet Shop Boys. Pogues singer Shane MacGowan was born on Christmas Day, so hopefully one year we can send it to number one, and then we won't have to get him a present.

WRITE YOUR WINNER IN BOX 3 ON THE WALLCHART

DRIVING HOME FOR CHRISTMAS vs SILENT NIGHT

So 'Fairytale Of New York' was never a number one single. But how about Chris Rea's 'Driving Home for Christmas'? It's certainly one of the best-loved Christmas hits, but its chart performance is fairly remarkable. It first entered the chart in 1988 and peaked at only number 53. It then reappeared on the chart in 2007, reaching 33. In 2008 it was number 53 again, and in 2009 it reached number 40. There was another dip in 2010 as it reached only 67, then it rallied to number 36 in both 2011 and 2012. In 2013 it was back to number 53 again, then 43 in 2014. In 2015 it finally broke the top 30 for the first time at number 29, and in 2016 it reached its highest ever chart placing of number 26. Its chart progress matches almost exactly the original inspiration for the song, a long, slow journey to Middlesbrough. At the current rate 'Driving Home for Christmas' will eventually get to number one in 2047.

The words to 'Silent Night' were composed in 1818 by a young Austrian priest, Father Joseph Mohr. He decided he wanted the song to be performed in his church, and so took it to Franz Xaver Gruber, a schoolmaster friend of his who lived in a nearby village. Gruber wrote a melody and guitar accompaniment, and the two men performed the carol together for the first time on Christmas Eve 1818. Bing Crosby's recording of 'Silent Night' is the third-biggest-selling single in music history. Mohr and Gruber didn't have any other hits.

WRITE YOUR WINNER IN BOX 4 ON THE WALLCHART

SANTA CLAUS IS COMIN' TO TOWN vs MARY'S BOY CHILD

Every year I enact my very own version of 'Santa Claus is Comin' to Town'.

He's making a list, he's checking it twice
And despite that, he still has to go back to Sainsbury's because he forgot the sprouts, the gin, and the little cocktail sausages on sticks that Mum likes

'Mary's Boy Child' was written by Jester Hairston, and was originally a calypso number for a friend's birthday party, entitled 'He Pone and Chocolate Tea'. Years later Hairston was asked to write a Christmas song for a local choir and, remembering his old tune, wrote new lyrics. Harry Belafonte heard the new song being performed by the choir and asked for permission to record it. In 1957 Belafonte's version was UK Christmas number one, selling over one million copies. In 1978 Boney M released a version of the song. This also reached Christmas number one, and sold nearly two million copies. On hearing about this later success, Hairston, who was seventy-eight at the time, remarked, 'God bless my soul. That's tremendous for an old fogey like me'.

WRITE YOUR WINNER IN BOX 5 ON THE WALLCHART

6
DO THEY KNOW IT'S CHRISTMAS?
vs HARK! THE HERALD ANGELS SING

'Do They Know It's Christmas?' has now been number one in four different recordings. There was the original from 1984, which sold over three million copies. That was followed by Band Aid II in 1989, featuring a slightly 'poppier' line-up including Big Fun, Kylie Minogue, and Technotronic, with Chris Rea on guitar and Luke Goss on drums. Then Band Aid 20 in 2004, which went slightly indie, and featured Chris Martin, Snow Patrol and Ms Dynamite, with Thom Yorke from Radiohead on piano and Danny Goffey from Supergrass on the drums. Finally, Band Aid 30 reached number one in 2014, with a cast including YouTubers such as Alfie Deyes and Zoella alongside One Direction, Ed Sheeran and Emile Sandé.

The words to 'Hark! The Herald Angels Sing' were written by Charles Wesley, although his first line was actually 'Hark! How all the welkin rings', 'welkin' being archaic English for 'heavens'. It was his collaborator George Whitefield who pointed out that this sounded rubbish and that kids just didn't really say 'welkin' any more. He suggested 'Hark! The herald angels sing' instead, and the rest is carol history. Whitefield seems to have been the Midge Ure to Wesley's Bob Geldof.

WRITE YOUR WINNER IN BOX 6 ON THE WALLCHART

7 STAY ANOTHER DAY vs SANTA BABY

'Stay Another Day' was Christmas number one in 1994 for East 17. It kept Mariah Carey's 'All I Want for Christmas is You' off the top spot. Tough competition, although the rest of the top ten that Christmas week included the Mighty Morphin Power Rangers, Zig and Zag, Jimmy Nail and 'Cotton Eye Joe' by Rednex.

'Santa Baby' has most famously been a hit for Eartha Kitt, Kylie Minogue and Miss Piggy. The full list of all the presents requested in the song reads: fur coat, a light-blue convertible, a yacht, the deed to a platinum mine, a duplex apartment, a number of blank cheques and a ring. What she actually ended up with was a Jo Malone candle, the new Hilary Mantel book, and a National Trust gift membership.

WRITE YOUR WINNER IN BOX 7 ON THE WALLCHART

8 WHITE CHRISTMAS vs CHRISTMAS WRAPPING

Bing Crosby's 'White Christmas' is quite simply the biggest-selling record of all time. There is some dispute as to where Irving Berlin wrote the song, with two separate hotels, the La Quinta in Hollywood and the Biltmore Arizona, both claiming the glory.

'Christmas Wrapping' by US new-wave band The Waitresses has never risen higher than number 45 in the UK charts, but was famously covered by the Spice Girls as the B-side to their 1998 Christmas number one 'Goodbye'. Kylie Minogue and Iggy Pop also recorded a cover of the song for the album *Kylie Christmas*. The writer of the song, Chris Butler, was amazed to find an Ohio house in 2004 which he considered to be an incredible bargain. After happily moving in, not able to believe his good fortune, until he was informed it was the former home of American serial killer Jeffrey Dahmer, but went ahead and bought it anyway.

WRITE YOUR WINNER IN BOX 8 ON THE WALLCHART

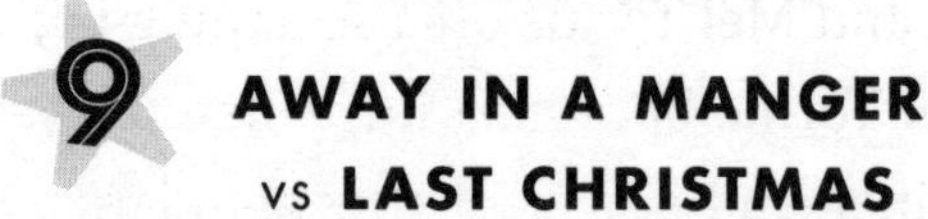

9 AWAY IN A MANGER vs LAST CHRISTMAS

For many years 'Away in a Manger' was believed to be a song written by Martin Luther for his children, and was even called 'Luther's Cradle Hymn'. However, it is now believed to be an entirely American composition, though no one knows exactly who wrote it. Probably not Van Halen. It is the only Christmas song whose title still makes some sense if you put the word 'Pret' in the middle of it.

Respectfully to the spurned suitor who is the subject of 'Last Christmas', if anybody ever gave you their heart by wrapping it up and sending it, you would probably want someone to take it off your hands on Boxing Day too. To be fair she would have given it away even quicker than that if the Forensics Office had been open on Christmas Day.

WRITE YOUR WINNER IN BOX 9 ON THE WALLCHART

10 THE CHRISTMAS SONG vs WONDERFUL CHRISTMASTIME

'The Christmas Song', most commonly subtitled as 'Chestnuts Roasting on an Open Fire', was written in just forty minutes, by Robert Wells and Mel Tormé on a scorching-hot Californian day in 1945. Mel Tormé became a huge star, far better known as a US entertainer and singer of jazz standards. In 1966 he married the British actress Janette Scott, which meant that, for the eleven years that their marriage lasted, Mel Tormé's mother-in-law was Thora Hird.

Paul McCartney holds the record for most Christmas number one singles in history. He scored four with The Beatles, and then a fifth when 'Mull Of Kintyre' was number one for Wings in 1977. 'Wonderful Christmastime' was the closest he ever came to a solo Christmas number one, peaking at number six. Among the songs which kept it off the top were Pink Floyd's 'Another Brick in the Wall', 'Rapper's Delight' by The Sugarhill Gang, and 'Day Trip To Bangor' by Fiddler's Dram.

WRITE YOUR WINNER IN BOX 10 ON THE WALLCHART

11 MISTLETOE AND WINE vs STOP THE CAVALRY

'Mistletoe and Wine', Cliff Richard's 1988 Christmas number one, has very unusual songwriting credits. Its three writers were Jeremy Paul, a writer on *Upstairs Downstairs*, Leslie Stewart, who has written episodes of *Peak Practice* and *Holby City*, and Keith Strachan, who went on to make another fortune when he and his son wrote the theme tune to *Who Wants to Be a Millionaire?*.

Jona Lewie had already had one surprise hit single in 1980 with 'You'll Always Find Me in the Kitchen at Parties', and his record label decided that 'Stop The Cavalry' might just have a crack at the Christmas market. It hadn't been written as a Christmas song, it was an anti-war protest song, but the brass band and the line 'wish I was at home for Christmas', convinced them it would have a chance. It is still a Christmas standard nearly forty years later, even if it was beaten to the Christmas number one slot by 'There's No One Quite Like Grandma', another famously anti-war protest song.

WRITE YOUR WINNER IN BOX 11 ON THE WALLCHART

12 ALL I WANT FOR CHRISTMAS IS YOU vs GOD REST YE MERRY GENTLEMEN

'All I Want for Christmas is You' is such a timelessly brilliant song, it feels somehow like it has been around since the sixties. It was, in fact, written in 1994 by Mariah Carey and Walter Afanasieff, after Carey's manager and then husband, Tommy Mottola, had suggested she release a Christmas album. Afanasieff initially thought it was risky, but is probably glad that he backed down, as 'All I Want for Christmas is You' is now the eleventh best-selling single of all time. It has sold over 14 million copies, spent 78 weeks in the UK chart, and is estimated to have earned over $50 million in royalties.

'God Rest Ye Merry Gentlemen' is one of the oldest carols still sung, with its origins sometime in the sixteenth century, but even with over 500 years of history it hasn't sold as many copies as 'All I Want for Christmas is You'. The 'merry' in the title refers to the 'rest' and not to the 'gentlemen', and so the title should always be written and sung as 'God Rest Ye Merry, Gentlemen' and not 'God Rest Ye, Merry Gentlemen'. Every day is a school day, right?

WRITE YOUR WINNER IN BOX 12 ON THE WALLCHART

13 WINTER WONDERLAND vs IN THE BLEAK MIDWINTER

These two songs pretty much sum up the two different British reactions to snow. 'Winter Wonderland' covers our excitement at snowballs, sledging, days off school and catching snowflakes on our tongues. 'In the Bleak Midwinter' meanwhile, neatly sums up the fact that the trains don't work, the council forgot to grit the road, and your boiler has chosen this exact moment to give up the ghost. In other words, the difference between being a child and being an adult.

WRITE YOUR WINNER IN BOX 13 ON THE WALLCHART

14 MERRY XMAS EVERYBODY vs IT'S BEGINNING TO LOOK A LOT LIKE CHRISTMAS

Slade's 1973 Christmas number one 'Merry Xmas Everybody' really kickstarted the tradition of Christmas pop hits. Before Slade, there hadn't been a Christmas-themed number one since 'Mary's Boy Child' in 1957. Slade's Noddy Holder took the melody for the chorus from an old song he'd written called 'Buy Me a Rocking Chair'.

'It's Beginning to Look a Lot Like Christmas' was written by Meredith Wilson, and was presumably inspired by visiting any UK high street retailer from about 18th October onwards.

WRITE YOUR WINNER IN BOX 14 ON THE WALLCHART

15 LET IT SNOW! vs FROSTY THE SNOWMAN

You will be familiar with this sort of thing by now, but 'Let It Snow' was written in California in the height of summer. Its composer, Jule Styne, also composed 'Diamonds are a Girl's Best Friend' and 'Three Coins in the Fountain', while its lyricist, Sammy Cahn, was responsible for lots of Sinatra's work, including 'Come Fly with Me' and 'Love and Marriage'.

'Frosty the Snowman' was written for Gene Autry, who was keen to follow up the phenomenal success of 'Rudolph the Red-Nosed Reindeer' with another huge Christmas hit. It did the trick, and has since been covered by everyone from Bing Crosby to the Beach Boys, and the Jackson 5 to the current King of Christmas, Michael Bublé.

WRITE YOUR WINNER IN BOX 15 ON THE WALLCHART

16 ______________ VS ______________

Now for the wild-card battle. Please choose any song that makes you feel like Christmas is on its way. It could be a carol I've missed, such as 'O Little Town Of Bethlehem', or a traditional song I've left out, perhaps 'Have Yourself a Merry Little Christmas'? You could choose a classic Christmas pop hit. I left out Elton John's 'Step Into Christmas' and 'Christmas Time (Don't Let The Bells End')' by The Darkness. Or you could just choose a song which reminds you of Christmas, and of the ones you love, whether they are near or far away.

WRITE YOUR WINNER IN BOX 16 ON THE WALLCHART

CHRISTMAS SONGS

THE WORLD CUP OF EVERYTHING

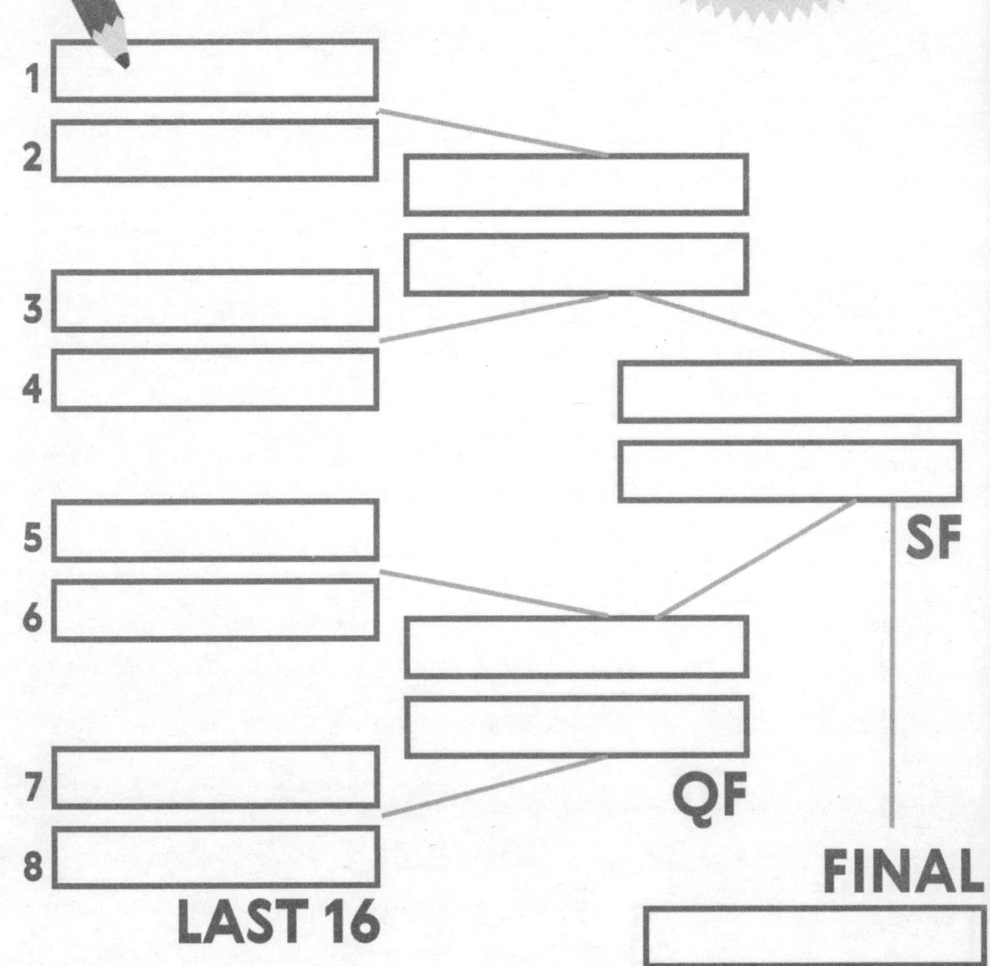

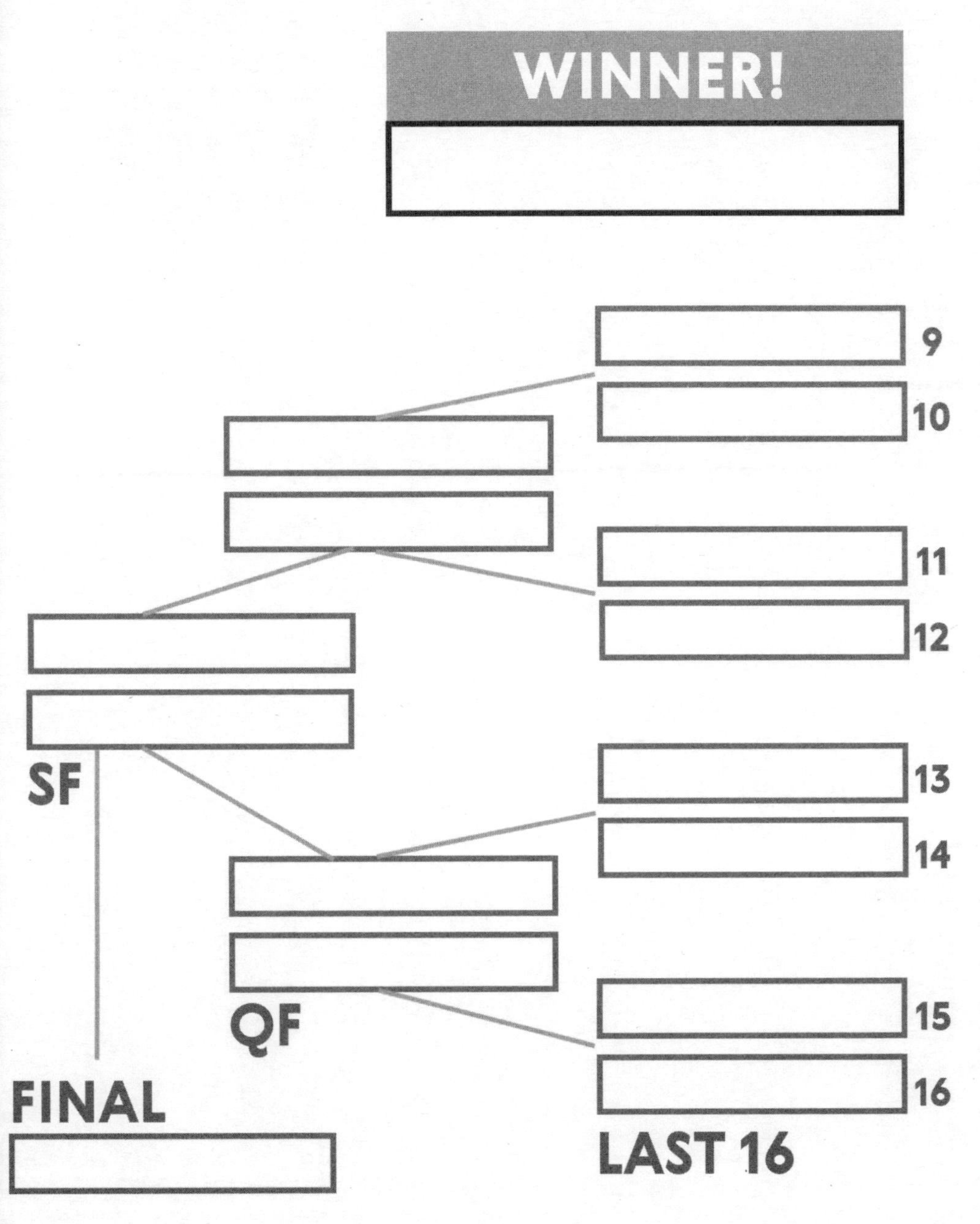
WINNER!
9
10
11
12
SF
13
14
QF
15
16
FINAL
LAST 16

WORLD CUP OF EVERYTHING

So you now have fourteen World Cup winners, you have lost most of your friends due to arguments about Frazzles, and you have created family rifts that will last for generations and will always be spoken of, in hushed terms, as 'The Unfortunate Chocolate Hobnob Incident'.

The way I see it, things can't get any worse, right? So why don't we take all of your winners from the different World Cups and pit them against each other? A battle to find the very best of the very best, the Ultimate Champion.

Who, or what, will win the World Cup of Everything?

I have given a lot of thought to what my winners of the

fourteen World Cups in this book would be, and these would be my champions. Please don't judge me.

WORLD CUP OF . . .

CHOCOLATE – Maltesers
ANIMALS – Dogs (Sorry cat people. And meerkat people)
CRISPS – Wotsits (in a fight to the death with Frazzles)
RESTAURANTS – Nando's
BRITISH BANDS – The Beatles
SWEETS – Fizzy cola bottles
AMERICANS – Muhammad Ali
BRITISH SITCOMS – *Porridge* (also won the World Cup of *Porridge*)
DISNEY FILMS – *Toy Story*
DRINK – Diet Coke (well, Coke Zero, because, you know, I'm an idiot)
CHRISTMAS FILMS – *It's a Wonderful Life*
BISCUITS – Jaffa Cakes (I know, I know, don't start)
GAME SHOWS – *Family Fortunes* (beat *University Challenge* in a quick-fire final round)
CHRISTMAS SONGS – 'Fairytale of New York'

Like me, you should now have fourteen winners to fill in on your World Cup of Everything wallchart. If you have exactly the same fourteen winners as me, then feel free to get in touch and we'll get married.

You may have noticed that we will need sixteen competitors for this knockout battle, and so we are two short. Well, in all the World Cups so far you have had two wild-card spaces to fill in with your own choices. There are also two wild-card spaces here, but this time it's my turn to choose. I have chosen two things which haven't featured in any of our World Cups so far, but which both represent the finest things about our country, namely our sense of humour and our creative innovation. So, to join your fourteen winners in the World Cup of Everything, here are my two wild-card picks:

MORECAMBE & WISE
MINT VIENNETTA

Good luck to all your winners. Thank you so much for reading this book, and thank you so much for voting and arguing about such lovely, inconsequential nonsense. Do please tweet me with your World Cup of Everything winners; I look forward to hearing how *Blackadder* got on against Mint Viennetta in the final.

EVERYTHING

THE WORLD CUP OF EVERYTHING

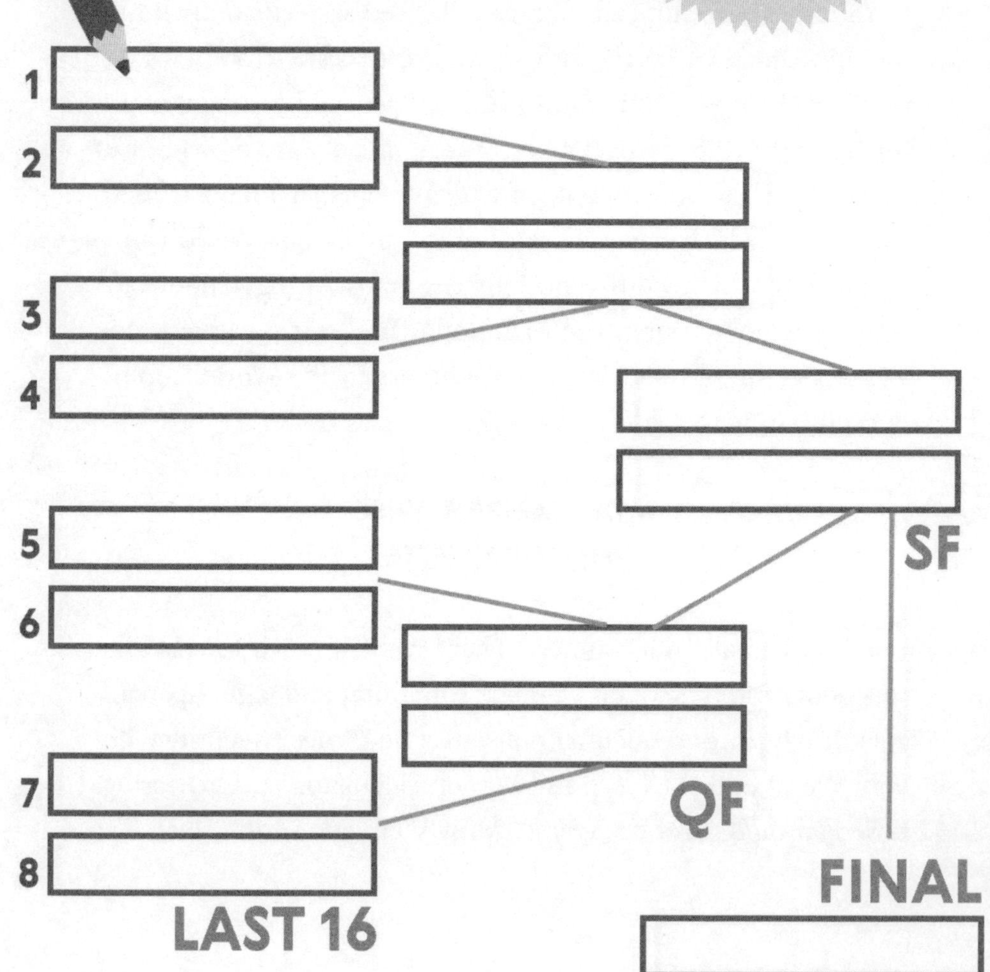

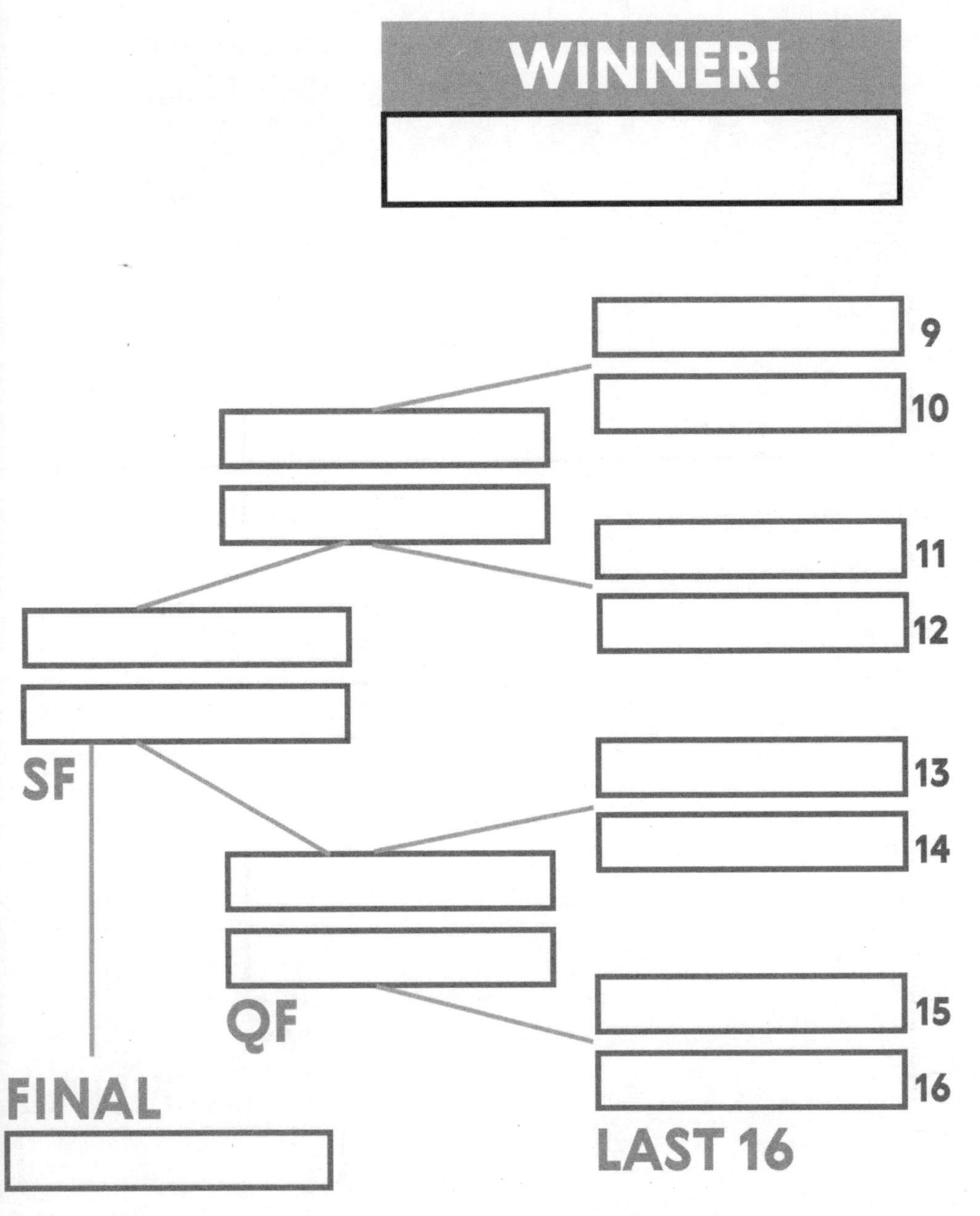

WINNER!
9
10
11
12
SF
13
14
QF
15
16
FINAL
LAST 16

WORLD CUP OF ANSWERS

WORLD CUP OF CHOCOLATE

1. DAIRY MILK
2. GALAXY
3. MALTESERS
4. KITKAT
5. SNICKERS
6. WISPA
7. MARS
8. TWIRL

WORLD CUP OF ANIMALS

'THE WEAKEST MINK'

1. BEAR GRYLLS
2. TIGER WOODS
3. SAM FOX
4. ANGELA EAGLE
5. ANTHONY MCPARTLIN
6. LIONEL MESSI
7. HIPPOCRATES
8. BEATRIX POTTER
9. NEWT GINGRICH
10. SEAL

PET SOUNDS!

1. PIG
2. FROG
3. MOUSE
4. DOG
5. COW
6. SHEEP
7. PARROT
8. ROOSTER

TOP FIVE PET NAMES

DOGS

1. MAX
2. BUDDY
3. MOLLY
4. MAGGIE
5. JAKE

CATS

1. MOLLY
2. CHARLIE
3. TIGGER
4. POPPY
5. OSCAR

WORLD CUP OF CRISPS

CHINESE CHALLENGE!

REAL CRISPS:
CUCUMBER
ROASTED SQUID
TOMATO CHICKEN
BLUEBERRY
NUMB & SPICY HOT POT

NAME THAT CRISP!

1. HULA HOOPS
2. FRAZZLES
3. QUAVERS
4. DISCOS
5. SKIPS
6. NIK NAKS
7. WOTSITS
8. PRINGLES
9. SQUARES
10. MINI CHEDDARS

WORLD CUP OF RESTAURANTS

I HONESTLY DON'T HAVE A CLUE HOW OLD GREGGS IS

1. HARRY RAMSDEN'S
2. GREGGS
3. MCDONALD'S
4. KFC
5. PIZZA EXPRESS
6. NANDO'S
7. YO! SUSHI
8. JAMIE'S ITALIAN

TRUE DISHES:

McFALAFEL

MUNG BEAN ICE CREAM

McD CHICKEN PORRIDGE

McTOAST

STROOPWAFEL McFLURRY

WORLD CUP OF BRITISH BANDS

BANDS TRANSLATED INTO FRENCH

1. DEPECHE MODE
2. ORCHESTRAL MANOEUVRES IN THE DARK
3. RADIOHEAD
4. EAST 17
5. WET WET WET
6. SUGABABES
7. THE ROLLING STONES
8. TAKE THAT
9. COLDPLAY
10. MANIC STREET PREACHERS
11. THE TREATMENT
12. LITTLE MIX
13. BLUR
14. THE SMITHS
15. ELBOW

ONE-HIT WONDERS!

1. MATCHSTALK MEN AND MATCHSTALK CATS AND DOGS BY BRIAN AND MICHAEL
2. VIDEO KILLED THE RADIO STAR BY THE BUGGLES
3. TURNING JAPANESE BY THE VAPOURS
4. THE ONE AND ONLY BY CHESNEY HAWKES
5. INSIDE BY STILTSKIN
6. SPACEMAN BY BABYLON ZOO
7. TUBTHUMPING BY CHUMBAWUMBA
8. YOUR WOMAN BY WHITE TOWN
9. BRIMFUL OF ASHA BY CORNERSHOP
10. JCB SONG BY NIZLOPI

WORLD CUP OF SWEETS

SWEET SLOGANS

1. FRUIT GUMS
2. FRUIT PASTILLE
3. REFRESHERS
4. MAYNARDS WINE GUMS
5. MURRAY MINTS
6. SPANGLES (YES REALLY)
7. SKITTLES
8. TIC TAC

9. TOFFOS
10. HARIBO

LOVE HEARTS

TRUE MESSAGES

GROW UP

SKYPE ME

JUST SAY NO

LUV U 24/7

YOLO

WORLD CUP OF AMERICANS

BIGGEST-SELLING ARTISTS

1. THE BEATLES
2. GARTH BROOKS
3. ELVIS PRESLEY
4. LED ZEPPELIN
5. EAGLES
6. BILLY JOEL
7. MICHAEL JACKSON
8. ELTON JOHN
9. PINK FLOYD
10. AC/DC (WELL DONE)

11. GEORGE STRAIT
12. BRUCE SPRINGSTEEN
13. AEROSMITH
14. THE ROLLING STONES
15. BARBRA STREISAND
16. MADONNA
17. MARIAH CAREY
18. METALLICA
19. WHITNEY HOUSTON
20. VAN HALEN

SPORTS TEAMS

1. NEW YORK
2. CHICAGO
3. CLEVELAND
4. ATLANTA
5. LOS ANGELES
6. BOSTON
7. HOUSTON
8. PITTSBURGH
9. SEATTLE
10. WASHINGTON DC

SPELLING

THEATER, STORY, ANNEX, ORGANIZATION, PROGRAM, GRAY, MUSTACHE, PRIZED, MATTE, ALUMINUM, ARTIFACT, DREAMED, MARVELOUS, JEWELRY, FAVORITE, JEWELED, AX, CENTER, VISE, ANALYZED, SKILLFUL, SPECIALTY, LEARNED, CIPHER, BEHAVIOR, FIBER, TRAVELING, SAVIOR, AIRPLANE, FUELING, PLOWS, ARMOR, WOOLEN, PAJAMAS, COZY, DEFENSE, ACKNOWLEDGMENT, VALOR, KILOMETER, TIRES, DISKS, SMOLDERING, AUTHORIZATION, CANCELED, VITTLES, DONUT, LICORICE, HUMOR, CIVILIZATION, MANEUVER

WORLD CUP OF BRITISH SITCOMS

NAME THE SITCOM!

1. DAD'S ARMY
2. RED DWARF
3. PORRIDGE
4. 'ALLO 'ALLO!
5. FATHER TED
6. FAWLTY TOWERS
7. ABSOLUTELY FABULOUS
8. ONLY FOOLS AND HORSES
9. DINNERLADIES
10. BREAD

CATCHPHRASE

1. I DON'T BELIEVE IT!: VICTOR MELDREW – *ONE FOOT IN THE GRAVE*
2. LOVELY JUBBLY!: DEL BOY – *ONLY FOOLS AND HORSES*
3. GO ON GO ON GO ON GO ON GO ON GO ON GO ON: MRS DOYLE – *FATHER TED*
4. I'M FREE!: MR HUMPHRIES – *ARE YOU BEING SERVED?*
5. I HAVE A CUNNING PLAN: BALDRICK – *BLACKADDER*
6. LISTEN VERY CAREFULLY, I SHALL SAY THIS ONLY ONCE: MICHELLE DUBOIS – *'ALLO 'ALLO!*
7. NO NO NO NO NO NO NO NO NO NO YES: JIM TROTT – *VICAR OF DIBLEY*
8. HAVE YOU TRIED TURNING IT ON AND OFF AGAIN?: ROY – *THE IT CROWD*
9. HI-DE-HI CAMPERS! HO-DE-HO!: GLADYS PUGH – *HI-DE-HI!*
10. WE'RE DOOMED!, DON'T PANIC!, STUPID BOY: PRIVATE FRAZER, CORPORAL JONES, CAPTAIN MAINWARING – *DAD'S ARMY*

MUCH TOO GEEKY CHALLENGE

1. DEAR JOHN
2. TERRY & JUNE
3. BOTTOM
4. FATHER TED
5. RAB C. NESBITT

6. JUST GOOD FRIENDS
7. WAITING FOR GOD
8. AS TIME GOES BY
9. SPACE-D
10. GIMME GIMME GIMME
11. GOODNIGHT SWEETHEART
12. BLACKADDER
13. A FINE ROMANCE
14. IT AIN'T HALF HOT MUM
15. ARE YOU BEING SERVED?

WORLD CUP OF DISNEY

HIGHEST-GROSSING ANIMATIONS

1. FROZEN
2. MINIONS
3. TOY STORY 3
4. FINDING DORY
5. ZOOTOPIA
6. DESPICABLE ME 2
7. THE LION KING
8. FINDING NEMO
9. SHREK 2
10. ICE AGE: DAWN OF THE DINOSAURS
11. ICE AGE: CONTINENTAL DRIFT

12. THE SECRET LIFE OF PETS
13. INSIDE OUT
14. SHREK THE THIRD
15. SHREK FOREVER AFTER

ACTORS IN DISNEY FILMS

1. TOM HANKS
2. JAMES EARL JONES
3. CAMERON DIAZ & EDDIE MURPHY
4. PAUL NEWMAN
5. IDINA MENZEL
6. LOUIS PRIMA
7. ELLEN DEGENERES
8. JOHN GOODMAN & BILLY CRYSTAL
9. SAMUEL L. JACKSON
10. THE ROCK

WORLD CUP OF DRINKS

'PINTLESS'

1. CIDER
2. COFFEE
3. TANGO
4. GIN
5. SEVEN-UP

6. MILK
7. LEMONADE
8. PINA COLADA
9. FANTA SIA
10. GIN
11. MILKSHAKE
12. TEQUILA

PUB CRAWL CHALLENGE

1. THE RED LION
2. THE CROWN
3. THE ROYAL OAK
4. THE WHITE HART
5. THE SWAN
6. THE WHITE HORSE
7. THE KING'S ARMS
8. THE QUEEN'S HEAD
9. THE COACH AND HORSES
10. THE BLACK HORSE
11. THE ROSE AND CROWN
12. THE PRINCE OF WALES
13. THE FOX AND HOUNDS
14. THE KING'S HEAD
15. THE WHEATSHEAF

WORLD CUP OF CHRISTMAS FILMS

FAKE CHRISTMAS FILMS

REAL FILMS:

SANTA WITH MUSCLES

JACK FROST 2 – REVENGE OF THE MUTANT KILLER SNOWMAN

WHAT WOULD JESUS BUY?

SANTA CLAUS CONQUERS THE MARTIANS

NATIVITY 3 – DUDE, WHERE'S MY DONKEY?

CHRISTMAS FILM CAST MEMBERS

1. ELF
2. THE MUPPET CHRISTMAS CAROL
3. LETHAL WEAPON
4. HOME ALONE 2
5. THE HOLIDAY
6. DIE HARD
7. SCROOGED
8. WHITE CHRISTMAS
9. LOVE ACTUALLY
10. TRADING PLACES
11. ARTHUR CHRISTMAS
12. A CHRISTMAS CAROL

CHRISTMAS WORD ASSOCIATION

1. PRESENTS
2. TURKEY
3. SANTA
4. TREE
5. FAMILY
6. BOOZE/ALCOHOL/DRINK
7. SNOW
8. JESUS
9. EVE
10. CAROLS

WORLD CUP OF BISCUITS

BROKEN BISCUITS

1. BOURBON
2. RICH TEA
3. PINK WAFER
4. DIGESTIVE
5. FIG ROLL
6. GINGER NUT
7. CHOCO LEIBNIZ
8. WAGON WHEEL
9. CHOCOLATE FINGER

10. CUSTARD CREAM
11. PARTY RING
12. SHORTBREAD FINGER

AUSTRALIAN BISCUITS

REAL BISCUITS:

PASSIONFRUIT CREAMIES

HONEY JUMBLES

ICED VOVOS

TIC TOCS

CARAMEL CROWNS

WORLD CUP OF GAME SHOWS

FOREIGN TITLES

1. WHO WANTS TO BE A MILLIONAIRE?
2. THE PRICE IS RIGHT
3. FAMILY FORTUNES
4. COUNTDOWN
5. DEAL OR NO DEAL
6. THE WEAKEST LINK
7. CELEBRITY SQUARES
8. THE MILLION POUND DROP

9. BLOCKBUSTERS
10. POINTLESS

GAME SHOW HOSTS

1. FAMILY FORTUNES
2. CATCHPHRASE
3. CELEBRITY SQUARES
4. BLOCKBUSTERS
5. FIFTEEN TO ONE
6. COUNTDOWN
7. YOU BET!
8. THE PRICE IS RIGHT
9. TREASURE HUNT
10. CALL MY BLUFF
11. ASK THE FAMILY
12. KNIGHTMARE

WHAT DO CHALLENGES MAKE? PRIZES!

1. NICE TO SEE YOU TO SEE YOU NICE – BRUCE FORSYTH
2. IS THAT YOUR FINAL ANSWER? – CHRIS TARRANT
3. QUESTION OR NOMINATE? – WILLIAM G. STEWART
4. COME ON DOWN! – LESLIE CROWTHER
5. YOU ARE THE WEAKEST LINK, GOODBYE – ANNE ROBINSON

6. NOTHING IN THIS GAME FOR TWO IN A BED – JIM BOWEN
7. HIGHER OR LOWER? – BRUCE FORSYTH
8. I'VE STARTED SO I'LL FINISH – MAGNUS MAGNUSSON
9. IT'S GOOD BUT IT'S NOT RIGHT – ROY WALKER
10. OUR SURVEY SAID! – BOB MONKHOUSE
11. POT AS MANY BALLS AS YOU CAN – JOHN VIRGO
12. I'LL HAVE A P PLEASE BOB – TO BOB HOLNESS

WORLD CUP OF CHRISTMAS SONGS

CHRISTMAS NUMBER ONES

1. I WANT TO HOLD YOUR HAND BY THE BEATLES
2. GREEN GREEN GRASS OF HOME BY TOM JONES
3. ERNIE THE FASTEST MILKMAN IN THE WEST BY BENNY HILL
4. MERRY XMAS EVERYBODY BY SLADE
5. THERE'S NO-ONE QUITE LIKE GRANDMA BY ST. WINIFRED'S SCHOOL CHOIR
6. SAVE YOUR LOVE BY RENEE AND RENATO
7. MISTLETOE AND WINE BY CLIFF RICHARD
8. MR. BLOOBY BY MR. BLOBBY
9. 2 BECOME 1 BY SPICE GIRLS
10. CAN WE FIX IT BY BOB THE BUILDER
11. MAD WORLD BY MICHAEL ANDREWS & GARY JULES
12. KILLING IN THE NAME BY 3RAGE AGAINST THE MACHINE

TOP TEN CAROLS

1. OH HOLY NIGHT
2. SILENT NIGHT
3. IN THE BLEAK MID-WINTER
4. HARK! THE HERALD ANGELS SING
5. O COME ALL YE FAITHFUL
6. IN THE BLEAK MID-WINTER
7. O LITTLE TOWN OF BETHLEHEM
8. ONCE IN ROYAL DAVID'S CITY
9. CAROL OF THE BELLS
10. JOY TO THE WORLD

ACKNOWLEDGEMENTS

The World Cups I run on Twitter are to raise money for an incredible charity, Childs-i Foundation. They do extraordinary work with displaced children in Uganda, on a shoestring budget. If at any point during this book you do win a bet, do feel free to visit www.childsifoundation.org and bung them a couple of quid. Thank you!